The Life of
ANTHONY WOOD
in His Own Words

Anthony Wood and his arms,
*W. Burghers delineavit et sculpsit, c.*1691. Mezzotint, redone in 1712.

THE LIFE OF
ANTHONY WOOD
IN HIS OWN WORDS

Edited by
NICOLAS K. KIESSLING

Bodleian Library
UNIVERSITY OF OXFORD

First published in 2009 by the Bodleian Library
Broad Street, Oxford OX1 3BG

www.bodleianbookshop.co.uk

ISBN   978 1 85124 308 2

Cover design by Dot Little
Designed and typeset in Monotype Janson by illuminati, Grosmont
Printed in Great Britain by the MPG Books Group, Bodmin and King's Lynn

British Library Catalogue in Publishing Data
A CIP record of this publication is available from the British Library

CONTENTS

ACKNOWLEDGEMENTS

THE National Endowment for the Humanities provided funds for the research for this edition during 2004 and 2005. Since I first began work on the Oxford antiquarian Anthony à Wood in 1992, I have had numerous persons give generously of their time. For this latest project, those who advised and encouraged me included J.B. Bamborough, Giles and Lisa Barber, Jim Bell, Tom Birrell, Mark Bland, Trevor Bond, Mary Clapinson, Bill Clennell, Ann Gustard, Michael Hanly, Ralph Hanna III, Misako Himura, William Hodges, Clive Hurst, Julie Ann Lambert, Olav Lausund, Stanton Linden, the late Paul Morgan, Robert Schmiel, Paul Slack, David and Bridget Sturdy and Al von Frank. The staff at the book delivery counter in Duke Humfrey's, Alan Carter, Russell Edwards and Jean-Pierre Mialon, deserve praise for their extraordinary labours on my behalf. Most important has been my wife, Karen, who has been my faithful and insightful critic and without whom I would neither have begun nor have finished this edition. While in Oxford I was a Senior Visiting Member of Linacre College, and I thank the Principal and colleagues at the College for their constant welcome. Anyone working with Anthony à Wood or his milieu is indebted to the great Andrew Clark, whose eight monumental volumes on Wood are a marvellous resource for later scholars.

INTRODUCTION

Anthony wood, or Anthony à Wood, as he called himself from 1662, was born in Postmasters' Hall on Merton Street, Oxford, on 17 December 1632 and died in the same house on 29 November 1695. He was an undistinguished undergraduate at Merton College; neither a genius, nor a brilliant stylist, nor a creative thinker. His older brother, a fellow of Merton, saw a rather grim future for him. His mother held a similar opinion and, as he recalled in his *Diarie*, 'would several times forsooth propose to me the trade of a Tinner or Tin-man or a man that makes Kitchen-ware, Lanthorns'. All that changed in the summer of 1656, when a copy of *The Antiquities of Warwickshire* by William Dugdale came to the Bodleian Library. Wood wrote of his response in his *Secretum*:

> my pen cannot enough describe how A. Wood's tender affections, and insatiable desire of knowledg, were ravish'd and melted downe by the reading of that book — What by musick and rare books that he found in the public Library his life at this time and after was a perfect Elysium.[1]

Wood was on his way to becoming Oxford's most famous, most cited, most maligned, and most controversial antiquarian of the seventeenth century. For virtually every single day of the rest of his life, he directed incredible energy towards the study of the records of his city, county, and university. He followed the patterns of research established by such antiquarian scholars as John Leland, William Camden, William Burton and Brian Twyne, and the direction of contemporary scholars such as William Dugdale and John Fell, to become the historian of Oxford and its university. His two publications during his lifetime concerned the history of the university. The first was the massive two-volume *Historia et antiquitates universitatis Oxoniensis* (1674), translated from English into Latin at the command of the person who financed its publication, John Fell, then Vice-chancellor of the university and in control of the university press; and the second was the even more massive two-volume *Athenæ Oxonienses* and *Fasti*, a controversial bio-bibliography containing the lives of over 1,500 graduates and persons associated with the university.[2] Equally important publications were posthumous. His literary executor Thomas Tanner arranged Wood's manuscript notes for a second edition of the *Athenæ* (1721) with the addition of five hundred new lives. John Gutch published Wood's English version of the *Historia*, *The History and Antiquities of the University of Oxford* (4 volumes, 1786–96); Andrew Clark arranged Wood's notes on the city of Oxford for the *Survey of the Antiquities of the City of Oxford* (3 volumes, 1889–99); and Clark gathered Wood's notes in his collection of almanacs, books and manuscripts for *The Life and Times of Anthony Wood, Antiquary, of Oxford, 1632–1695, described by Himself* (5 volumes, 1891–1900).

The occasion for writing *The Diarie of the Life of Anthony à Wood Historiographer and Antiquarie of the most famous Universitie of Oxford*, which Wood later revised and renamed *Secretum Antonii*, was the severe criticism he received after the publication of the *Athenæ Oxonienses*. The most damaging attack came in the form of a libel suit initiated by Henry Hyde, second Earl of Clarendon, in defence of his father Edward Hyde, the first Earl of Clarendon. Wood in two different biographies had stated that the old Earl had required bribes for offices during the Restoration. Wood was in jeopardy of losing everything, most importantly his reputation and status in Oxford and at the University. He defended himself in the public arena by preparing three documents in which he tried to demonstrate that he was a trusted, hard-working, modest, selfless antiquarian who had printed truthful histories of the University and its members. Two of these were published in 1692 and 1693: 'To the Reader', a preface to the *Athenæ*, and *A Vindication of the Historiographer of the University of Oxford*.[3] The third was his *Diarie*, a narrative written from a first-person point of view. He continued to work on the *Diarie* only at intervals after 1693. Of higher priority were his revisions of and additions to the *Athenæ*. It was not until nearer the end of his life, in late 1695, that he directed his attention once more to the *Diarie*. He then determined to rewrite it, changing to the more objective third-person point of view, adding details, refining the argument, and extending the narrative to 1672. He retitled it *Secretum Antonii*. The revision occupied him in his last weeks, and he thrice altered passages in the first version, the *Diarie*, to allude to his impending death in the *Secretum*. For example, when he referred to his notes on William Burton's *Description of Leicestershire*, he changed 'which I have laying by me at this time' to 'which he had lying by him in his last dayes'.[4] He wrote the last entries within five days of his death on 29 November when he had a bittersweet reconciliation with his sister-in-law, Mary Drope Wood. This meeting settled a quarrel which had begun twenty-five years earlier, in 1669, when she had banished him from the table of their common home on Merton Street. Anthony told of this banishment and the 'reconciliation' in his entry of June 1669: 'AW was dismist from his usual and constant Diet, which for many yeares he had taken in the House where he was borne, and then lived, by the rudeness and barbarity of a brutish woman, of which she afterwards repented, when too late', that is, when he was at death's door.[5]

Wood died shortly after he reached the entry of July 1672 in the *Secretum*, though he had before him rough copy to continue the narrative well beyond that date. He several times referred to future entries, as 'You will heare more hereafter', and 'see in Oct. 1674'.[6] But this rough copy is missing and in the text below selected entries from his almanacs, notes and manuscripts focus on the major events of his life from 1672 to 1695. The narrative is followed by two letters, one by Arthur Charlett, the Master of University College, and another by Thomas Tanner, then the chaplain of All Souls and one of the executors of Wood's estate, which recount Wood's physical and mental condition during his last days, and a copy of his signed will, which is now in the National Archives (Public Record Office).

The manuscript of the *Secretum* ended up in the possession of Tanner, who allowed Thomas Hearne, an Oxford scholar and antiquarian, to borrow it. Hearne published an edition in 1730. Bodley's Librarian, William Huddesford, republished Hearne's edition in 1772, and the manuscript was re-edited in 1813 by Philip Bliss and again in 1891–1900 by Andrew Clark. This is the first critical edition, in that it records the changes Wood made when he prepared the second version.[7]

ABBREVIATIONS
AND CONVENTIONS

Athenæ	*Athenæ Oxonienses. An exact History of all the Writers and Bishops ... in the most ancient and famous University of Oxford, from ... 1500, to the End of the Year 1690. ... To which are added, the Fasti* (London, for T. Bennet, 1691–92). The two later editions are referenced by 1721 or 1813–20.
AW	The abbreviation used by Wood for himself is retained.
Dating	Wood began the new year on 25 March, in Julian old style, rather than in the Gregorian new style. The year between 1 January and 24 March is given as, e.g., 1674/5 until 25 March, when 1675 is used. Wood's dates in Julian style, approximately twelve days behind Gregorian new style, are retained.
f. 1ʳ, f. 1ᵛ	The recto and verso folio page numbers of the copy text, Tan, f. 1ʳ to f. 69ʳ, are entered in the margins.
Foster	Joseph Foster, *Alumni Oxonienses, 1500–1714* (Oxford, 1891–92).
Har	British Library, MS. Harley 5409.
Historia	Anthony à Wood, *Historia et antiquitates universitatis Oxoniensis* (Oxonii, e Theatre Sheldoniano, 1674).
History	(1786) A. Wood, *The History and Antiquities of the College and Halls*, ed. John Gutch, 2 vols (Oxford, 1786, 1790).
	(1792) A. Wood, *The History and Antiquities of the University of Oxford*, ed. John Gutch, 2 vols (Oxford, 1792, 1796).
LAW	N.K. Kiessling, *The Library of Anthony Wood* (Oxford Bibliographical Society, 2002).
LT	*The Life and Times of Anthony Wood, Antiquary, of Oxford, 1632–1695, described by Himself*, ed. Andrew Clark, 5 vols (Oxford Historical Society, 1891–95).
MS.	or MSS. Wood's abbreviations for manuscript or manuscripts.
ODNB	*Oxford Dictionary of National Biography*, online edition, 2008.
Oxôn	The form of Oxonia or Oxonium Wood used most often in the Tanner manuscript; his usage is retained.
Tan	Bodleian Library, MS. Tanner 102.
WCO	*Wood's City of Oxford*, ed. Andrew Clark, 3 vols (Oxford Historical Society, 1889–99).

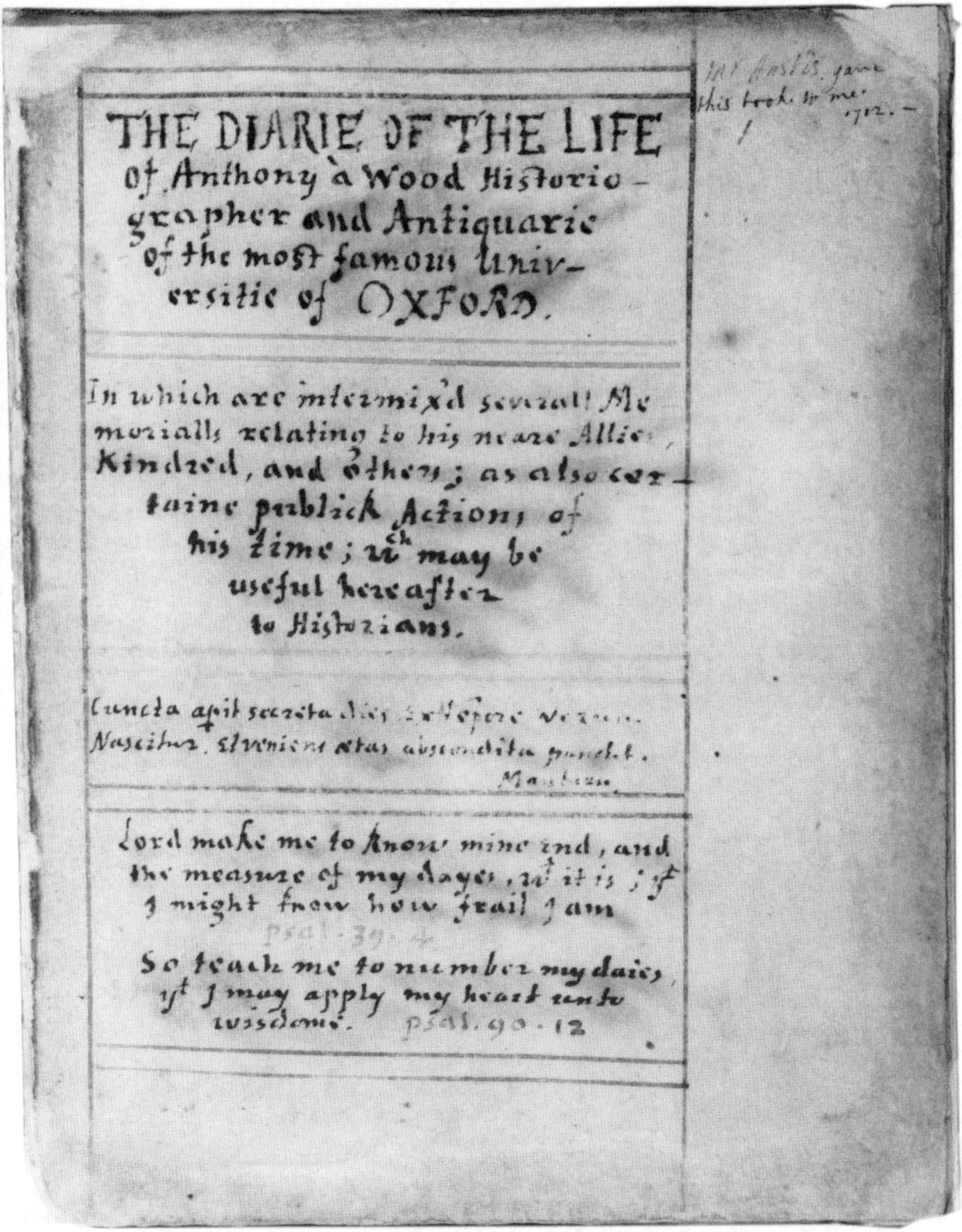

PLATE I   Title page of *The Diarie of the Life of Anthony à Wood*, British Library, MS. Harley 5409, f. 1ʳ. W. Dugdale used the Mantuan quotation, 'The day reveals all secrets. At the right time the truth arises, and the coming age reveals what is concealed', on the title page of his *Antiquities of Warwickshire* (1656). Edward Harley records this gift from John Anstis in a MS. note, top right.

Dom. 1632.
An. Reg. 8. Car. I

Dec. 7

Anthony Wood

or à Wood son of Tho.
Wood or à Wood Bachelaur of Arts & of the civil law,
was borne in an antient stone-house opposite to ye west front
of merton coll. in the collegiat parish of S. John Bapt.
de merton, situat & being within ye universitie of
Oxford, on munday the seventeenth day of decēb.
(S. Lazarus day) at about 4 of the clock in the mor-
-ning: which stone house, with a backside and garden adjoyning, was bought by his Father of John
Lant master of Arts of the Univ. of Oxon, q. Decēb.
6. Jac. 1. Dom. 1608, & is held by his family of Merton
coll. before mention'd.

Dec. 23

He was christned or taken into the bosome of the
church: At which time he had to his godfathers Anthony Clopton Bachelaur of Divinity & Fellow of Corp.
Christi College, and Edward Dawson Dr of physick
of Lincolne College: And to his godmother mris Catherine Fisher the wife of Will. Seymoure of Oxon
an Attorney; and afterwards the first wife of
Tho. Rowney an Attorney also of the same place:
father by his second wife to Thom. Rowney esq.
High-sheriff of Oxfordshire, an. 169

Dom. 1633
An. 9. Car. I

He was altogether nursed by his mother (of whome shal
be mention made under the yeare 1666) and by none
else: For as she nursed his 3 eld. brothers, so she nursed
him (whom she found very quiet) and the two next
yt followed.

Dom. 1634
An. 10 Car. I

July

At ye sumer Assizes held in the guild hall of the citie
of Oxon, appeared with a comission frō ye King,
Georg Owen & Will. Ryley Officers of Arms, to visit

PLATE 2   First page of the *Secretum Antonii*,
Bodleian Library, MS. Tanner 102, f. 1ʳ.

SECRETUM ANTONII

PLATE 3   Wood's residence, Postmasters' Hall, on Merton Street.

Anno $\left\{\begin{array}{l} \text{Domini 1632}^2 \\ \text{Regni 8 Caroli I} \end{array}\right.$

17 Dec. Mon. ANTHONY WOOD or à Wood[3] son of Tho*mas* Wood or
à Wood Bachelaur of Arts and of the civil law, was borne in an
antient stone-house opposite to the forefront of Merton coll*ege*
in the collegiat Parish of S. John Bapt*ist* de Merton, situat and
being within the Universitie of Oxford, on Munday the sevententh
day of Decemb*er* (S. Lazarus day) at about 4 of the clock in the
morning an*no* 1632: which stone house, with a Backside and Garden
adjoyning, was bought by his Father of John Lant Master of Arts of
the Univ*ersity* of Oxôn, 8. December. 6. an*no* Jac*obi* 1. Dom*ini* 1608,[4]
and is held by his family of Merton coll*ege* before mention'd.

23 Dec. Sun. He was christned or taken into the bosome of the church:
At which time he had to his Godfathers Anthony Clopton
Bachelaur of Divinity and Fellow of Corp*us* Christi College, and
Edward Dawson D^r of Physick of Lincolne College: And to his
Godmother M^ris Catherine Fisher the wife of William Seymoure
of Oxon, an Attorney; and afterwards the first wife of Tho*mas*
Rowney an Attorney also of the same place, father by his second
wife to Thom*as* Rowney esq*uire* High-Sherriff of Oxfordshire,
an*no* 1691.

$$\text{Anno} \left\{ \begin{array}{l} \text{Domini } 1633 \\ 9 \text{ Caroli I} \end{array} \right.$$

He was altogether nursed by his Mother (of whome shal be mention made under the yeare 1666)[5] and by none else: For as she nursed his 3 elder brothers, so she nursed him (whom she found very quiet) and the two next that followed.[6]

$$\text{Anno} \left\{ \begin{array}{l} \text{Domini } 1634 \\ 10 \text{ Caroli I} \end{array} \right.$$

July.   At the summer Assize[7] held in the Guild hall of the Citie of Oxôn, appeared with a Commission from the King, Georg Owen and Will*iam* Ryley Officers of Armes, to visit and take an account of   f. 1ᵛ all the Armes and Pedegrees of the Gentry of Oxfordshire. And to add authority to their Commission, 'twas read in the open court before the Judg, Justices and country Gentrie. This Memoire I here set downe becaus Mʳ Wood's Father (of whom I shall make mention[8] under the yeare 1642) was warn'd among the Gentrie to appeare before the said Officers or Heralds with his Armes and Pedegree and to have them entred into their Books; but he forsooth pleading the privilege of the University, or that he was a privileged person, and so consequently exempted, as he pretended (but false) *E curia Marischalli*,[9] he did not appeare in his owne behalf, tho he did in the behalf of the Petties of Tetsworth, and entred what he knew of that family the Armes, Matches and Issue of three or more Descents,[10] being desired so to do by Maximilian Pettie, who gave him the Fees, and he the Heralds. It was afterwards to Mʳ *Anthony* Wood when he came to understand those things a great Trouble to him that his father did not enter three or more Descents of his owne Familie, which he had then been better able to doe, than those of the Familie of his wife (Pettie). And the reason is, because that his Father dying when he was yong, those things which he knew of his family dyed with him, and his son could never obtaine them from any other person of his kindred, nor can he yet from

4

any place of Record, unless he take a journey into Lancashire from whence his Grandfather came about the beginning of the raigne of Queen Elizabeth.[11]

Anno $\begin{cases} \text{Domini } 1635 \\ \text{11 Caroli I} \end{cases}$

This yeare he had the small pox so much that he was for a time blinded with them.

1 Aug. Mon. A Fine of 30[li] was set by the Warden and Fellowes of Merton College when his Father renewed his lease of the old stone-house wherin his son *Anthony* Wood was borne (called antiently Portionists or Postmasters hall) for 40 yeares, and for a common Inn called the Flowr de Luce situat and being in the parish of S. Martin ad Quadrivium in Oxôn. (which Inn his Father had bought of Richard Theed Gentleman on the eleventh of September 14. Jacobi I. Domini 1616) and at the same time a Lease of the Garden opposite to S. Albans hall was let to his father for 27 yeares.

f. 2[r]

Anno $\begin{cases} \text{Domini } 1636 \\ \text{12 Caroli I} \end{cases}$

29 Aug. Mon. The King, Queen, Prince Rupert, many of the Nobility and others came from Woodstock into Oxôn: a little before which time he was conveyed in a servants Armes, with his father and mother going to the Lodgings of Dr Thomas Iles Canon of Christ Church, whence being conveyed to the Mount in his Garden[12] looking into Fish street he saw the King, Queen, and the rest riding downe the said street into Christ Church great Quadrangle. This was the first time that he ever saw the said King, and Queen and the first time that he ever saw such a glorious Traine as that was, which he would often talk of when he was a man.

30 Aug. Tue. They were entertained by the Universitie, and by D[r] Laud Archbishop of Canterbury at S. Johns College.[13]

31 Aug. Wed. They departed — See the whole story of this entertainment in *Hist et Antiq. Univ. Oxon*, lib. 1, sub an*no*. 1636; which Hist*ory* was written by M*r* A*nthony* Wood ==.[14]

Anno { Domini 1637
13 Caroli I

He was put to school to learne the psalter — And about that time playing before the Dore of his fathers House neare Merton Coll*ege*, one of the Horses called Mutton belonging to Tho*mas* Edgerley the University Carrier, rode over him (as he was going to be watered) and bruis'd his head very much. This caused a great heaviness for some time after in his head and perhaps a slowness in his apprehending with quickness things that he read or heard; of which he was very sensible when he came to reason.[15]

Anno { Domini 1638
14 Caroli I

In the beginning of this yeare his eldest Brother Thomas Wood (who was borne at Tetsworth in Oxfordshire) became one of the students of Christ Church, by the favour of D*r* Tho*mas* Iles, he being then 14 yeares of age — See more of him under the yeares 1642 and 1651.

f. 2*v*

Anno { Domini 1639
15 Caroli I

He was in his Bible and ready to go into his Accedence.[16]

1639/40. 8 Mar. Sun. His yonger Brother John Wood died, and was buried the day following in Merton Coll*ege* Church.

Anno { Domini 1640
16 Caroli I

He was put to a Latine School in a Little House neare to the church of S Peter in the Baylie and opposite to the street called

6

the North Baylie, which leads from New inn to the Bocherew.
The name of his Master he hath forgot, but remembers that he was
Master of Arts and a Preacher, by a good Token that one of the
Beadles of the Universitie did come with his silver staff to conduct
him from the said Little House (a poore thing God wot) to the
church of S. Marie, there to preach a Latin Sermon he thinks, for it
was on a working or school day) before the Universitie.[17]

$$\text{Anno} \left\{ \begin{array}{l} \text{Domini 1641} \\ \text{17 Caroli I} \end{array} \right.$$

He was translated to New Coll*ege* schoole, situated between the
west part of the chappell and E*ast* part of the cloyster, by the
advice, as he usually conceived, of some of the Fellowes of the
said coll*ege* who usually frequented his Fathers house. One John
Maylard Fellow of the said coll*ege* was then or at least lately the
Master (afterwards Rector of Stanton S John neare Oxon) and after
him succeeded Joh*n* Davys one of the chaplaynes of the said House,
whome he well remembers to be a quiet man.

Nov.   His Grandmother Penelopie, the widdow of Capt. Rob*ert* Pettie
or Le Petite Gent*leman* (his mothers Father) died with greif at or
neare Charlemount in Ireland, the seat of her Nephew William
Viscount Caulfield, occasion'd by the barbarous usuage of her
intimate acquaintance (but a bigotted Papist) S[r] Philim O Neale,
who acted the part of an Arch-Traytor and Rebell when the
grand rebellion broke out in that Kingdome 23 October 1641. This
Penelopie was the daughter of Richard Taverner Lord of Wood-   f. 3[r]
Eaton in Oxfordshire, by his second wife, Mary, dau*ghter* of S[r] John
Harcourt K[t], of the antient and noble Family of the Harcourts of
Stanton-Harcourt in the said Countie. She was borne at Wood-
Eaton in the beginning of Sept. 1566, and when shee was about 21
yeares of age (being then a most comlie and proper person, as most
of the Taverners were then, and in after times, some of whome
he does remember) shee was married to his Grand-Father Robert
Pettie before mention'd, then Lord of Wyfald or Wiveold, and of

other lands neare to Henlie in Oxfordshire and a Tenant to Eaton Coll*ege*, of a very good Farme at Cotsford neare to Bister in the said Countie.

1641/2. Mar. In the beginning of March his brother Robert, who had lately been taken from the Free-school at Thame, left Oxôn in order to goe to France with Charles Dufore of Montillet a kind of a merchant at Bloys. After he was setled there, the said Charles was to send his son Dennis to Oxôn to live with Roberts Father by way of exchange for Robert, but the Troubles in England soon after following, Charles Dufore refused to send his son. Wherefore Rob*ert* Wood continuing at Bloys and in other places in the Kingdome of France till the beginning of 1647 (at which time he was neare 17 yeares of age) he return'd to his native place of Oxôn, but had utterlie forgotten his mother tongue, which was a great Trouble to his Brethren to make him understand what they spoke to him. — [18]

$$\text{Anno} \left\{ \begin{array}{l} \text{Domini 1642} \\ \text{18 Caroli I} \end{array} \right.$$

In the beginning of this yeare the 2^d brother of AWood,[19] named Edward became one of the Portionists or Postmasters of Merton Coll*ege* under the Tuition of Mr Ralph Button.

Aug. Upon the publication of his Majesties Proclamation for the suppressing of the Rebellion[20] under the conduct and command of Robert Earl of Essex, the members of the Universitie of Oxôn began to put themselves in a posture of Defence, and especially for another Reason, which was that there was a strong Report that divers companies of soldiers were passing thro the country as sent from London by the Parliament for the securing of Banbury and Warwick — Dr Pink of New Coll*ege*, the Deputy-Vicechancellour,   f. 3^v called before him to the public schooles all the privileged mens Armes to have a view of them: where not onlie privileged men of the Universitie and their servants, but also many scholars appeared,

bringing with them the furniture of Armes of every coll*ege* that
then had any. Mr Woods Father had then Armour or Furniture
for one man, viz a Helmet, a Back and Breast-piece, a Pyke and
a Musquet and other Appurtenances: And the eldest of his men-
servants (for he had then three at least) named Thomas Burnham
did appeare in those Armes when the scholars and privileged
men trained; and when he could not train, as being taken up with
business, the next servant did traine: and much adoe there was to
keep Thomas Wood the eldest son, then a Student of Chr*ist* Ch*urch*
and a youth of about 18 yeares of age, from putting on the said
Armour and to traine among the scholars. — The said scholars and
privileged men did somtimes traine in New Coll*ege* Quadrangle
in the eye of Dr Rob*ert* Pink the Dep*uty*-Vicechancellour,[21] then
Warden of the said coll*ege* — And it being a novel matter, there
was no holding of the school-boyes in their school in the cloyster
from seeing and following them. And Mr Wood remembred well
that some of them were so besotted with the Training and activitie
and gayitie therein of some yong scholars, as being in a longing
condition to be one of the Traine, that they could never be brought
to their Books againe. It was a great Disturbance to the Youth of
the citie, and Mr Woods Father foresaw that if his sons were not
removed from Oxôn, they would be spoyl'd.

23 Oct. Sun. The great Fight at Edghill in Warwickshire called Keynton-
Battle between the Armies of K*ing* Ch*arles* 1 and his parliament was
began.

Upon the first Newes at Oxôn that the Armies were going to
fight, Mr Woods eldest brother Thomas before mentiond left his
Gowne at the Towns end, ran to Edghill, did his majestie good
service, return'd on horse-back well accountred, and afterwards was
made an Officer in the Kings Army — See more in *Athenae et Fasti
Oxon*, written by AWood lib. 2. p. 692.

29 Oct. Sat. The King with his Army of Foot, prince Rupert and pr*ince*
Maurice his two Nephews, prince Charles and James Duke of York,
his two sons entred into Oxôn.

Nov. His fathers house opposite to Merton College was taken up for   f. 4^r
the quarters of John Lord Colepeper Master of the Rolls and of the
privie Councill to his Majestie. Whereupon Mr Woods Father with
his Familie removed to a little House in his Backside, which he
about 2 or 3 yeares before had new built.

    About the same time his Majesty caused his Magazine to be put
into New College Cloister and Tower &c. Whereupon the Master
of the school there, with his scholars (among whome AWood was
one) were removed to the choristers chamber at the East-end of the
common Hall of the said College. It was then a dark nasty Room
and very unfit for such a purpose, which made the scholars often
complaine, but in vaine.

1642/3.   19 Jan. Thur. His Father Thomas Wood or à Wood before mentiond
died, being Thursday about 4 of the clock in the Morning, to the
very great grief and reluctancy of his wife and children — He died
in his House in the Backside before mention'd in the room over the
Kitchin: and being a fat and corpulent man, and therefore his Body
could not keep, he was buried between 8 and 9 of the clock at night
on the same day in the north part of Merton College outer-chappell
or church, neare to the graves of James Wood his younger brother,
who died in Sept. 1629 and John Wood his son, whome I have
mention'd under the yeare 1639. This Thomas Wood (father to AW)
was borne at Islingdon neare London in January 1580, was bred in
Grammar learning in those parts, became a student in Broadgates
hall (now Pembroke College) in the yeare 1600, afterwards one of the
Clerks, I think, of Corpus Christi College: and as a member of that
House he was admitted Bachelor of Arts on the 15 of March 1603.
Before which time he had taken to wife an antient and rich maid
called Margaret, daughter of Hugh Wood of Kent (of the family of
the Woods of Waterbury in that county) and sister to Robert Wood
a Haberdasher of Hats living at the Plow and Harrow on Ludgate
Hill in London and to Henry Wood living in Kent. They were
married at Wood-Eaton in Oxfordshire where shee lived in the
House of Richard Taverner Esquire (uncle to Thomas Wood his
second wife.)

About which time the said second wife named Mary (who was   f. 4^v
borne in the said House) being then a child of about two yeares old,
Tho*mas* Wood would often take her out of the cradle, dandle her in
his Armes, and would several times say, that he hoped shee would
live to be his second wife, which accordingly came to pass, and
was mother to AWood. — By and with the money which Tho*mas*
Wood had with the said Margaret, and the 500^{li} which his parents
bequeathed to him, he grew rich, purchased the House wherein
AWood was borne, with its appurtenances, also the great Inne
called the Flour de Luce which I have before mention'd, Land in
Tetsworth, now valued at 45^{li} per an*num* and Lands and Tenements
in other places. In the yeare 1618 the said Tho*mas* Wood was
actually created Bach*elor* of the Civil Law, had some employment
in that facultie, and after the death of his said first wife, which
hapned at Tetsworth 14 July 1621 he took to wife Mary Pettie alias
La Petite mother to AWood (the same who had been the child in
the Cradle before mentiond) by whome having a good portion and
growing richer thereupon, he was fined in October 1630 for refusing
the honour of Knighthood, a matter then lately brought up to
obtaine money for his majesties use. This money which was paid by
all persons of 40^{li} per an*num* that refused to come in and be dub'd
Knights was called Knighthood-money.[22] This Tho*mas* Wood was
son of Richard Wood, who, when a youth, was brought to Islingdon
by Rob*ert* Wood his uncle and Godfather, as the tradition goeth in
the family: who giving him good breeding, he ever after lived in
good Fashion. The posterity of the said Robert, who have Lands
and Tenements to this Day in Islingdon live at Kingston upon
Thames in Surrey; where, and elswhere they have an Estate that
amounts to 2000^{li} per An*num*, and have been several times offer'd
the degree of Baronet.

$$\text{Anno} \begin{cases} \text{Domini 1643} \\ \text{19 Caroli I} \end{cases}$$

It was much lamented by the Relations of the Father and Mother
of AW that he and his brother Christopher were left yong when

their father dyed, and that no body was left (because of the raging
of the civil warr) to take care of them, only a woman. His eldest
Brother Thomas, whome I shall mention under the yeare 1651, was   f. 5ʳ
then a rude and boisterous soldier: His second brother Edward, was
now a yong scholar of Trinity Coll*ege* (lately of Merton) and did
in this or in the next yeare beare Armes for his Maj*esty* within the
Garrison of Oxôn, and was so farr from being a Governour or Tutor
to others, that he could scarcely govern himself; and his 3ᵈ Brother
Robert was in France in the thirteenth yeare of his age. In this
condition he continued, and yet went to schoole at New Coll*ege*, but
by the great Hurry and noise that was this yeare in Oxôn, and by
the absence of his Master, he and his brother lost much time.

    This yeare the Plate which had been given to A. Wood at
his christning by his Godfathers and Godmother, which was
considerable, was (with all other plate in Oxôn) carried by his
Majesties command to the mint at New Inne, and there turned into
money to pay his Majesties Armies.[23]

Anno { Domini 1644
       20 Caroli I

29 May. On Wednesday being the Eve of the Ascension Robert Earl of Essex
    Generalissimo of the Parliament Forces and Sʳ Will*iam* Waller
    going with their Forces from Abendon over Sandford Ferry, and
    so thro Cowley and over Bullington Green (to the end that they
    might go towards Islip) faced the city of Oxôn for several Houres,
    whilst their carriages slipt away behind them. This gave some
    Terror to the Garrison of Oxon, his Maj*esty* being then therein,
    and great Talke there was that a Siege would suddenly follow.
    Mʳ AWoods mother therefore resolving that he and his brother
    Christopher should be removed out of harmes way she sent them
    with an horse and man into the Country: And because the Infection
    was then in Oxôn she order'd that they should be conveyed to
    Tetsworth, ten miles distant from Oxôn; where they continued for
    a fortnight or more in the House of Rich*ard* Sciense then called
    the Catherine Wheel, now a great new built Inn of Bricke (1683)

at the lower end of Towne. There I say they continued till it was
thought that they had no infection about them,[24] and then they
were conveyed two miles on one Side of Tetsworth, to a Merkate
Towne called Thame, and there they were set downe and conveyed   f. 5ᵛ
into the Vicaridge House neare to and on the north side of the
church, where they were very lovingly received by the Vicar Mʳ
Thom*as* Henant and his wife Elizabeth one of the Daughters of
Leonard Pettie Gent*leman*, kinsman to the mother of A*nthony* and
C*hristopher* Wood; in which house their three elder Brothers had
before sojourn'd while they went to the Free-school in Thame,
founded by John Lord Williams of Thame. Afterwards they were
entred into the said school, there to be educated till they were fit
to be Academians or Apprentices. The Master of that school was
William Burt Master of A*rts*, somtimes Fellow of New Coll*ege*, who
before had married Elizabeth, one of the Daughters of Maximilian
Pettie of Thame and Tetsworth, kinsman to their Mother. Which
Will*iam* Burt was afterwards Schoolmaster of Wykehams school
neare Winchester, Warden of the Coll*ege* there and Dʳ of Divinity.
The Usher of the said school was one David Thomas Bach*elor* of
Arts of Jesus Coll*ege* who before had married a Maid of ordinary
Note but handsome. Shee had several yeares lived in the parish
where A*nthony* and C*hristopher* Wood were borne, and her sirname,
I think was Price, having been brought up under her kinswoman or
Aunt called Joane Evans who kept a publick house now knowne by
the name of the Magpie, in the same parish.

The said D*avid* Thomas was afterwards the second Master of
the Free-school at Dorchester in Oxfordshire, founded by Joh*n*
Feteplace Esq*uire*, and at length Master of a well endow'd School at
Leycester, the chief Towne in Leycestershire, where he continued
till the time of his Death, in Aug. 1667, having before obtained a
comfortable Estate by the great paines he took in pedagogie and by
the many sojourners that he alwaies kept in his House.

It was observ'd by the Vicar Mʳ Henant while AWood sojourned
in his house that the said AWood was very sedulous, was alwaies
up and readie the first in the House, and alwaies ambitious of being

first in the school in the morning; and if any way hindred, he would be apt to cry and make a noise to the disturbance of the family, as Mr Henant hath several times told him when he was Master of Arts.

AWood did partly remember that he was much retired, walked mostly alone, was given much to thinking and melancholy; which somtimes made his nights rest so much disturb'd, that he would walk in his sleep (only with his shirt on) and disturb and fright people of the House when they were going to their respective Beds, two or 3 houres after he had taken up his rest. This also, besides his owne memorie, he hath been often told by his cozen Henant the wife, who lived at Great Milton neare Oxôn in the house of his cozen John Cave after her husbands death.

f. 6^r

On Sunday the 8 of Octob*er* hapned a dreadfull fire in Oxôn,[25] such an one (for the shortness of the time wherein it burned) that all Ages before could hardly paralel. It began about two of the clock in the afternoon in a little poore house on the south side of Thames street (leading from the north gate to High Bridg) occasion'd by a Foot-soldier's roasting a Pigg which he had stoln. The wind being verie high and in the north, blew the Flames southward very quick and strangly and burnt all Houses and Stables (except S. Maries Coll*ege*) standing between the back-part of those houses that extend from the north Gate to S. Martins church on the east, and those Houses in the north Baylie called New inn Lane on the west: then all the old Houses in the Bocherew (with the Bocherew it self) which stood between S. Martins church and the church of S. Peter in the Baylie; among which were two which belong'd to AWoods Mother, besides the Stables and back-houses belonging to the Flowr de Luce, which were totally consumed to her great Loss and so consequently to the Loss of her sons, as they afterwards evidently found it.

$$\text{Anno} \begin{cases} \text{Domini 1645} \\ \text{21 Caroli I} \end{cases}$$

While AWood and his brother Christopher continued at Thame, you cannot imagine what great Disturbances they suffer'd by the soldiers of both parties, somtimes by the Parliament soldiers of Aylesbury somtimes by the Kings from Borstall house and somtimes from the Kings at Oxôn and at Wallingford Castle. The f. 6ᵛ chiefest Disturbances and Affrightments that they and the family wherein they lived, endured, were these.

On the 27 of January being Munday, an*nus* 1644 Colonel Tho*mas* Blagge Governour of Wallingford Castle roving about the country very early with a Troop of stout Horsmen consisting of 70 or 80 at most, met with a partie of Parliamenteirs or Rebells of at least 200 at Long Crendon about a mile northward from Thame: which 200 belong'd to the Garrison of Aylesburie, and being headed by a Scot called Colonel Crafford, who, as I think, was Governour of the Garrison there, they pretended that they were looking out quarters for them. I say that Col*onel* Blagge and his partie meeting with these Rebells at Long Crendon, fought with, and made them run, till his men following them too eagerly were overpowr'd with multitudes that afterwards came in to their assistance; (almost treble his number) at which time he himself with his stout captaine —— Walter (they two only) fought against a great many of the Rebells for a long while together; in which encounter the brave colonel behaved himself as manfully with his sword, as ever man did, slashing and beating so many fresh Rebells with such Courage and Dexterity, that he would not stirr, till he had brought off all his owne men, whereof the Rebells kild but two, (not a man more) tho they took sixteen; who stayed too long behind. Captain Walter had six Rebells upon him, and according to his custome fought it out so gallantly, that he brought himself off with his Colonel and they came home safe to Wallingford with all their men except 18. Col*onel* Blagge was cut over the face, and had some other hurts but not dangerous.

After the Action was concluded at Crendon, and Blagge and his men forced to fly homeward, they took part of Thame in their way: And AW and his Fellow-Sojournours being all then at Dinner in the Parlour with some strangers there, of whome their Master Burt and his wife were of the number, they were all alarum'd with their f. 7ʳ

approach: and by that time they could run out of the House into
the Backside to look over the Pale that parts it from the common
Road, they saw a great number of Horsmen posting towards Thame
over Crendon Bridge, about a stones cast from their House (being
the out and only House on that Road before you come into Thame)
and in the head of them was Blagge with a bloody Face, and his
party with Captain Walters following him. The number as was
then guessed by AW and those of the family, was 50 or more, and
they all rode under the said pale and close by the House. They
did not ride in Order, but each made shift to be foremost; and one
of them riding upon a shelving ground opposite to the Dore, his
Horse slip'd, fell upon one side and threw the Rider (a lusty man)
in AWoods sight — Colonel Crafford, who was well hors'd and at
a pretty distance before his men in pursuite, held a pistol to him,
but the Trooper crying quarter, the Rebells came up, rifled him
and took him and his Horse away with them — Crafford rode on
without touching him, and ever or anon he would be discharging
his pistol at some of the Fag-end of Blaggs Horse, who rode thro
the west end of Thame, called Priest-end leading towards Ricot.

Whether Crafford and his men followed them beyond Thame,
I think not, but went into the Towne and refreshed themselves
and so went to Aylesbury. — I find one Laurence Crafford the
sixth son of Hugh Crafford (of the same family, which is noble,
of Kilbourne) to have been borne in his fathers Castle at Jordan
hill neare Gloscow in Scotland, on the Calends of November 1611,
and to have received some education in Glascow. Afterwards it
appeares that he went beyond the seas and served in the warrs for
eleven yeares under Gustavus and Christianus Kings of Sweedland,
in Germany, and afterwards for the space of three yeares he was
a Protobune of Horse[26] under Charles Lewis Elector Palatine. In
1641 he was sent into Ireland by the Parliament of England to fight   f. 7ᵛ
against the Rebells, where he served in the quality of a Tribune
for two yeares, and in 1643 he was sent for from thence by the
Parliament of England and made *Legatus secundus*, Major generall,
under Edward Montague Earl of Manchester, and afterwards in the

16

Scotch Expedition. At length when the Scots besieged Hereford, he
was kil'd with a Bullet shot from the works, on the 17 of Aug*ust* 1645
aged 34 yeares: whereupon his body being carried off to the city of
Glocester, it was buried there in the larg chappel at the east end of
the choire, called our Ladies chappel, within the Cathedral there,
and soon after had a very fair Monument set or fastned on the
north wall neare to his Grave, containing the proportion of a man
to the middle (or the Bust of a man) in white Marble, with a short
staff in his right hand. Which monument continuing in its luster
till after the restoration of K*ing* Ch*arles* 2, it was then ordered to
be plucked downe by the Bishop, Deane and prebends[27] — This
Laurence Crafford seems to be the same person with Colonel
Crafford before mention'd, who I think was Governour of Aylesbury
in Buck*inghamshire* for a time. As for Colonel Blagge,[28] who was
borne of an antient and gentile familie in Suffolke he suffered much
between the declension of the Kings cause and the restoration of
K*ing* Ch*arles* 2, by exile and several imprisonments; but after the
king was restored he was rewarded with the Governourship of
Yarmouth and other things in Norfolk; yet being just setled and
in capacity of spending the remainder of his Dayes in ease and
quietness, he died to the great grief of his family and relations
within the City of Westminster, on the 14 of Nov*ember* 1660 aged
47 yeares: whereupon his body was buried in the great North Isle
joyning to the church of S. Peter (commonly called the Abbey
church within the said citie).

    The next great Disturbance whereby AW and his Fellow
Sojournours were alarum'd at Thame, was this. In the latter
end of Apr*il* 1645 a famous Buckinghamshire commander called
Capt*ain* —— Phips the Rag-man was in Thame with 20 Horse
and Dragoons to guard their committee for the excise (the chief of
which committee were Goodman Heywood, and Goodman Hen
the Butcher his servant) and tarrying there two dayes or more, S[r]   f. 8[r]
Will*iam* Campion Governour of Borstall house having received
notice of them, sent out his Captaine Lievetenant called Capt*ain*
—— Bunce with a partie of 20 Horse; who instantly marching

thither over Crendon Bridg as it seems and so by the Vicaridge House, drove them thro the Towne of Thame. Whereupon Phips and his committee flying pretty fast till they came to the Bridg below Thame Mill (which is eastward and a little by north about a stones-cast from the Vicars house) they faced about hoping to make good the bridge with their Dragoons. But this valiant Captaine Bunce after he had received a volley from Phips and his partie (which touched only one common soldier slightlie) charged over the Bridg, and with his pistols shot one of them dead and beat them off the Bridge, so as they all ran away, but lost just half their number: for besides him that was killed, there were nine taken, whereof two were Capt. Phips himself and his Lievtenant, ten only escaping, most of which had marks bestowed on them.

Capt*ain* Bunce returned safe to Borstall with 9 prisoners, 10 Horses, six fire-lock Musquets and 4 case of Pistols. This is that Bunce who shot the pillaging Scot cal'd Major Jecamiah Abercromy (belonging I think to Aylesbury Garrison) neare Stretton-Audley in Oxfordshire; which entring deep into his side, fell from his Horse on the 7 of March 1644:[29] so that being carried off prisoner, with others, to Borstall House, died there soon after full of sorrow for his activity in the Rebellion against K*ing* Ch*arles* 1.

Another great Alarme to the juvenile muses in the Vicaridge house, particularly to AW, was this Colonel Rich*ard* Greaves a most confiding Presbyterian laying couchant for a considerable time in Thame with a great partie of Horse (upon what account I can not tell) in the beginnning of Sept*ember* 1645, it was known among the chief Officers in Oxôn: Whereupon Col*onel* Will*iam* Legge the Governour thereof resolving to beat up him and his partie, he sent 400 Horse from Oxôn commanded by Col*onel* David Walter (High-Sherriff of the countie) and Col*onel* Rob*ert* Legge the Governours Brother. These, with 60 Musquettiers of the Governours Regiment (commanded by Captaine —— Burgh) marched forth from Oxôn in the afternoon of Saturday Sept. 6, and before they came neare to Thame, they divided into two Bodies, the Van headed by Col*onel* Walter and the Reer by Col*onel*

f. 8ᵛ

18

R*obert* Legge. They found the Towne very strongly barricaded
at every Avenue: notwithstanding which, Major Scrope Medcalf
(Maj*or* to Coll*onel* Rob*ert* Legge) gallantly led up the forlorne
hope, charged the Rebells Guards, and maintained his ground so
handsomly, that Major Aglionby coming up to his assistance, the
Rebels were beat off the Guards, so as Maj*or* Medcalfe with 7
Troopers leapt from their Horses, and removing the Carts opened
the Avenue. This done, the two gallant Majors charged the Rebells
up thro the street, doing execution al the way to the Market-place,
where Col*onel* Greaves himself stood with about 200 Horse drawn
up; but Col*onel* Walter being ready with the other Troops (viz his
owne, that of Col*onel* Tooker and that of Major Trist) gave the
Rebels such a charg as made them fly out of the Towne; and after
pursuing the fugitive Rebels, drove them above half a mile from
Thame. In the meane while Coll*onel* Legge, who with the Reere
guarded the Towne and Avenews least other of the Rebells, (being
in all 800) should break in and defeat the whole, now drew into
the Towne, that others might have secure time to search Houses
and Stables: orders were given and 'twas done accordingly. After
which they all drew out of the Towne and marched away with
their Horses and Prisoners.

Before they had gone two miles, at least 200 Rebels were got
in their Reere, but then Col*onel* Legge charged them so gallantly,
that the Rebels ran back, much faster than they came on. Yet farr
had they not gone, before these vexed Rebels came on againe and
then also Col*onel* Legge beat them so farr back, that they never
attempted to come on againe. In this last charge that most hopeful
yong Gentleman Capt*ain* Hen*ry* Gardiner (son of Sr Tho*mas*
Gardiner his Majesties Sollicitor Gen*eral*) was unfortunately shot
dead; a youth of such high incomparable courage, mix'd with such   f. 9^r
abundance of modesty and sweetness, that wee cannot easily match
him, unless with his brave Brother, yong Sr Thomas Gardiner;
which two are now buried both in one grave in the Cathedral of
Christ church in Oxon; whither they were brought with much
universal sorrow and affection.

Besides this gallant Gentleman, no Officer was killed, only 3
common soldiers, nor scarce any hurt only Maj*or* Medcalfe shot
in the Arme. The Rebels dropt plentifully in the street and in
the Fields, and Colo*nel* Greaves escaped very narrowly, being
run into the Body, and at first thought to have been slaine. The
Rebells being thus beaten, his Majesties Forces brought away those
prisoners they had taken; which, besides common Troopers, were 27
Officers: among whome were their Adjutant-General —— Puide,[30]
their Provost-General Marshall (or Prov*ost* Marshall General)
and their chief Engineer, four Captaines as Capt*ain* Hanson, Joh*n*
Thornhill, *James* the elder &c. Seven Lievtenants, viz. Wilmot,
Hughes, Bagnall, Lampert, Canne, Wilson, Crompton, and three
Cornets Bradshaw, Brooks and Symons. There were also taken
13 Sergeants, quartermasters and Corporalls, and a great deal of
money was found in the Rebels Pockets: (having lately received
Advance-money). Many Armes also were taken and between two
and three hundred good Horse, besides three colours; two whereof
had Mottos. The one was *Non Reos Res* and the other was *Patria
poscente paratus.*[31]

This Alarm and Onset was made by the Cavaliers from Oxôn
about break of day on Sunday Morning Sept*ember* 7, before any of
the Rebels were stirring. But by the Alarm taken from the Sentinel
that stood at that end of the Towne leading to Oxôn, many of
them came out of their Beds into the Market place without their
Doublets; whereof Adj*utant* Gen*eral* Puide was one, who fought
in his shirt. Some that were quarter'd neare the Church, as in
Vincent Barry's house between it and the School, and in the Vicars
house (where AW then sojourn'd) fled into the church (some with
their Horses also) and going to the top of the Tower would be
peeping thence to see the cavaliers run into the Houses where they
quarter'd, to fetch away their Goods.

f. 9ᵛ

There were about 6 of the Parliament Soldiers (Troopers) that
quarter'd in the Vicars House, and one being slow and careless
was airing and warming his Boots, while they were fighting in the
Towne: and no sooner he was withdrawne, into the garden I think,

20

but some of the Cavaliers who were retiring with their spoyle
towards Borstall (for they had separated themselves from those
that went to Oxôn) ran into the Vicars House and seized on cloaks
and goods of the Rebels, while some of the said Rebels who had
lock'd themselves up in the church were beholding out of the church
windows what they were doing.

On the day before (Saturday) some of the said Rebels[32] that
lodg'd in the said House had been progging for Venison, in Thame
Park I think, and one or two pasties of it were made, and newly put
into the Oven before the Cavaliers entred into the House. But so it
was that none of the said Rebels were left at eleven of the clock to
eat the said pasties, so their share fell among the school-boyes that
were sojournours in the said House.

As for the beforemention'd Adjutant General Puid, he had leave
within 3 dayes after he was brought to Oxôn, to depart upon his
Parol; yet wanted the civility either to returne himself, or to release
the Gentleman, (or any other) that he had promised in exchange for
him. Such and no better is the Faith and Humanity of the Rebels.[33]

Besides these, were other Alarms and Skirmishes, which being
frequent and of little concern, yet much to the schoolboyes, who
were interrupted thereby, I shall forbeare the recital of them. They
had also several times Troopers from Borstal, who would watch
and be upon the Guard in the Vicaridge house (the out-house
northward from Thame as I have before told you) and continue
there a whole night together, while some of their partie were upon
London Road neare Thame to lay in wait for provision or wine   f. 10[r]
that came from London towards Aylesbury, or to any persons
thereabouts that took part with the Rebells. Some of these Troopers
would discourse with the school-boyes that lived in the House
(being of the number of six or somtimes more) while they were
making their Exercise in the Hall against the next day. Some of
them, AW found to have Grammar learning in them, as by the
questions they proposed to the Boys: and others having been, or
lived in Oxôn knew the Relations of AW, which would make them
shew Kindness to him and his Brother. But that which AW observ'd,

was, that the Vicar and his wife were alwaies more kind to the
Parl*iament* Soldiers or Rebells, than to the Cavaliers, as his Master
W*illiam* Burt and his wife were, having been alwaies acquainted
with and obliged to the families of the Ingoldesbies and Hamdens
in Buckinghamshire and other Puritanical and factious Families
in the said countie; who, while yong had been mostly bred in the
said school of Thame, and had sojourned either with the Vicar
or Master: But as for the Usher Dav*id* Thomas, a proper stout
Welshman, AW alwaies took him to be a good Loyallist, as indeed
he was.

$$\text{Anno} \left\{ \begin{array}{l} \text{Domini 1646} \\ \text{22 Caroli I} \end{array} \right.$$

Wednesday Jun*e* 10, the Garrison of Borstall was surrendred for the use
of the Parliament. The schoolboys were allowed by their Master
a free libertie that Day and many of them went thither (4 miles
distant) about 8 or 9 of the clock in the morning to see the forme
of surrender, the strength of the Garrison and the soldiers of each
partie. They, and particularly AW, had instructions given to them
before they went, that not one of them should either tast any liquor,
or eat any provision in the Garrison; and the reason was, for feare
the royal partie, who were to march out thence should mix poyson
among the liquor or provision that they should leave there. But as
AW remembred he could not get into the garrison, but stood as
hundreds did without the works, where he saw the Governour S^r
Will*iam* Campion, a little man, who upon some occasion laid flat
on the ground on his belly to write a letter, or Bill, or the form of a
Pass, or some such thing.

24 June. Wednesday and Midsomer day, the Garrison of Oxon, which was
the chiefest Hold the King had, and wherein he had mostly resided
while the civil warr continued, was surrendred for the use of the
Parliament, as most of his Garrisons were this yeare, occasion'd
by the fatal Battle of Naesby, which hapned in the last yeare,
wherein the King and his partie were in a woful manner worsted.

In the evening of the said Day, many of the Kings Foot-partie
that belonged to the said Garrison came into Thame, and layd
downe their Armes there, being then a wet season. Some of whome
continuing there the next day, AW went into the Towne to see
them. He knew some of their Faces and they his, but he being a
Boy and having no money, he could not then relieve them or make
them drink: yet he talked with them about Oxford and his Relations
and acquaintance there; for the doing of which he was check'd when
he came home.

    In the latter end of Aug*ust* or beginning of Sept*ember* following
his brother Edw*ard* Wood Bach*elor* of Arts and Scholar of Trinity
Coll*ege*, came on Foot from Oxôn with Leonard Pettie the brother
of the wife of his cozen Henant the Vicar, and another scholar
to see him and his Brother, the Vicar and the Master, and their
wives. They continued at least two Nights in the Vicars house
and great kindness was expressed by them towards AW and his
brother Christop*her* whom, the next day, the said Edward told,
that they were soon after to return to Oxôn, that their mother had
much suffer'd in her estate by the late dreadful Fire in Oxôn and
therefore was not able to maintaine them any longer at school in
Thame &c. AW seemed very sorry at this News, because he was
well and warme where he was, had good companie, and seem'd
to have a fix'd love for the place, even so much that he did never
afterwards care to hear of New Coll*ege* School to have given him
scholastical education; but applied all he had to that of Thame &c.[34]
But there was no Remedy for go he must, and go he did with his   f. 11[r]
Brother after Michaelmas following on a horse or horses that were
sent for them.

    After his returne to the house of his Nativity, he found
Oxford empty, as to scholars, but pretty well replenish'd with
Parliamentarian Soldiers. Many of the Inhabitants had gained great
store of wealth from the Court and Royallists that had for several
yeares continued among them, but as for the yong men of the City
and University he found many of them to have been debauch'd
by bearing Armes and doing the Duties belonging to Soldiers, as

watching, warding, and sitting in Tipling-Houses for whole Nights
together. His mother put his Brother Christopher to School in Oxon
and himself to the Tuition of his brother Edward of Trinity college,
to whom he went once or twice in a day to receive instruction,
and alwaies spent every afternoon in his chamber, which was a
cockleloft over the common gate of that college.

While he continued in this condition, his Mother would alwaies
be soliciting him to be an Apprentice, which he could never endure
to heare of: And somtimes she would tell him that she would set
him out to an Attorney or Sollicitor, and he remembred well that
she often mention'd Mr John Theyer a Sollicitor (of whom shall
be mention made under the yeare 1668) as a fit master for him, but
still he drew back and turn'd his eare. Nay she was so silly that
she would several times propose to him some inferior mechanical
Trade,[35] because she found him to have a mechanical head, and
alwaies at leisure times very active in framing little trivial things or
Baubles.

Anno { Domini 1647
{ 23 Caroli I

26 May. Wed. AWood was matriculated as a Member of the University and
a gentlemans son — [36] This was done by his brother Edward, who
obtained a certificate that he was matriculated, from Matthew Cross
the superior Beadle of Law, which he kept by him to the time of
his death[37] — But afterwards when he was Masters of Arts and had
a full sight of the matriculation Books he could not find his name
regestred in any of them.

18 Oct. St Lukes day and Munday he was entred into the Buttery-Book of   f. 11^v
Merton college, being about that time made by Mr Edward Copley
Fellow of that House, his postmaster,[38] and put into the chamber
under him in the great quadrangle. He had not then any Tutor in
that College, but continued still under the Instruction of his Brother
Edward in Trinity College.

At that time Christmas appearing, there were Fires of charcole made in the common hall on Allsaints Eve, Allsaints day and night, on the Holydayes, their nights and eves between that time and Christmas day. Then on Christmas eve, Christm*as* day and holy dayes and their nights and on Candlemas eve, Candlemas day and night.

At all these Fires every night, which began to be made a little after five of the clock, the senior Under-Graduats would bring into the hall the Juniors or Freshmen between that time and six of the clock, and there make them sit downe on a Forme in the middle of the Hall, joyning to the Declaiming-Desk: which done, every one in order was to speake some pretty Apothegme, or make a Jest or Bull, or speake some eloquent Nonsense, to make the company Laugh: But if any of the Freshmen came off dull, or not cleverley, some of the forward or pragmatical Seniors would Tuck them, that is set the nail of their Thumb to their chin, just under the lower Lipp, and by the help of their other Fingers under the Chin, they would give him a mark, which somtimes would produce Blood. On Candlemas day,[39] or before (according as Shrovetuesday fell out) every Freshman had warning given him to provide his speech to be spoken in the publick Hall before the Under-Graduats and servants on Shrove-Tuesday night that followed, being alwaies the time for the observation of that ceremony. According to the said summons AWood provided a Speech as the other Freshmen did.

1647/8. Shrove-Tuesday: Feb*ruary* 15, the Fire being made in the common hall before 5 of the clock at night the Fellowes would go to supper before six, and making an end sooner than at other times, they left the Hall to the libertie of the Undergraduats, but with an Admonition from one of the Fellowes (who was then Principal of the Undergraduats and Postmasters) that all things should be carried in good Order. While they were at supper in the Hall, the Cook (Will Noble) was making the lesser of the brass Pots ful of Cawdel[40] at the Freshmans charge; which, after the Hall was free from the Fellowes, was brought up and set before the Fire in the

f. 12^r

said Hall. Afterwards every Freshman according to seniority was
to pluck off his Gowne and Band, and if possibly to make himself
look like a scoundrell — This done they were conducted each after
the other to the high Table and there made to stand on a Forme
placed thereon; from whence they were to speak their speech with
an audible Voice to the company: which, if well done, the person
that spoke it was to have a cup of cawdle and no salted Drinke;
if indifferently, some Cawdle and some salted Drink, but if dull
nothing was given to him but salted Drink, or salt put in college
Beere, with Tucks to boot. Afterwards when they were to be
admitted into the Fraternity, the senior Cook was to administer to
them an Oath over an old shoe, part of which runs thus — Item tu
jurabis quod penniless bench not visitabis &c (Penniless bench is a
seat joyning to St Martins church apud quadrivium, where Butter
women and Hucksters use to sit.)[41] the rest is forgotten and none
there are that now remembers it. After which was spoken with
gravity, the Freshman kist the shoe, put on his gowne and band and
took his place among the Seniors.

Now for a diversion and to make you Laugh at the Folly and
simplicity of those times, I shall entertaine you with part of a
speech which AWood spoke while he stood on the Forme placed on
the Table, with his gowne and band off and uncovered.

Most reverend Seniors[42]
"May it please your Gravities to admit into your presence a
kitten of the Muses, and a meer Frog of Helicon to croak the
cataracts of his plumbeous cerebrosity before your sagacious
ingenuities. Perhaps you may expect that I should thunder out
Demicannon words, and level my sulphurious Throat against my
Fellowes of the Tyrocinian Crew, but this being the universal
judgment of wee fresh water Academians, behold as so many
Stygian Furies, or ghosts risen out of their winding sheets wee
present our selves before your Tribunal, and therefore I will not
fulminate nor tonitruate[43] words nor swell into Gigantick Streins:
such towring ebullitions do not exuberate in my Aganippe, being

f. 12^v

at the lowest ebb. I have been no chairman in the committee of Apollo's creatures, neither was I ever admitted into the cabinet councils of the Pyerian Dames, that my Braines should evaporate with high Hyperboles, or that I should bastinado the Times with a tart Satyr of a Magic Pen. Indeed I am but a fresh water soldier under the banners of Phœbus, and therefore cannot as yet set quart-pots or double Juggs in Battalia, or make a good shot in sack and claret, or give Fire to the pistoletto Tobacco Pipe, charg'd with its Indian powder; and therefore having but poor skill in such service, I were about to turne Heliconian Dragooner, but as I were mounting my dapper Nagg, Pegasus, behold Shrovetuesday night arrested me, greeting me in the name of this honorable Convocation to appeare before their Tribunal and make answer for my self, which most wise Seniors shall be in this wise.

I am none of those May-pole-Freshmen that are tall Cedars before they come to be planted in the Academian Garden, who are fed with the papp of Aristotle at twenty or thirtie yeares of age, and suck at the Duggs of their Mother, the University, tho they be huge[44] Colossus's and youths rampant.

These are they who come newly from a country Bagg-pudding and a good brown Loaf to deal with a Penny-commons, as an Elephant with a poor Fly, tumbles it and tosses it, and at last gives him a chop. These are the Mertonian counterscullers that tug as hard for postmasters place, as a Dog at Mutton —

I am none of the University Blood-Hounds that seek for preferment, and whose noses are as acute as their eares, that lye perdue for places, and who good saints[45] do groan till the Visitation comes — These are they that esteem a Tavern, as bad as Purgatory, and wine more superstitious than holy water: and therefore I hope this honorable convocation will not suffer one of that Tribe to tast of the sack, least they should be troubled with a vertigo and their heads turne *round* —

f. 13[r]

I[46] never came out of the country of Lapland — I am not of the number of Beasts — I meane those Greedie Doggs and

Kitchin-Haunters, who noint their chops every night with greese
and rob the cook of his Fees &c."

Thus he went forward with smart Reflections on the rest of the
Freshmen and some of the servants which might have been here
set downe, had not the speech been borrowed of him by several of
the Seniors who imbezeld it — After he had concluded his speech
he was taken downe by Edm*und* Dickenson one of the Bachelaur-
commoners of the House; who with other Bachelaurs and the
Senior Under-Graduats made him drink a good Dish of Cawdle,
put on his gowne and band, placed him among the seniors and gave
him Sack.

This was the way and custome that had been used in the college
time out of mind, to initiate the Freshmen; but between that time
and the restoration of K*ing* C*harles* 2 it was disused, and now such a
thing is absolutely forgotten.

Anno $\left\{ \begin{array}{l} \text{Domini } 1648 \\ 24 \text{ Caroli I} \end{array} \right.$

The Visitors appointed by Parliament having sate several times in
the Lodgings of S*r* Nath*aniel* Brent Warden of Merton Coll*ege* in
the last yeare, but to little purpose, they proceeded this yeare with
very great rigour, to the ruin of the Universitie. The members of
every coll*ege* were all summoned to appeare on a certaine day, and
somtimes two or 3 colleges or more appeared in one day, and if
they did not give in a positive answer whether they would submit
to them and their Visitation, as appointed by Parliament, they were
forthwith ejected.

Friday (May 12) The members of Merton College appear'd, and when
AW was called in (for the members were called in one by one, he
was ask'd this question by one of the Visitors — *Will you submit to
the authority of Parliament in this Visitation?* to which he gave this
answer, and wrot it downe on a paper lying on the Table as he was

f. 13*v*

28

directed — *I do not understand the business, and therefore I am not able to give a direct Answer.*[47]

Afterwards his Mother and Brother Edward, who advised him to submit in plaine Termes, were exceeding angry with him and told him that he had ruined himself and must therefore go a begging. At length by the intercession of his Mother made to Sr Nathan*iel* Brent (who usually cal'd her his little Daughter, for he knew her and us'd to set her on his knee when shee was a Girle and a Sojournour in her husbands house during the time of his first wife) he was conniv'd at and kept in his place, otherwise he had infallibly gon to the Pot.

Aug.

His eldest Brother Tho*mas* Wood, who had served in the quality of Lievtenant of Horse for his Majestie during the warr, did, after the warr was terminated, returne to his Coll*ege* of Ch*rist* ch*urch* and there received the profits of his place; but about the beginning of Aug*ust* this yeare, he very abruptly left the Universitie, went into Ireland, and finding out his School-Fellow Colonel Hen*ry* Ingoldesby became an Officer in his Regiment to fight against the Rebells there. The reason of his sudden Departure was this: viz. that he being one of the Prime Plotters of the remaining Cavaliers in Oxôn, to seize on the Garrison, Visitors, and all the Arms they could find, to the end that they might joyne themselves to others that had plotted in the same manner in other Parliament Garrisons, to relieve the distressed Cavaliers that were besieg'd in Colchester, the Plot was discovered by one or more of them when they were in their cups; which made every one shift for themselves as well as they could, but some being taken, one of them named Edward Adams a Barber was upon the point of being hang'd, having mounted the ladder in order thereunto on the signe post of the Catherine Wheel in Magdalen Parish (in which Inn they had layd the Foundation of their Plot. Mr Francis Croft, whome AW found to be one of the chaplaynes of Merton Coll*ege* at his first comming thereunto, was deeply engaged in the said Plot. He was a high-flone Cavalier and a boon companion, and was the man that gave to

f. 14^r

every person that was concern'd in the Plot the Oath of Secrecy:
which being done they were to write theire names in his little
paper-book which he usually carried in his pocket; but if they could
not write they were to set their mark, and he to add their names to
it. At the first discovery of the plot Mr Croft fled, and some of the
Parliament soldiers of the garrison supposing that he might be in
his chamber, which joyned to that chamber, which was afterwards
the common Room belonging to Merton Coll*ege*, they broke open
his Dore, searched but found the Bird flown. This being done early
in the morning, his Dore stood open most of the day following,
and AW with some of the Juniors going into it, saw it all adorn'd
with Escocheons, which he (Mr Croft) had got by burying several
persons of Quality in Merton Coll*ege* Church and elswhere during
the abode of the Kings and Queens courts in Oxon, but these, his
Books and bedding were not then touched.

6 Nov. Mon. Edward Wood before mentiond, Bach*elor* of Arts and scholar
of Trin*ity* Coll*ege* (who before had submitted to the Visitors)
was with others admitted Probationer-Fellow of Merton Coll*ege*.
— They were severely examin'd and in due course elected and
admitted: which was done by the favour of the Warden S^r N*athaniel*
Brent the Arch-Visitor, yet all that were then admitted, submitted
to the Visitors. Some Admissions of Fellowes that followed were
done by the sole Authority of the committee and Visitors. Soon
after E*dward* Wood being setled in the Bay-Tree chamber in the
first quadrangle next to the Gate of Merton Coll*ege*, AW was put
into the Cockloft over him. So then and after his trudging to
Trin*ity* Coll*ege* to receive his instruction was sav'd.

$$\text{Anno} \begin{cases} \text{Domini } 1649 \\ \text{1 Caroli II} \end{cases}$$

AWood's mother (Mary Wood) being much out of purse in
reedyfying the stables and out-Houses of the Flowr de Luce, and
in repairing the Inn it self, she gave off House-keeping and taking
her son Christopher and a Maid with her, went to Cassington

neare Woodstok and sojourned in a fair stone-house then inhabited
by one John Tipping lately sequestred from the Vicaridg of
Shabbington in Buck*ingh*amshire, neare to Thame, who had married
an Oxford Gentlewoman the dau*ghter* of one Willi*am* Dewey who
had been acquainted with M^{ris} Wood from her childhood. In the
same House did then sojourn Mr Joh*n* Lucas lately senior Fellow of
New College, and Mr Rich*ard* Sherlock lately chaplain of the said
college, but now (1649) curat of Cassington. AWood did often retire
thither to see his Mother and somtimes lodge there for a night
or two. Mr Sherlock was civil to him and would give him good
instruction and talk fatherly to him. Mr John Goad was then Vicar
of Yarnton, a mile distant from Cassington; (to whom Christo*pher*
Wood went dayly to School) and being a suffering Cavalier did go
often to the said Mr Tippings house to visit his brother-sufferers.

   This person AW did often see there and received Instruction
from him in many particulars and found him an exceeding loving
and tender man. AW did not then in the least think to write
the Lives of the said Rich*ard* Sherlock and the said Jo*hn* Goad,
as afterwards he did, or to live to see them well promoted, and
become eminent Authors. But so it was that length of time and
sufferings made them forget such a little thing as AW was, and
much adoe he had to make Dr Sherlock know and understand him,
when 20 yeares after this time he sent to him Letters to Winwick
in Lancashire (one of the fattest Parsonages in England) to let him
have an Account of himself, to be put in *Hist. et Antiq. Universit.
Oxon*^{(a):48} At which time finding him shie in answering his Letters,
he was forced at Length, when he saw where the Fault lay, to tell
him that he was the son of that little woman (M^{ris} Wood) that
somtimes sojourn'd with him in the same House at Cassington,
wherin he also had sojourn'd; and then he was very free with AW
and answer'd his Letters.

   In like manner also when AW was consulting 30 yeares
after this time the *Athenæ et Fasti Oxon*, he sent to Mr Goad at
Merchant Taylors School in London for some account of himself
and writings, and found him very shie, but giving him the like

Answer that he gave to Dr Sherlock, he was very free afterwards
in his communications, and received from him ful[(b)49] satisfaction,
expressing himself, as Sherlock before did, verie joyfull, and
congratulated themselves that they should live, to see such a little
Junior that they had knowne him to be, to become an Author
and a publisher of several folio's for the good and benefit of the
commonwealth of Learning.

Mr Anthony Hodges Rector of Wytham in Berks (a mile distant
from Cassington) would often come among these Royallists at M^r
Tippings House and there make them Merry — [50] He was a very
good scholar and fit in many respects to oblige posterity by his Pen,
but delighting himself in Mirth, and in that which was afterwards
called Buffooning and Bantering, could never be brought to set pen
to paper for that purpose. He was the Mirth of the Company and
they esteem'd him their *Terræ filius*.[51]

1649.   Dec. John Blanks a hansome yong man and contemporarie with AW
in Mer*ton* Coll*ege* being sent for home to keep his christmas, AW
went with him to the House of his Father James Blanks Gent*leman*
Impropriator of Bledlow in Buck*inghamshire*, neare to Thame in
Oxfordshire, where he continued more than a weeke. The church
there stands upon a rising ground, and at the end of the chancel, is
a larg deep place, having on its sides Bushes and Brambles growing.
At the bottome of this deep place issues out one or more springs
and gives the original to a little River. Between the end of the
chancel and the brink or edg of this deep place is contain'd as much
ground as the space of six paces of a man. AW then heard several of
the Inhabitants repeat two old verses that had gon from man to man
these many yeares, which run thus

He that lives and stil abide
Will see the chancel fal in the Lyde.

This deep place is with them cal'd the Lyde, and the ground
between the Brink of it and the end of the Chancel doth sensibly
weare away, so that if some care in time be not taken, the proverbial
verses may prove true.[52]

In the church here were some Armes in the Windowes, and
an inscription or two on grave stones, of which AW toke notice
according to his then capacity, but afterwards obtained a better
method of taking them. These things are here set downe; because
they were the first matters of that nature that AW took notice of —

1649/50. Jan. In the latter end of January he sent a generous Requital to Mʳ
James Blanks for the great civilities he shew'd unto him during his
being in his house last Christmas.

1649/50. 16 Feb. Sat. His brother Edward who was his Tutor, thinking it
fit that he should chang him for another, he was put under the
Tuition of Clinton Maund an Irish man borne of English Parents,
as being descended from the Maunds of Chesterton neare Bister
in Oxfordshire. He was a Bach*elor* Fellow, well growne in yeares,
but a grand Presbyterian, alwaies praying in his chamber, and
when Master of Arts preaching abroad — AWoods brother was
pevish and would be ever and anon angry if he could not take or
understand Logical Notions as well as he. He would be somtimes
so angry that he would beat him and turne him out of his chamber;
of which, complaining to his Mother, she was therefore willing that
Anthony should take another Tutor.

$$\text{Anno} \begin{cases} \text{Domini } 1650 \\ \text{2 Caroli II} \end{cases}$$

In the beginning of this yeare AW was made one of the Bible
Clerks by the Favour of Sʳ Nath*aniel* Brent the warden, for these
reasons (1) Because the Visitors cal'd into question the right of the
Fellows of the said Coll*ege* their bestowing of the postmasters places
(2) Because a Clerks place was better than that of a postmaster,
tho since not, because that Benefactions have been after this time
bestowed to make the postmasters places better. There was then
no duty in the chappel for the clerks, because the common prayer
and sacraments in the chap*el* were put downe, and but very little
Attendance there was for them in the Hall.⁵³

5 Apr. Fri. He answer'd Generals in the public schools, and James Bricknell his chamberfellow and clerk of Merton Coll*ege* opposed him.[54]

22 Apr. Mon. He left the cockleloft over his Brothers Chamber in the first Quadrangle and removed to the Chamber in the little or old Quadrangle, opposite to the Exchequer Chamber, which was appointed for the Clerks.

Aug.   In the latter end of Aug: several Juniors of Mert*on* Coll*ege* as   f. 16ʳ
Joh*n* Blanks, Brian Ambler, AWood &c. got horses and rode to Wallingford in Berks*hire* purposely to see the castle there, being then about to be demolished. They were in number about eight, and when they came to desire the Guards to let them come into the Castle, they refused to doe it, for no other reason as the scholars supposed, but that their number was too great and may have some Designe upon them. Col. Arth*ur* Evelin, was then, as it seems the Governour, but was not at home, otherwise, as 'tis believed they might have had entrance. So going back to the Towne of Wallingford, they dined there and return'd to Oxôn.

14 Dec. Sat. One Anne Green a servant Maid, was hang'd in the Castle of Oxôn, for murdering her Bastard=child, begotten by Jeffry Reade Grand-son to Sʳ Tho*mas* Read of Duns-Tew in Oxfordshire. After she had suffer'd the Law, she was cut downe, and carried away in order to be anatomiz'd by some yong Physitians, but they finding life in her, would not venter upon her, only so farr, as to recover her to life. Which being look'd upon as a great wonder, there was a Relation of her Recovery printed, and at the end several Copies of Verses made by the yong Poets of the Universitie were added. See more in the next yeare.[55]

1650/1. 16 Jan. Thur. Twelve Postmasters of Merton Coll*ege* were expel'd by the Visitors, viz. Joh*n* Blanks, John Wright, Brian Ambler, Rich*ard* Philipps &c. Some of which, who were *godly youths*, as Georg Pricket, Steph*en* Richmond, Willi*am* Stane &c. they afterwards restored to, and confirmed them in their places. So that had

AW continued Postmaster a little longer, he had without doubt received his quietus. As for John Blanks, he afterwards retired to his Fathers House and became an Attorney: John Wright after the Kings restoration became Master of the Kings School at Worcester; Brian Ambler a minister in Shropshire, and Richard Philips upon a second Answer given in to the Visitors, was kept in, and after he had taken a Degree in Arts, he became a mortified and pious Minister in Shropshire &c.

1650/1. 22 Jan. Wed. Edward Wood Fellow of Merton College was for f. 16ᵛ
divers pretended miscarriages and misdeameanors suspended by the Visitors from his commons and all profits from his place, as also from being Tutor in that College untill farther Order.⁵⁶ The miscarriages were first for entertaining strangers at his chamber with more wine than 'twas thought convenient (2) For drinking the Kings Health at Medley neare Oxôn, two yeares before, with some of his contemporaries of Trinity Coll &c. — which suspension was occasion'd by the uncharitable Information made to the Visitors by Thomas Franke a junior Fellow of Merton College who now did lay in wait, as 'twere to bring the said College into distraction and trouble.

This Thomas Franke, after all his obsequious Flatteries, fals Tales, cringing to the Presbyterians and Independents, and his being actually in Armes in the Troop raised by the University of Oxôn against King Charles. 2 at Worcester, anno 1651, had the impudence after the restoration of the said King to turn about, and for his money to get the Rectory of Cranfield in Derbyshire;⁵⁷ whilst others that had been great sufferers for his Majesties cause and had no money were forced to shark and live as Opportunity served. He was a most vile person and not fit to live in a society; yet, if I am not mistaken, he did, when he used to retire to the college, after he had been setled at Cranfield, express some repentance of what he had done to the injury of several of the Society before Mʳ Peter Nicolls and John Powell Senior, Fellowes of the said College.

This yeare Jacob a Jew opened a Coffey house at the Angel in
the parish of S. Peter in the East, Oxôn, and there it was by some,
who delighted in Noveltie, drank — When he left Oxon he sold it
in Old Southampton buildings in Holborne neare London, and was
living there 1671 — See in 1654.[58]

Anno { Domini 1651
{ 3 Caroli II

7 Apr.   Mon. A fine of thirtie pound[59] was set by the Warden and Fellowes
of Merton Coll*ege* for M^ris Wood (mother to AW) to pay, by way of
renewing, for the housing and gardens against Merton Coll*ege* and
for the Flour de Luce and its appurtenances in S. Martins Parish;
which was soon after paid.

About the same time the second Impression of the Pamphlet   f. 17^r
concerning Ann Green, with the verses at the end, was published
with its old Title viz *Newes from the Dead: or a true and exact
Narration of the Miraculous Deliverance of Ann Green* &c. At the end
of this Impression are several copies of verses added, which were
not in the first Impression, among which is one printed under the
name of AWood, beginning thus

I'le stretch my Muse but that a verse
I'le hang upon thy living Hearse.
Chime in yee wits and rhyme a knell
For Death her self is lately fell &c.[60]

Dec.   Thom*as* Wood eldest brother to AW died of the Flux at Drogheda
commonly called Tredagh in the month of Decembe*r*[61] — He was
borne at Tetsworth neare to Thame in Oxfordshire, where his
Father then had a Farme, on the 24 May 1624, educated mostly
in the Free school at Thame under his kinsman Mr *William* Burt,
was made student of Ch*rist* Church in 1638 as I have before told
you, and afterwards was the first, or one of the first yong scholars
in Oxon that threw off his gowne and ran to Edghill Battle — see
more under the yeare 1642. At his returne thence he was actually

created Bach*elor* of Arts among soldiers that had done service at the
said Battle:[62] and then his Father seeing that he could not persuade
him from being a soldier, he bought a Horse, Armes, cloaths &c. set
him up for a Trooper, and got him a place to ride in the Troop of
Captaine Thomas Gardiner of Cudesdon neare Oxon. Afterwards
he became a stout and desperat soldier, was in several Battles, and
besieged in divers Garrisons, particularly, if I am not mistaken, at
Basing in Hampshire, and was made a Lievtenant of Horse. When
the warr was terminated, and the Kings cause utterlie vanquish'd,
he return'd to his College, was actually created Master of Arts,
an*no* 1647,[63] but in the next yeare being deeply engaged in the
Cavaliering Plot, as I have told you under that yeare, (1648) he to
avoid being taken and hanged for it, fled into Ireland, where finding
out his quondam School-Fellow at Thame called Col*onel* Hen*ry*
Ingoldesbie, he became a Lievtenant in his Regiment, afterwards a
Captaine, and, as I have heard, had a commission a little before his   f. 17^v
Death, to be a Major. About a yeare before that time, viz. in 1650 he
returned for a time to Oxon to take up his Arrears at <u>Ch</u>*rist Church,*
and to settle his other Affaires; at which time being often with
his Mother and Brethren, he would tell them of the most terrible
assaulting and storming of Tredagh, wherein he himself had been
engaged. He told them that at least 3000, besides some women and
children, were, after the Assaliants had taken part, and afterwards
all the Towne, put to the sword on the 11. and 12. of Sept*ember* 1649;
at which time Sr Arth*ur* Aston the Governour had his Braines
beat out, and his body hack'd to pieces. He told them that when
they were to make their way up to the Lofts and Galleries in the
church, and up to the Tower where the enimy had fled, each of the
Assaliants would take up a child, to use as a Buckler of Defence
when they ascended the steps to keep themselves from being shot
or brain'd.

   After they had kil'd all in the church, they went into the Vaults
underneath, where all the flower and choicest of the women and
ladies had hid themselves. One of these a most hansome Virgin,
arraid in costly and gorgeous Apparel kneel'd downe to Tho*mas*

Wood with Teares and Prayers to save her Life: And being strucken
with a Profound Pitie, took her under his Arme, went with her out
of the church, with intentions to put her over the Works and to let
her shift for her self; but then a soldier perceiving his Intentions,
he ran his sword up her belly or Fundament. Whereupon Mr Wood
seeing her gasping, took away her money, Jewells &c. and flung her
downe over the works &c.

In the latter end of 1680 when the Parliament sate at Oxôn
AWood was walking with Sr Hen*ry* St Georg Clarentius King of
Armes in the school-quadrangle — Sr Hen*ry* then meeting with
Coll*onel* Hen*ry* Ingoldesbie before mention'd, telling him who AW
was, AW thereupon did discourse with him concerning his Brother
Thomas: and among several Things that the Colonel told him was
that Thomas was a good soldier, stout and ventrous, and having an
Art of Merriment called Buffooning, his company was desired and
loved by the Officers of his Regiment. He told him then he buried
him in a church at Tredagh answerable to his quality, but could not
tell him when he died — This Tho*mas* Wood was a tall, proper,
and robust man, like his Father, but black and swarthy, unlike in
that to any of his Brethren, or Father.

This yeare AW began to exercise his natural and insatiable   f. 18^r
genie he had to musick — He exercised his Hand on the Violin
and having a good eare to take any tune at first hearing, he could
quickly draw it out from the violin, but not with the same tuning
of strings that others used. He wanted understanding Friends and
money to pick him out a good master, otherwise he might have
equald in that Instrument and in singing any person then in the
Universitie. He had some companions that were musical, but they
wanted instruction as well as he.

Anno $\left\{ \begin{array}{l} \text{Domini 1652} \\ \text{4 Caroli II} \end{array} \right.$

Friday July 2 AWood was examin'd for the Degree of Bac*helor* of Arts
in the Natural Philosophy School, by Will*iam* Browne M.A of

Magd*alen* Coll*ege* a Native of Oxôn. He had before answer'd twice
under a Bachelaur among the crowd in the Divinity School, and
once if not both the times, under Matth*ew* Bee a Determining
Bachelaur of Universitie Coll*ege* in the Lent-time 1650/1: which
M*atthew* Bee was afterwards minister of Windlebury neare Bister
in Oxfordshire: And on the 6 of the same month he was adm*itted*
Bach*elor* of Arts.

26 July. Munday, and Shabington Wake as it seems, he rode in the company
of a Mimick and Buffoon called Tho*mas* Williams; and the horse
of AW being bad, or else that he was no good Rider he had a fall
and put out his —— Arme[64] When he came to Shabbington he put
off his Doublet and found his Arme swel'd and exceeding tender.
Th*omas* Williams who had been bred an Apothecary, would needs
persuade him that his Arme was not out of Joynt, only bruised, and
so applyed a cloath and oyle to it; yet notwithstanding this he could
not use it, which caus'd all his mirth to be turn'd into Melancholy.
In this condition he continued about a week there, rode to Thame,
eat and drank, but with little comfort or rest, and at length came
home in a most afflicted condition.

10 Aug. Tues. After he had been at home some dayes he was advised to go
to —— Adams a Lock-smith living in Catstreet who was an expert
Bone-setter, to the end that he might look upon it, and see what
was to be done. He spoke mildly to AW when he look'd on his
Arme, gave him sweet words and told him all was well. At length
casting AW's head aside Adams fastned one of his hands above and
the other below the Elbow, pluck'd the Arme straight and set it. But
the paine being great and unexpected (because that the veines and
arteries had been shrunk) he fell into a great sown, and could see
nothing but green before his eyes. Adams then laid him upon the
Bed, gave him cordials and put him to sleep. Afterwards he found
himself at ease, and better every day, but never before that time or
since, knew what sowning was or is.

    Thomas Williams before mention'd had an Estate of Land,
Houses and Money left to him by his Father, but never would

f. 18ᵛ

Follow his Trade, onlie live a loos life and took all advantages to
do it *gratis*. Afterwards when AW came to understand the world
better, he found him a Debaucher of Youth, and not fit to live in an
Universitie among Gentlemen. His usual way was, that after he had
let out money to any man, he would hang upon him, eat and drink
in his House: And if he could meet with any of his acquaintance,
whose nature was easie, he would take him with him to eat, drink
and lodg on the Debter: and to this Farmer of Shabington to whome
he had lent money, did he go to hang upon him, and take AW with
him, as he afterwards understood.

In the latter end of Aug*ust* or beginning of Septemb*er* AW went
to angle with Will*iam* Stane of Mert*on* Coll*ege* to Wheatley Bridge
and nutted in Shotover by the way. The day was hot and AW
sitting and standing some houres in Fishing he got an Ague, came
home faint and dry, with the loss of an Appetite of eating. It prov'd
a quartan Ague, and an houre or two before it came on him he
would be exceeding prone to vomit, and what in the Well-Days his
stomach had contracted, he would on the sick-day vomit it out with
great wretching and payne. This brought his Body low, but made
him grow much taller: and much physick and slops being taken in
the winter following, yet he could find no remedy. At length he was
advised to retire into the country to take better Ayre than in Oxôn,
follow the plow, and use what exercise he could there to shake the
Ague off.

1652/3. Tuesday (Feb. 15) AW went to Cassington before mention'd, and
because Mr Tipping and his wife had quitted their Quarters in that
Towne, he took up his Quarters at the next dore, in the house of an   f. 19^r
honest and sufficient Farmer called Francis Bolter; whose house tho
thatched, yet AW had a very fair Chamber therein with a chimney
and a place to lay his books in.

21 Feb. AW had a very sad Dreame in his sleep. He was in a melancholy
place, had no companion &c.

His body was much out of Order, and on those nights, wherein
he had his hot Fit (for his cold fit would come with extreame

vomiting about 5. or 6 at night) he would have disconsolate
Dreames, which would make him melancholy on the dayes
following.

While he continued in the country, he followed the plow on his
Well-Dayes and sometimes plowed. He learnt there to ring on the
six Bells then newly put up: and having had from his most tender
yeares an extraordinary ravishing Delight in musick, he practiced
privately there, without the help of an Instructer, to play on the
Violin. It was then that he set and tuned his strings in Fourths, and
not in Fifths according to the manner: And having a good Eare
and being ready to sing any Tune upon hearing it once or twice,
he would play them all in short time with the said way of Tuning,
which was never knowne before.

4 Mar. Fri. His Landlord did once perswade him to drink his Ague away:
and thereupon going to the Alehouse an Houre or two before it was
to come, they set hand to Fist and drunk very desperatly. But then
vomiting all up before it made any continuance in his stomach, or
before it got up in his head, he was forced, after he had spent three
shillings to lead his Landlord home, notwithstanding he had put in
Mr Woods Cup Tobacco. — This country man (a merry Fellow and
one that pretended to wit) thought that the Ague was a little Spirit
or Devil that had got within AW; and therefore when hot weather
came he would have him go into the water and drowne it, or go
to Oxôn in a Boat and so shift it from him into the water and row
hastily from it, and leave it to shark for it self. AW told him this was
a Pythagorean Opinion of his: at which hard word being startled,
he thought it was none of AW's, but the little Devil within him that
sent it out of his Mouth &c. In this condition he continued, till the
weather was alterd, and grew hotter, and then his Ague and fits
grew less, yet when cold weather came againe it would be apt to   f. 19^v
return, and would have fastned on him againe had he not prevented
it by taking Physick.

Saturday March 12 his brothers Edw*ard* and Robert Wood, with Mr Tho*mas*
Cole steward of Merton Coll*ege* were with him to comfort him

in his disconsolate condition — They dined with him and then
departed.

$$\text{Anno} \begin{cases} \text{Domini } 1653 \\ 5 \text{ Caroli II} \\ 0/1 \text{ \{Oliveris Protectoris} \end{cases}$$

After he had spent the summer at Cassington in a lonish and retir'd
condition he return'd to Oxôn; and being advised by some persons,
he entertain'd a Master of Musick to teach him the usual way of
playing on the Violin, that is by having every string tuned 5 notes
lower than the other going before. The Master was Charles Griffith
one of the Musitians belonging to the city of Oxôn, whom he
thought then to be a most excellent Artist, but when AW improv'd
himself in that Instrument, he found him not so. September 8
Thursday, he gave him 2ˢ–6ᵈ entrance and 10ˢ quarterly. This
person after he had extreamly wondred how he could play so
many Tunes as he did by Fourths, without a Director or Guide,
he then tuned his violin by Fifts, and gave him Instructions how
to proceed, leaving then a Lesson with him to practice against his
next comming.

The last yeare, after he was entred into the publik Library[65]
(which he took to be the happiness of his Life, and into which he
never entred without great veneration) he could do but little in
it, because he was entred but a little while before his Ague took
him. But this yeare being a constant student therein he became
acquainted with the places in the Arts Library, (for no farther could
Bachelaurs of Arts then goe) where the books of English Historie and
Antiquities stand. He lighted upon *The Description of Leycestershire*,   f. 20ʳ
written by Will*iam* Burton: and being exceedingly delighted with
the performance, he did this, or in the yeare following, take notes
thence and make collections from it, which he had lying by him
in his last dayes. He took great Delight in reading *The Display of
Heraldry*, written by John Guillim, and in other books of that faculty,
written by John Bossewell, John Ferne &c. and endeavour'd, to draw
out and trick Armes with his pen.[66] And afterwards when he came to

ful yeares, he perceived it was his natural Genie and could not avoid
them. Heraldry, Musick and Painting did so much crowd upon him
that he could not avoid them; and could never give a reason why he
should delight in those studies, more than in others, so prevalent
was nature, mix'd with a generosity of mind, and a hatred to all
that was servile, sneaking or advantagious for lucre sake.[67] — His
brother Edw*ard* Wood was much against these studies, and advised
him to enter on those that were beneficial, as his mother did — He
had then a gentile companion of the same Coll*ege* (*John* W*arnford*)
who delighted in vertuous studies as he did, and would walk several
times with him in shady recesses and retired walkes, to each others
content, but the same *John* W*arnford* being a Gent*leman* of a good
Descent and an heir to an Estate of 700[li] per an*num* at least, he went
afterwards to London, mixed himself with idle company that flatter'd
and admired him, and at length debauch'd him; which did not a little
Trouble to AW.[68]

Nov. His kinsman Charnel Pettie Esq*uire* an old Puritan and an honest
and quiet man became High-sherriff of Oxfordshire — His Estate
was at Tetsworth and elswhere, but lived now at Stoke-Lyne neare
to Bister, the Inheritance of his Daughters son named Ralph Holt,
who being a Minor, the said Charnel Pettie was his Guardian.

$$\text{Anno} \begin{cases} \text{Domini } 1654 \\ 6 \text{ Caroli II} \\ 1/2 \ \{ \text{Oliveris Protectoris} \end{cases}$$

f. 20[v]

25 July. Tues. —— Hussey and —— Peck, two Gentlemen that were lately
Officers in the Kings Army were hang'd in the Castle-yard in Oxôn
to the great Reluctancy of the generous Royallists then living in
Oxôn — They were out of commission and employ, and had no
money to maintain them which made them rob on the high-way.
After a tedious imprisonment in the Jayle at Oxon, they were
condemn'd to dye by that inveterate Enimy to the Royal Partie John
Glynn serjeant at law, who this yeare went Oxford circuit.

Hussey was the Eldest, had received some Marks of honour in his Face, and no doubt in his Body also, and died penitent. Peck who was yonger, was proper, robust and seemed a stout man. He died resolute and not so penitent as Hussey. As soon as they were cut downe, they were carried away by some Royallists, and Hussey was on the same day at night buried by them in the Church of S. Peter in the Baylie. This was the first or 2ᵈ Execution that AW ever saw, and therefore it struck a great Terror into him to the disturbance of his Studies and Thoughts — They were exceedingly pittied by all men.

10 Aug. Thur. AW was examined for the Degree of Master of Arts by Will*iam* Bull of Trinity, afterwards Fellow of Allsouls Coll*ege*.
— The other Examiners were Georg Weldon of Magd*alen* Coll*ege* and Joh*n* Whitehead of Exeter Coll*ege*, who examin'd the rest of the class. — He had certificats by him for the performance of other Lectures, but they are imbezld and lost.

Cirques Jobson a Jew and Jacobite, borne neare Mount-Libanus sold coffey in Oxôn in an House between Edmund hall and Queen coll*ege* corner — see in the yeare 1650 and 1655.[69]

By his sedulous and close studying in the publick Library, and by conversing with Books not used by the Vulgar Students, especially MSS, he was taken notice of by Mʳ Tho*mas* Barlow the Head-Keeper of the said Library; who began thereupon to express some kindness towards him, with the offering his assisting hand.   f. 21ʳ

Latter end of 1654. AW having by this time obtain'd proficiency in musick, he and his companions, *William* Bull, *Edmund Gregory*, *John Trap*, *Georg Mason* were not without silly Frolicks — not now to be maintaind — [70]

$$\text{Anno} \left\{ \begin{array}{l} \text{Domini } 1655 \\ 7 \text{ Caroli II} \\ 2/3 \text{ \{ Oliveris Protectoris} \end{array} \right.$$

25 Apr. Wed. Edw*ard* Wood eldest brother to AW and fellow of Merton coll*ege* was installed junior Proctor of the Univ*ersity* of Oxôn.

44

Whereupon he soon after appointed AW his collector in Austins;[71] which office he kept till he was admitted Master of Arts.

3 May.   Thur. AW made his first Declamation in the Natural Philosophy School for the Degree of Master of Arts — The subject was *Bonum quoddam quilibet efficiat, Optimi autem solum perseverant.*[72]

16 May.   Wed. AW made his 2ᵈ Declamation in the said schoole — And his subject was *Utrum prestantius esset Ciceronis libros comburere, quam Mortem subire?*[73]

22 May.   Tues. Edward Wood died to the great Reluctancy of his Friends and Relations, in his Mothers house against Merton College, being the fourth week of his proctorship — He was administred to in his last dayes by Ralph Button his quondam Tutor, now Canon of Christ church. He died of vomiting Blood and consumption with it, and made a most religious End.

24 May.   Thur. His body was carried into the Common hall of Merton College, where the Society and such Masters of Arts that were pleased to come to pay their last respects to him, had gloves, wine and bisket in abundance, as also had the Doctors, Heades of Houses   f. 21ᵛ
and his brother Proctor Samuel Bruen, to which last Edward Wood had bequeathed money to buy him a mourning gowne. Afterwards his body being carried to Merton College Church; there was a sermon preached for that occasion by his aforesaid quondam Tutor; which being not extant, I cannot refer you to it. His Hearse was adorn'd, with escocheons and verses; among which last was a copie made by his acquaintance Dʳ Barton Holyday Archdeacon of Oxford, an antient Poet,[74] running thus

> Upon the death of his vertuous and prudent Friend
> Mʳ Edward Wood, in the beginning of his
> Proctorship of the Universitie of Oxôn
> Chosen he was a Censor of the Times:
> He chose to dye, rather than View the Crimes.
> The Cynique's Lanterne he farr wiser thought

That for an honest Man at high-noon sought.
Then bring a Midnight Sinner to the Light
Whose darker Actions do outshade the night.
Friend thou was wise, with honour thus to dye,
Fame is thy Epitaph, thy Tombe the Skye.[75]

12 Oct.   Fri. A handsome Maid living in Catstreet, being deeply in love
with Joseph Godwin a junior Fellow of New Coll*ege*, poyson'd her
self with Rats-bane — This is mention'd because it made a great
wonder that a Maid should be in love with such a person as he who
had a curld shag-pate, was squint ey'd and purblind[76] and much
deform'd with the smal pox. He was the son of a Father of both his
names, who was a Bookseller at the upper end of Catstreet, and
before he had been translated to Winchester School had been in the
same Forme with AW at New Coll*ege* School.

17 Oct.   Wed. On the Vigil of S Luke, part or half of the Roof of the south
part of Merton coll*ege* outer-Chappel, joyning to the Tower, fell
within the church about 9 of the clock at night, and broke all
the stones laying on the Floor, of which some were Monumental
Stones. Afterwards when the Ruins were taken away, AW retriev'd
the brass plates that were fixed on them, and transcrib'd and sav'd   f. 22[r]
the Inscriptions on them, which he afterwards printed in his *Histor.
et Antiq. Univ. Oxon.* lib. 2. p. 91.[77]

17 Dec.   Mon. He was admitted Master of Arts, being then his birthday, and
at the same time he was admitted ad Regendum=[78] — It was his
intention to be admitted 2 or 3 dayes after he had last declaim'd, but
being troubled with the aking of a Tooth, he drew it, which caused
a swelling in his cheek, and that a Tumour, and that a Lancing
therof, which made him unfit to appear in public.

1655/6.   In the beginning of March he published five sermons of his brother
Edw*ard* Wood lately deceased, which he had preached before the
Universitie.[79] He dedicated them to D[r] Jonathan Goddard Warden
of Merton Coll*ege*, and sent to him a very fair copie of them bound
in blew Turkey-Leather, with their leaves gilt — I sent the Book

by the carrier to London, and James Bricknell, M.A., his quondam chamberfellow presented it in his (AWoods) name to the said warden living in Gresham College.

In this yeare[80] Arthur Tillyard an Apothecary and great Royallist sold coffey publickly in his House against All-soules Coll — He was encouraged so to do by som Royallists now living in Oxôn, and by others who esteem'd themselves either *Virtuosi* or *Wits*; of which the chiefest number were of Allsouls College as Peter Pett, Thomas Millington, Timothy Baldwin, Christopher Wren, Georg Castle, William Bull &c. There were others also, as John Lamphire a Physitian lately ejected from New College, who was somtimes the natural Droll of the Company, the two Wrens, Sojounours in Oxon, Mathew and Thomas sons of Dr Wren Bishop of Ely &c. This coffey house continued till his Majesties Returne and after, and then they became more frequent, and had an Excise set upon Coffey.

$$\text{Anno} \begin{cases} \text{Domini } 1656 \\ 8 \text{ Caroli II} \\ 3/4 \ \{ \text{ Oliveris Protectoris} \end{cases}$$

f. 22ᵛ

By this time AW had genuine skill in Musick, and frequented the weekly meetings of Musitians in the house of William Ellis late Organist of S. Johns College, situat and being in a House opposite to that place whereon the Theater was built. The usual company[81] that met and performed their parts were (1) John Cock M.A. fellow of New College by the Authority of the Visitors. He afterwards became Rector of Heyford-Wareyne near Bister, and marrying with one of the Woodwards of Woodstock, lived an uncomfortable life with her (2) John Jones M.A. Fellow of the said college, by the same Authority (3) Georg Crake M.A. of the said college also by the same Authority — He was afterwards drownd, with Brome, son of Brome Whorwood of Halton neare Oxôn, in their passage from Hampshire to the Isle of Wight 5 Sept. 1657 (4) John Friend M.A. fellow also of the said House and by the same Authority — He died in the country anno 1658 (5) Georg Stradling M.A. fellow of Allsouls College an admirable Lutinist and much respected

by Wilson the Professor (6) Ralph Sheldon Gent*leman* a Rom*an*
Catholick of Steple-Barton in Oxfordshire, at this time living
in Halywell neare Oxôn, admired for his smooth and admirable
way in playing on the Viol. He died in the city of Westminster
—— 1659 and was buried in the chancel of the church of S. Martin
in the Fields (7) Thom*as* Wren a yonger son of Matthew Wren
Bishop of Ely, a sojournour now in the house of Franc*es* Bowman
Bookseller living in S. Maries Parish in Oxon. (8) Tho*mas* Janes
M.A. of Magd*alen* Coll*ege*, would be among them, but seldome
played. He had a weekly meeting in his chamber at the coll*ege*,
practiced much on the Theorbo Lute, and Gervace Westcote being
often with him as an Instructor, AW would somtimes go to their
meeting and play with them.

    The Musick Masters who were now in Oxôn and frequented
the said meeting, were (1) Will*iam* Ellis Bach*elor* of Musick, owner
of the House wherein the meeting was. He alwaies play'd his part
either on the Organ or Virginal — (2) D*r* Joh*n* Wilson the public
Professor, the best at the Lute in all England. He somtimes play'd
on the Lute, but mostly presided the consort (3) —— Curteys
a Lutinist lately ejected from some choire or Cath*olic* church.
After his Majesties restoration he became gent*leman* or singing
man of Ch*rist* church in Oxôn (4) Tho*mas* Jackson a Bass-Violist;   f. 23*r*
afterwards one of the choire of S Johns coll*ege* in Oxôn (5) Edw*ard*
Low Organist lately of Ch*rist* church: He play'd only on the Organ;
so when he performed his part, M*r* Ellis would take up a Counter-
Tenor Viol and play, if any person were wanting to performe that
part. (6) Gervase Littleton alias Westcot, or Westcot alias Littleton,
a violist — He was afterwards a Singing man of S. Johns coll*ege* (7)
Will*iam* Flexney, who had belonged to a Choire before the warr —
He was afterwards a Gent*leman* or Singing-man of Ch*rist* Ch*urch*
— He playd well upon the Bass viol and somtimes sung his part.
He died 6 Nov*ember* 1692 aged 79 or thereabouts (8) Joseph Proctor
a yong man and a new commer: he died soon after as I shall tell
you anon. — John Parker one of the Universitie musitians would
be somtimes among them, but M*r* Low, a proud man, could not

endure any common Musitian to come to the Meeting, much less
to play among them. — Among these I must put Joh*n* Haselwood
an Apothecary, a starch'd formal Clisterpipe, who usually playd
on the Bass-viol and somtimes on the counter-Tenor. He was very
conceited of his skil (tho he had but little of it) and therefore would
be ever and anon ready to take up a viol before his betters: which
being observed by all, they usually call'd him *Handlewood*. As for
other musitians who were about this time Beginners, you shall have
the names of them under the yeare 1658.

22 July.   Tues. Joseph Proctor died in Halywell, and was buried in the
middle of the church there. He had been bred up in the faculty of
Musick by M*r* Joh*n* Jenkyns the Mirrour and wonder of his Age for
Musick, was excellent for the Lyra-viol and Division-Viol, good at
the Treble-Viol and Treble=violin, and all comprehended in a man
of three or 4 and twentie yeares of age. He was much admired at
the meetings, and exceedingly pittied by all the faculty for his loss.

    This summer came to Oxôn *The Antiquities of Warwickshire* &c.
written by Will*iam* Dugdale, and adorn'd with many cuts. This
being accounted the best book of its kind that hitherto was made
extant, my pen cannot enough describe how A. Wood's tender   f. 23ᵛ
affections, and insatiable desire of knowledg, were ravish'd and
melted downe by the reading of that book — What by musick and
rare books that he found in the public Library his life at this time
and after was a perfect Elysium.

29 Oct.   Wed. In the latter end of Octob*er* he began to survey and transcribe
the monumental Inscriptions and Armes in the several parochial
churches and college chappels within the city and Universitie of
Oxon.

1656/7.   10 Jan. Sat. AW, his mother, and his two Brothers Rob*ert* and
Christopher Wood gave 5ˡⁱ to Merton coll*ege*, towards the casting
of their five Bells into eight — These five were antient Bells, and
had been put up into the Tower at the first building thereof, in the
time of D*r* Hen*ry* Abendon Warden of Merton Coll*ege,* who began

to be warden in 1421. The Tenor or great Bell (on which the name
of the said Abendon was put) was supposed to be the best Bell
in England, being, as 'twas said, of fine mettal silver found. The
generality of people were much against the altering of that Bell,
and were for a Treble to be put to the five, and so make them six:
And old Sarjeant Charles Holloway, who was a very covetuous man
would have given money to save it and to make the five, six, Bells,
that is to put a Treble to them. But by the Knavery of Thom*as* Jones
the Sub-Warden (the Warden being then absent) and —— Derby
the Bell-Founder, they were made eight, and D*r* Joh*n* Wilson D*r* of
Musick had a Fee from the college to take order about their Tuning.

Jan*uary*. Whereas AW had before learned to play on the Violin by the
Instruction of Charles Griffith, and afterwards of Jo*hn* Parker one
of the Universitie Musitians, he was now advis'd to entertaine one
Will*iam* James a Dancing Master, by some accounted excellent
for that Instrument, and the rather, because it was said, that he
had obtained his knowledg of Dancing and Musick in France. He   f. 24*r*
spent in all half a yeare with him and gained some improvement
from him, yet at length he found him not a compleat Master of his
facultie, as Griffith and Parker were not; and to say the Truth there
was yet no compleat Master in Oxôn for that Instrument, because
it had not been hitherto used in Consort among Gentlemen, only
by common Musitians, who played but two parts. The Gentlemen
in privat meetings which AW frequented playd three, four and five
parts all with Viols, as Treble-Viol, Tenor, Counter-Tenor and Bass,
with an Organ, Virginal or Harpsicon joyn'd with them: And they
esteemed a Violin to be an Instrument only belonging to a common
Fidler, and could not endure that it should come among them for
feare of making their meetings seem to be vaine and fidling. But
before the restoration of K*ing* Ch*arles* 2 and especially after, Viols
began to be out of Fashion, and only Violins used, as Treble-Violin,
Tenor and Bass-Violin; and the King according to the French mode
would have 24 Violins playing before him, while he was at Meales,
as being more airie and brisk than Viols.

$$\text{Anno} \left\{ \begin{array}{l} \text{Domini 1657} \\ \text{9 Caroli II} \\ \text{4/5 } \{ \text{ Oliveris Protectoris} \end{array} \right.$$

27 Mar. Fri. At the funeral of Jane Wickham the widdow, and
somtimes the second wife of Will*iam* Wickham of Garsingdon
neare Oxôn Gent*leman*. Shee was buried in the Chancel of the
church there by the Remaines of the said *William* Wickham. This
woman was sister to Hen*ry* Brome of Clifton neare Banbury in
Oxfordshire (of the same Familie with the Bromes of Halton) and
died in Oxon, 25 March. AW did not then survey the monuments
in Garsingdon church, because of the company there, but rode
immediatly home to Oxôn —

30 Apr. Thur. He began his perambulation of Oxfordshire: And the
Monuments in Wolvercot church were the first that he survey'd and
transcrib'd —

14 May. Thur. All the eight Bells of Merton Coll*ege* did begin to ring
— And he heard them ring very well at his approach to Oxon in
the evening, after he had taken his Rambles all that Day about the
country to collect Monuments — The Bells did not at all please
the curious and critical Hearer. However he plucked at them often
with some of his Fellow-Colleagues for recreation Sake. They were
all afterwards re-cast and the Belfry wherein the Ringers stood
(which was a little below the Arches of the Tower, for while the
five hanged the Ringers stood on the ground) being built of bad
Timber, was plucked downe also, and after the Bells were put up
againe, this Belfry, that now is, above the Arches, was new made
and a window broke thro the Tower next to Corp*us* Ch*risti* Coll*ege*
was made to give light.

f. 24ᵛ

4 Aug. He began to peruse and run over all the Manuscript collections of
the great Antiquary John Leland that are reposed in the Archives
of Bodlies Library — He was exceedingly delighted in them, was
never weary of them, but collected much from them.

14 Aug. In his rambles about the country, he went to Dorchester seven
miles distant from Oxôn to see his old Master David Thomas,
who, from being Usher of Thame School, was now the Head-
Master of the free school at Dorchester, founded by John
Feteplace esquire an old Bachelaur. — He had succeeded in that
Office John Drope lately Fellow of Magdalen College who was
the first Master appointed by the Founder. AW could not but
here acknowledge his owne weakness, you may call it folly if you
please, as being startled at his first sight of this most antient City,
famous for its being a station of the Romanes, for its entertaining
S. Birinus, and afterwards for giving him burial &c. The church
is larg and antique, and hath contained many Monuments of
Antiquity, which are since spoyled and defaced. Those that
remaine, he took an account of, as also of the Armes in the
windowes, and tricked out with his pen the Ichnography of the
church, cloyster and buildings adjoyning. And at his departure M^r
David Thomas gave him some Roman coynes found within the
Libertie of Dorchester.

5 Sept. Brome Whorwood lately Gentleman Commoner of S. Maries hall,
only son and heir of Brome Whorwood of Halton neare Oxôn,
was drown'd in his passage from Hampshire to the Isle of Wight.
— He had been at the Election of scholars at Winchester, and
being minded to see the Isle of Wight, did with George Crake of
New College hire a vessel that was leaky, which sunk by that time
they were half way in their journey — I^82 set this Memoire downe,
because AW had acquaintance with both of them. The mother of
the said Brome Whorwood who was drown'd, was Jane, daughter
and one of the two coheires of —— Ryther of Kingston upon
Thames in Surrey, somtimes surveyor of the stables to King James
I and daughter in law to James Maxwell Esquire one of the Gromes
of the Bed-chamber to King Charles I, as having married her
Mother after Rythers death. AW remembred her well, as having
often seen her in Oxon; she was red-hair'd as her son Brome was,
and was the most loyal person to King Charles I in his miseries, as

f. 25^r

any woman in England, as it appeares by several exploits that she
performed in Order to his preservation; among which I shall set
downe these two.

After his Majestie had been taken away from Holdenby he was
conveyed by easie removals to Hampton Court August 1647, at
which time the Citizens of London were very unruly, had alienated
their affections from the Parliament, were very averse to the Army,
and wholly enclin'd to his Majestie, as having a Designe to get him
among them, settle him in the Parliament House and so conclude
a Peace. His Majesty knew all this, and knew the Insolencies and
threatning of the Parliament Soldiers which they gave out to
destroy him, being animated so to do by the Cabal of Parliament
Officers sitting at Putney, which therefore made him think of an
escape from Hampton Court, if he could well know to what place
he could goe. Jane Whorwood knowing this, shee went to William
Lillie the Astronomer living in the Strand within the Libertie of
Westminster to receive his judgment about it, that is to say in what
quarter of the nation he might be most safe, and not be discovered
till himself pleased. When shee came to his dore, Lilly told her, he
would not let her come in, for he had buried a Maid-servant of the
plague very lately — *I feare not the plague but the pox*, saith shee.
So he let her in and went up staires. After Lillie had erected his
Figure, he told her that about 20 miles from London and in Essex,
he was certaine the King might continue undiscovered. Shee liked
his judgment very well, and being herself of a sharp judgment,
remembred a place in Essex, about that distance, where was an
excellent House and all conveniences for his reception &c. Away
shee went early next Morning to Hampton Court to acquaint his
Majestie; but see the misfortune, he either guided by his owne
approaching hard Fate, or misguided by John Ashburnham, went to
Tichfield in Hampshire and surrendred himself to Colonel Robert
Hammond Governour of the Isle of Wight. AW has heard from
William Lilly that Alderman ——— Adams of London sent to his
Majesty at Hampton Court a thousand pound in Gold: Five hundred
pound of which was put into Jane Whorwoods hands, who gave

f. 25ᵛ

Lilly for this and other Judgments 20^{li} of the same Money as the said Lilly usually reported.

Another loyal Exploit was this — His Majestie being in Caresbrok Castle in the said Isle of Wight, the Kentish men were then in Armes for him and joyn'd with the Lord George Goring. A considerable number of the best ships also revolted from the Parliament, and the citizens of London were forward to rise against the Parliament: whereupon his Majestie design'd an Escape thence if he could tell how. A smal ship was provided and anchored not farr from the castle to bring him into Sussex, and Horses were provided ready to carry him thro Sussex into Kent, and from thence to march immediatly to London, where thousands would have armed for him &c. These things being knowne among the Kings Friends, and particularly to Jane Whorwood, shee repaires againe to Lillie and acquaints him with the Matter: whereupon he got G. Farmer a most ingenious Locksmith dwelling in Bow Lane in London, to make a saw to cut Iron barrs asunder I meane to saw them, and Aqua Fortis besides — These things being quickly obtain'd, his Maj*esty* in a smal time did his worke. The barrs gave Libertie to him to go out, and he was out with his body till he   f. 26^r
came to his Breasts, but then his Heart failing he proceeded no farther; so afterwards he was kept closer — These things AW had from Will*iam* Lilly; who told him, (and so he afterwards found it among some of his notes) that the said Jane Whorwood came to him againe (upon the direction as he thought of Will*iam* Lord Say) to know from the perusal of his Figure, whether his Majestie should signe the propositions sent to him by the Parliament, so soon as they were read: to which Will*iam* Lillie consenting, and that it was his only way so to doe, which by her, or her letters, were communicated to his Majestie yet the said Lord Say (then one of the Commissioners from the Parliament for a peace) did, after his Majestie had communicated his Intentions to him what to doe, perswade him from signing the said propositions, telling him they were not fit for him to signe, that he (Say) had many friends in the H*ouse* of Lords, and some in the House of Commons, and he would

procure more, and then they would frame more easie propositions
&c. This perswasion of that unfortunate Lord occasion'd his Majesty
to wave the advice of Lilly and others &c. This Jane Whorwood is
the same Lady mentiond in the second volume of *Ath et Fasti Oxon*
p 523[83] where youl find that King Charles I. had put into her hands a
Cabinet of pretious Jewells to be by her kept till such time that he
should send for them; which he did a little before his Death: and
what passed thereupon you may see there. — But all these things
being spoken by the by, lets proceed.

16 Sept. Wed. AW went to Einsham to see an old kinsman called Thomas
Barncote — He was there wonderfully strucken with a veneration
of the stately yet much lamented ruins of the Abbey there, built
before the Norman conquest — He saw then there two high
Towers at the west end of the church, and some of the north walls
of the church standing. He spent some time with a melancholy
Delight in taking a prospect of the ruins of that place. All which,
together with the entrance or the Lodg, were soon after pul'd
downe, and the stones sold to build Houses in that Towne and
neare it — The place hath yet some Ruins to shew, and to instruct
the pensive Beholder with an exemplary Frailty.

24 Dec. Thur. At about eleven or twelve at Noon (Merton college Bells   f. 26ᵛ
being then ringing) William Bull Fellow of Allsouls college and
Henry Hawley fellow of Oriel, were with AW at his Lodging neare
Merton college, and smiling upon him and upon each other, they
told him, he must walk with them to S. Barthelmews Hospital neare
Oxôn and dine there with them and others of his acquaintance, but
would not tell him who they were, or upon what account — He
went forthwith with them and comming there about one of the
clock, who should he see there, newly up from his Bed and ready
but Edmund Gregory Bachelor of Arts, lately Gentleman Commoner
of Merton college, who, in the evening before had conveyed thither
a yong Gentlewoman of 15 yeares of age named —— Pottinger of
Choulesley near Wallingford in Berkshire, whome he had stole from
her parents. They were married early that morning in the chappel

of S. Barthelmews Hospital, which being done he bedded her for feare of a pursuit. The company sate downe to dinner between one and two of the clock in the Afternoon, after the Bridegroom had presented his Bride smiling to them. They tarried till 'twas dark and then went to Cuxham neare Watlington, where, or neare it his Father lived.

Afterwards this Edm*und* Gregory, who had a faire Estate left him by his Father, and had a good Estate with his yong wife, lived afterwards very high, farr beyond his Income, was High-sherriff of Oxfordshire in 1680; at which time being deeply in debt and beyond Recovery, his aforesaid wife died of Grief at Cuxham in June 1683. About which time M[r] Gregorie's Estate being all either sold or mortgag'd, he kept some small matter for himself retired to or neare Bagshot neare Windsor under a strang name, and died and was buried there.

1657/8. 14 Jan. Thur. He (AW) went with the Societie of Merton Coll*ege* to Haseley about 7 miles distant from Oxôn. being all invited to the funeral of Dr Edw*ard* Corbet Rector of that Towne,[84] who was then, and there (in the Chancel) buried — He had taken a view of the monuments there before —

12 Mar. Fri. Edm*und* Greg*ory* and his new wife in Oxôn — AW attended   f. 27[r]
them, shew'd them the public libr*ary*, Anatomy School &c.

17 Mar. Wed. Or therabouts his Cozen John Taverner son and heir of John Tav*erner* of Soundess neare Nettlebed in Oxfordsh*ire* Esq*uire*, died at Greys-Inn and was buried in S. Andrews church in Holborne neare London — His sister Mary the wife of John Harris of Silkstede neare to Winchester was his Heire.

23 Mar. Tues. He walked to Osney, where seeing a poore man digging in the Ruins, he shew'd AW a leaden impression or the seal of Pope John 23, which he bought of him —
William Byrd of Hallywell in the suburbs of Oxôn stonecutter, did in the latter end of this yeare find out the paynting or stayning

of Marble: A specimen of which he presented to the King after his restoration, as also to the Queen, and in 1669 to Cosmo Prince of Tuscany when in Oxôn.

In the latter end of this yeare Davis Mell the most eminent Violinist of London being in Oxôn, Peter Pett, Will*iam* Bull, Ken*elm* Digby and others of Allsoules as also AW did give a very handsome Entertainment in the Taverne cal'd The Salutation in S. Maries Parish Oxon, own'd by Tho*mas* Wood son of —— Wood of Oxon somtimes servant to the Father of AW — The company did look upon Mr Mell to have a prodigious hand on the Violin, and they thought that no person, as all in London did, could goe beyond him. But when Tho*mas* Baltser an Outlander, came to Oxon in the next yeare, they had other thoughts of Mr Mell, who tho he playd farr sweeter than Baltsar, yet Baltsar's hand was more quick and could run it insensibly to the end of the Finger-board.

$$\text{Anno} \left\{ \begin{array}{l} \text{Domini 1658} \\ \text{10 Caroli II} \\ \text{5 Oliveris} \\ \text{1 Richardis} \end{array} \right. \left\{ \text{Protectoris} \right.$$

f. 27^v

5 Apr.   Mon. Will*iam* George Bach*elor* of Arts and Student of Ch*rist* Church was buried in the chancel of Garsingdon church neare Oxon — This person had been Tutor to the children of Joh*n* Wickham of that Towne Gent*leman*, and when resident in the Universitie, was accounted a noted Sophister, and remarkable Courser[85] in the time of Lent in the publick schooles. He was poor and therefore ready to make the Exercise of dul or lazy scholars. He could not for want of money take the Degree of Master; yet the generality of scholars thought that if he had money, he would not, because otherwise he should not be accounted the best scholar of a Bach*elor* of Arts in Oxôn as he was. He look'd elderly and was cynical and hersute in his behavior.

13 Apr.   Easter-Tuesday Chr*istopher* Wood (brother to AW) was married to Elizabeth Seymour.

At Cuxham, with other of his acquaintance, in the House of Mr Gregory; where continuing 3 dayes, he went to several Townes to collect Monumental Inscriptions and Armes, as at Watlington, Brightwell &c.

19 Apr. Mon. Alderman John Nixon's school in the yard belonging to the Guildhall of Oxôn being finishd, the first Boyes made their entry; some of which were afterwards by the help of another school, Academians.

4 May. Tues. A maid was hang'd at Greenditch neare Oxôn, for murdering her Infant-Bastard — After shee was cut downe and taken away to be anatomiz'd, William Coniers a Physitian of S. Johns college and other yong physitians, did in short time bring life into her. But the Bayllives of the Towne hearing of it, they went between 12 and one of the clock at night to the House where she laid, and putting her into a coffin carried her into Broken hayes, and by a halter about her neck drew her out of it, and hung her on a Tree there. She then was so sensible of what they were about to do, that shee said *Lord have mercy upon me* &c. The women were exceedingly enraged at it, cut downe the Tree whereon shee was hang'd, and gave very ill language to Henry Mallory one of the Baillives when they saw him passing the streets, because he was the chief man that hang'd her. And because that he afterwards broke, or gave up his trade thro povertie (being a Cutler) they did not stick to say, that Gods Judgments followed him for the cruelty he shew'd to the poore maid — See Dr Plots *Natural History of Oxfordshire*, p. 197, 199.

f. 28^r

14 July. Wed. AW entertain'd two eminent Musitians of London named John Gamble and Thomas Pratt, after they had entertaind him with most excellent Musick at the Meeting House of William Ellis. Gamble had obtain'd a great name among the Musitians of Oxôn, for his book before publish'd entit*led Ayres and Dialogues to be sung to the Theorbo-Lute or Bass-Viol.*[86] The other for several compositions which they played in their consorts.

24 July. Sat. Tho*mas* Balsar or Baltzar a Lubecker borne, and the most
famous Artist for the Violin that world had yet produced, was now
in Oxôn, and this day AW was with him and Mr Edw*ard* Low lately
Organist of Ch*rist* Church at the Meeting-House of Will*iam* Ellis.
AW did then and there to his very great astonishment heare him
play on the Violin. He then saw him run up his Fingers to the end
of the Finger=board of the Violin, and run them back insensibly,
and all with alacrity and in very good Tune, which he nor any in
England saw the like before. AW entertain'd him and Mr Low with
what the House could then afford, and afterwards he invited them
to the Tavern, but they being engag'd to goe to other Company,
he could no more heare him play or see him play at that time.
Afterwards he came to one of the weekly meetings at Mr Ellis's
house and there played to the wonder of all the Auditory: and
exercising his Fingers and Instrument several wayes to the utmost
of his power, Wilson thereupon the public Professor, (the greatest
Judg of Musick that ever was) did, after his humoursome way, stoop   f. 28^v
downe to Baltzars Feet, to see whether he had a Huff[87] on, that is to
say to see whether he was a Devil, or not, because he acted beyond
the parts of Man.

About that time it was that Dr John Wilkins Warden of Wadham
Coll*ege*, the greatest curioso of his time, invited him and some of
the Musitians to his Lodgings in that coll*ege*, purposely to have
a consort and to see and heare him play. The Instruments and
Books were carried thither, but none could be perswaded there to
play against him in consort on the Violin. At length the company
perceiving AW standing behind, in a corner neare the dore they
haled him in among them, and play forsooth he must against him.
Whereupon he being not able to avoid it, he took up a Violin,
and behaved himself as poor Troylus did against Achilles. He was
abash'd at it, yet honour he got by playing with, and against such a
grand Master as Baltzar was. Mr Davis Mell was accounted hithirto
the best for the Violin in England, as I have before told you, but
after Baltzar came into England and shew'd his most wonderful
parts on that Instrument, Mell was not so admired, yet he played

sweeter, was a well bred Gentleman and not given to excessive drinking as Baltzar was.

30 Aug. Munday, a terrible raging wind hapned, which did much hurt — Dennis Bond a great Olivarian and Antimonarchist died on that Day, and then the Devil took Bond for Olivers appearance.[88]

3 Sept. Fri. Oliver Cromwell the Protector died — This I set downe, because some writers tell us that he was hurried away by the Devill in the wind before mention'd.

6 Sept. Mon. Richard Cromwell his son was proclaimed Protector at Oxon, at the usual places where Kings have been proclaimed — While he was proclaiming before S. Maries church dore, the Mayor, Recorder, Townclerk &c. accompanied by Col*onel* Unton Croke and his Troopers, were pelted with Carret and Turnip-tops by yong scholars and others who stood at a Distance.

f. 29ʳ

18 Oct. Mon. He went to Stoke-Lyne to give a visit to his kinsman Charnel Pettie, and his wife and other of his Relations there. He continued there till the 22 day of the said month: in which time he rode about the country adjoyning and collected several Monuments and Armes. He was at Cotsford in hopes to find a Monument there for his Grand-Father by his Mothers side, named Rob*ert* Pettie alias Le Petite Gent*leman*, but finding none, he searched in the Register and found that he was buried on the 10 of May 1612.

1658/9. 11 Feb. Fri. Nath*aniel* Crew M. A. and Fellow of Linc*oln* Coll*ege* brought to AW a Petition to present to the Parliament against standing Visitors in the University: To which, upon his desire, he set his hand &c. The Independents who called themselves now the Godly Party drew up another petition contrary to the former, and said 'twas for the cause of Christ &c. No person was more ready than Crew, a Presbyterian, to have the said Visitors put downe, notwithstanding he had before submitted to them, and had paid to them reverence and obedience.

12 Feb. Egg-Saturday, Edward Bagshaw M.A. and student of Ch*rist* ch*urch*
presented his Bachelaurs ad Determinandum,[89] without having on
him any formalities, whereas every Deane besides had formalities
on. Dr John Conant was then Vicechancellour, but took no notice of
Bagshaw.

    In this Lent, but the day when I cannot tell, AW went as a
stranger with Thom*as* Smith Master of Arts, (ejected his clerkship
of Magd*alen* Coll*ege* by the Visitors 1648) living now obscurely
in Oxon. I say he went with the said Mr Smith on a certaine
Morning to a private and lone house in or neare to, Bagley
Wood, between Oxon and Abendon, inhabited by the Lord of
Sunningwell called Hannibal Baskervyle Esq*uire*. The house called
Bayworth is an old House situated in a romancey place, and a   f. 29^v
man that is given to devotion and learning cannot find out a better
place. In this House AW found a pretty Oratory or chappel up
one pair of staires well furnish'd with velvet cusheons and carpets.
There had been painted windowes in it, but defaced by Abendon
soldiers (Rebells) in the grand rebellion. He also found there an
excellent Organ in the said Oratory: on which Mr Smith perform'd
the part of a good Musitian and sang to it. Mr Baskervyle was
well acquainted with him, and took delight to heare him play and
sing. He was civil to them but AW found him to be a melancholy
and retir'd man; and upon enquirie farther of the person he was
told that he gave the third or fourth part of his Estate to the
Poor. He was so great a cherisher of wandring Beggars, that he
built for them a larg place like a Barne to receive them, and
hung up a little Bell at his Back-dore for them to ring when they
wanted any thing. He had been several times indicted at Abendon
Sessions for harbouring Beggars. In his yonger Dayes while he was
a Student in Brasnose Coll*ege*, he would frequent the House of
his Kinswoman the Lady Scudamore, opposite to Merton Coll*ege*
Church: at which time the mother of AW being a Girle and a
Sojournour in his Fathers House neare to it, he became acquainted
with her: and when he knew that AW was her son, he was civil
to him, and AW afterwards frequented the house, especially in

the time of his son Tho*mas* Baskervyle, to refresh his mind with
a melancholy walke, and with the retiredness of the place, as also
with the shady Box-Arbours in the Garden.

In the latter end of this yeare (in Mar*ch*) scurvy Grass-Drink
began to be frequently drunk in the mornings as physick-Drinke.

All the time that AW could spare from his beloved studies of
English History, Antiquities, Heraldry and Genealogies, he spent
in the most delightful facultie of Musick, either instrumental or
Vocal: And if he had missed the weekly meetings in the House of
Will*iam* Ellis, he could not well enjoy himself all the week after.
All or most of the company, when he frequented that meeting, the
names of them are set downe under the yeare 16*5*6: As for those
that came in after and were now performers, and with whome
AW frequently playd, were these. (1) Charles Perot[90] M.A. Fellow
of Oriel Coll*ege*, a well bred Gent*leman* and a person of a sweet
nature (2) Christop*her* Harrison M.A. Fellow of Queens Coll*ege*,
a maggot-headed person and humourous: — He was afterwards
Parson of Burgh under Staynsmore in Cumberland, where he
died in the winter time an*no* 1694 (3) Kenelm Digby Fellow of
Alls*ouls* Coll*ege*. — He was afterwards LL. D*r*, and dying in the
said Coll*ege* on Munday night Nov*ember* *5* an*no* 1688 was buried
in the chappell there. He was a violinist, and the two former
Violists. (4) Will*iam* Bull Master of Arts, Bach*elor* of Phy*sics* and
Fellow of <u>Alls*ouls*</u> college; for the violin and Viol — He died 1*5*
Ju*ly* 1661 aged 28 yeares, and was buried in the chapel there (*5*)
Joh*n* Vincent M.A. Fellow of the said Coll*ege*, a violist — He went
afterwards to the Inns of Court and was a Barrester. (6) Sylvanus
Taylor somtimes Com*moner* of Wadh*am* Coll*ege*, afterwards Fellow
of Allsoules, and violist and songster — He went afterwards to
Ireland, and died at Dublin in the begining of Nov*ember* 1672. His
elder brother capt*ain* Silas Taylor[91] was a composer of musick
playd and sung his parts: and when his occasions brought him to
Oxon, he would be at the musical Meetings and play and sing his
part there (7) Hen*ry* Langley M.A. and Gent*leman* Com*moner* of
Wadh*am* Coll*ege*, a violist and songster — He was afterwards a

worthy Knight, lived at Abbey-Foriat neare Shrewsbury where
he died in 1680 (8) Samuel Woodford a commoner and M.A. of
the said Coll*ege*, a violist — He was afterwards a celebrated Poet,
beneficed in Hampshire and Prebendary of Winchester. (9) Franc*is*
Parry M.A. Fellow of Corp*us* ch*ri*sti coll*ege*, a violist and songster
— He was afterwards a traveller and belonged to the Excise Office
(10) Christop*her* Coward M.A. Fellow of *Corpus Christi* Coll*ege*
— a Violist and Division-violist[92] — He was afterwards Rector of
Dicheat in his native county of Somersetshire, proceeded D. of D.
at Oxôn. in 1694 — (11) Charles Bridgman M.A. of Queen coll and   f. 30ᵛ
of Kin to Sʳ Orlando Bridgman — He was afterwards Archdeacon
of Richmond — He died 26 Nov*ember* 1678 and was buried in the
chap*el* belonging to that Coll*ege*. (12) Nathan*iel* Crew M.A. Fellow
of Linc*oln* Coll*ege*, a Violinist and Violist, but alwaies played out of
Tune, as having no good eare — He was afterwards thro several
preferments Bishop of Durham (13) Matthew Hutton M.A. fellow
of Brasnose Coll*ege* — an excellent Violist — Afterwards Rector of
Aynoe in Northamptonshire — (14) Thom*as* Ken of New coll*ege* a
Junior — He would be somtimes among them and sing his part (15)
Christop*her* Jeffryes a junior Student of Ch*ri*st church, excellent at
the Organ and Virginals or Harpsichord, having been trained up
to those Instruments by his Father Georg Jeffryes Steward to the
Lord Hatton of Kirbie in Northamptonshire and Organist to K*ing*
Ch*arles* I at Oxon (16) Rich*ard* Rhodes another junior Student of
Ch*ri*st Church, a confident Westmonasterian,[93] a Violinist to hold
between his knees —

These did frequent the weekly meetings and by the help of
publick masters of musick, who were mixed with them, they were
much improv'd. Narcissus Marsh M.A. and fellow of Exeter Coll*ege*
would come somtimes among them, but seldome playd, because
he had a weekly meeting in his Chamber in the said coll*ege*, where
masters of musick would come, and some of the company before
mention'd. When he became Principal of S Albans hall he translated
the meeting thither and there it continued, when that meeting in
Mʳ Ellis's house was given over, and so it continued till he went

into Ireland and became M^r of Trin*ity* Coll*ege* at Dublin — He was afterwards Archb*ishop* of Tuam in Ireland —

After his Majesties restoration, when then the Masters of Musick were restored to their several places that they before had lost; or else if they had lost none, they had gotten then preferment, the weekly meetings at Mr Ellis's house began to decay, because they were held up only by scholars who wanted Directors and Instructors &c. so that in few yeares after, the meeting in that house being totally layd aside, the chief meeting was at M^r (then D^r) Marshes Chamber, at Exeter Coll*ege*, and afterwards at S. Albans hall, as before I have told you.

Besides the weekly meetings at Mr Ellis's house, which were first on Thursday, then on Tuesday, there were meetings of the scholastical Musitians every Friday night, in the winter time in some colleges; as in the chamber of Hen*ry* Langley, or of Samuel Woodford in Wadham coll*ege*, in the chamber of Christop*her* Harrison in Queens Coll*ege*, in that of Charles Perot in Oriel, in another at New Coll*ege* &c. to all which some Masters of Musick would commonly retire, as Will*iam* Flexney, Tho*mas* Jackson, Gervas Westcote &c. but these meetings were not continued above 2 or 3 yeares, and I think they did not go beyond the yeare 1662.

Anno $\begin{cases} \text{Domini 1659} \\ \text{II Caroli II} \end{cases}$

2 Apr.   Saturday he went to Stoke-Lyne neare Bister with his mother, a servant-mayd and a man, to give a Visit to his Cozen Charnel Petty Esq*uire* and other of his Relations there.

4 Apr.   Mon. He went to Middleton-Cheyney in Northamptonshire with his mother and other of his Relations at Stoke-Lyne, to visit his cozen Joh*n* Cave and those of his family — He continued there two or three Nights, in which time he took his Rambles to Banbury, visited the church and Antiquities there much broken and defaced: and thence to the antient and noble seat of Werkworth then lately belonging to the Chetwoods; of whom it had then, some yeares

f. 31^r

64

before, ben bought by Philip Holman of London Scrivener, who
dying in 1669 aged 76 was buried in the church there. One John
Lewes AW's kinsman conducted him thither where wee found the
eldest son and heir of the said Philip Holman named —— who was
lately return'd from his Travells, had changed his religion for that of   f. 31^v
Rome, and seemed then to be a melancholy and begotted convert.
He was civil to us and caused the church dore to be opened where
wee found several antient Monuments; the chiefest of which are
of the Chetwoods, which AW then transcrib'd with the Armes
on them. The Mannour House is a stately House, the antient
Habitation of the Chetwoods of Chetwood in Buck*inghamshire*:
part of which, viz. the former part, was built by the Chetwoods, the
rest by Philip Holman before mention'd. In the Gallery of the said
House are the Armes, Quarterings, Crests and Motto's of several of
the Nobility in England. At Banbury is a very fair church, but of 60
coates of Armes that were in the Windowes there before the warrs
began he could then see but 12 or 13. The Monuments there were
also wofully defaced in the late Civil warr, yet what remained he
transcrib'd and return'd to Middleton againe.

6 Apr.   Wed.[94] He returnd to Stoke-Lyne with a great deale of Company
(two coaches full) that went thence with him to Middleton.

7 Apr.   Thur. A fire hapned in Halywell in the suburb of Oxon, in the
house next on the East Side to that which Mr Alex*ander* Fisher had
lately built.[95] Mr John Lamphire the then Owner of it, was visiting
his Patients in the country, and lost his books, many of his Goods,
and some money.

9 Apr.   Sat. AW returned to Oxôn and brought with him a Tertian-Ague,
which held him ten Dayes, and in that time pluckd downe his body
much.

20 May Fri. At Dorchester and thence to Warborow to the house of Adam
Hobbes a Farmer, to desire leave to see a book in his Hands,
containing matters relating to the church of Dorchester. He denied

him the sight of it, but Hobbes being acquainted with Tho*mas* Rowney an Attorney of Oxôn, AW perswaded him to leave it in his hands for my use, which he did the next Mercate day that he came to Oxon. 'Twas a book in 4°, written on Parchment, in the raigne I think of Qu*een* Elizabeth, and in it he saw the larg will of Rich*ard* Beauforest, dat*ed* 13 July 1554 and proved the 8 of June 1555, whereby he gives the Abbey Church of Dorchester, which he had bought of the King to the Towne of Dorchester.

f. 32^r

2 June. Thur. A great meeting of the Anabaptists at Abendon, in order to make a Disturbance in the Nation.

20 July. Wed. His mothers house against Merton Coll*ege* was searched for Armes by a couple of Soldiers. Some other Houses were searched, and the stables of Colleges for Horses. This was done to prevent a rising of the Cavaliers here, and so the easier to suppress the rising of Sr George Booth and his partie in Cheshire and elswhere, on the first of August, which was the time when they were to appeare.

31 July. Sunday, a terrible wind hapned in the Afternoon while all people were at divine service. Two or three stones and some rough-cast stuff were blown from off the Tower of S. Martin alias Carfax: which falling on the leads of the church, a great alarm and out-cry was among the people in the church. Some cried Murder — and at that time a Trumpet or Trumpets sounding neare the Cross-inne dore to call the soldiers together because of the present plott, they in the church cried out that the day of judgment was at hand. Some said the Anabaptists and Quakers were come to cut their Throats, while the preacher Mr Georg Philips perceiving their Errour, was ready to burst with laughter in the pulpit to see such a mistaken confusion, and several of the People that were in the Galleries hanging at the bottom of them, were falling on the Heads of people crowding on the Floor to get out of the dores. This was on the very day before Sr Georg Booth and his party were to appeare in Cheshire — Colo*nel* Edw*ard* Massey at that time was to appeare in Glocestershire, but being taken he was put behind a Trooper,

f. 32^v

to carry him away to Prison. And as they were going downe a hill in the evening of this stormy day, the Horse Fell, and gave the Colonel an opportunity to shove the Trooper forward, and to make an escape into an adjoyning Wood.

In the beginning of Sept*ember* the library of the learned Selden was brought into that of Bodley. AW labour'd several weeks with Mr Tho*mas* Barlow and others in sorting them, carrying them up stairs and placing them.⁹⁶ In opening some of the books they found several pair of spectacles which Mr Selden had put in, and forgotten to take out and Mr Tho*mas* Barlow gave AW a pair, which he kept in memorie of Selden to his last day.

16 Sept. Fri. One ——— Kinaston a Merchant of London with a long Beard and Haire over-grown was at the Miter-Inn and faigning himself a Patriarch, and that he came to Oxford for a Modell of the last Reformation, divers Royallists repaired to him, and were blest by him, viz. Joh*n* Ball, Gilb*ert* Ironside and Hen*ry* Langley all of Wadham Coll*ege*. Bernard Rawlins a Glasier was also there and crav'd his blessing on his knees which he obtained. Joh*n* Harmar also the Greek Professor of the University appeared very formally and made a Greek Harangue before him. Whereupon some of the company who knew the design to be waggish, fell a laughing and betray'd the matter. It was a piece of waggery to impose upon the Royallists and such that had a mind to be blest by a Patriarch instead of an Archbishop or Bishop, and it made great sport for a time, and those that were blest were asham'd of it, they being more than I have set downe. Mr Will*iam* Lloyd⁹⁷ then living in Wadham Coll*ege*, in the quality of a Tutor to John Backhouse of Swallowfield in Berk*shire*, was the Author of this piece of waggery as he himself used to make his braggs. And because the Deane of Ch*rist* church Dr Owen and some of the Canons of that house and other Presbyterian Doctors resorted to him, or he to them for to draw up and give him a Modell, they were so much incensed, when they found the matter a cheat, that Lloyd was forced to abscond for the present, or, as he used to say, *run away*. This Mr Lloyd was

f. 34^r

afterwards successively Bishop of S. Asaph, Lichfield and Coventry. Georg Wharton the Astronomer did take notice of this matter in his Almanack an*no* 1661 and calls the Patriarch *Jeremias*, but puts the memoire under the XI of Sept*ember* which is false.

29 Sept. Thur. Michaelm*as* day the eldest brother then living of AW named   f. 33^v
Robert Wood was married to Mary Drope dau*ghter* of Tho*mas* Drope Bach*elor* of Div*inity* — It must be now knowne that when his Father died, he did by his will leave all his estate, except that at Tetsworth, to the longest liver of his children, and therefore Rob*ert* Wood being not in a capacity to settle a Joynture on his wife, having but the third part of the said estate which laid in Oxôn (because 3 of his sons were now living) AW did therefore upon Roberts request resigne the interest he had in the said estate, as surviver or longest liver if it should so happen; and this he did without any consideration given to him, which no body else would have done. Afterwards he did the like to his brother Christopher upon his request: which in after times did in a manner prove AWood's ruin, for he could hardly get his owne share from the children of his brethren.

24 Oct. Mon. AW began to peruse the Registers or Leiger books of S.   f. 34^r
Frideswides Priory, Osney and Einsham Abbeys, which are kept in Ch*rist* church Treasury. They were taken out thence by Mr Ralph Button Canon of the said House and reposed in his Lodgings in the cloyster there. To which Lodgings AW did recurr dayly till he had satisfied himself with them. It was an exceeding pleasure to him, and he took very great Delight to be poring on such books and collecting matters from them.

Oct. In this month Jam*es* Quin M.A. and one of the senior students of Ch*rist* church, a Middlesex man borne, but son of Walt*er* Quin of Dublin, died in a crazed condition in his Bedmakers House in Penyfarthing street, and was buried in the Cathedral of Ch*rist* ch*urch* — AW had some acquaintance with him, and hath several times heard him sing with great Admiration. His voice was a Bass, and he had a great command of it. 'Twas very strong and exceeding Trouling, but he wanted skill and could scarce sing in consort. He had been turn'd out of his students place by the Visitors, but being well acquainted with some great men of those times that loved Musick, they introduced him into the company of Oliver Cromwell the Protector, who loved a good Voice and instrumentall Musick well. He heard him sing with very great Delight, liquor'd him with sack, and in conclusion said, *Mr Quin you have done very well, what shall I doe for you?* To which Quin made answer with great complements, of which he had command with a great Grace, that *your Highness would be pleased to restore him to his Students place*, which he did accordingly, and so kept it to his dying day.

f. 34^v

26 Nov. Sat. His Acquaintance Henry Stubbe of Christ church sitting in the upper chamber of his Friend (William Sprigg Fellow of Lincoln college) opposite the Back gate of the Miter-Inn, a soldier standing there and discharging his Gun, the Bullet came thro Stubbe's haire and mis'd him narrowly.

Dec. In the latter end of this month, being Christmas-time, AW was at Cuxham in the house of Edmund Gregory — Mr William Bull, Mr Henry Hawley &c. were there also —

1659/60. In the beginning of February Henry Stubbe before mentiond was publickly complayn'd of in the Parliament House for palliating in print the wickedness and Roguery of Sr Henry Vane.[98]

13 Feb. Mon. Munday at night was great rejoycing in Oxôn for the news that then was brought that there should suddenly be a Free-Parliament. The Bells rang and Bonfiers were made, and some Rumps and Tayles of sheep were flung into a Bonfier at Queens College gate. Dr John Palmer a great Rumper, Warden of Allsouls college in the place of Dr Sheldon, being then very ill and weak, had a Rump throwne up from the street at his windowes. He had been one of the Rump parliament and a great Favourite of Oliver.

At this time AW being resolv'd to set himself to the study of Antiquities and do somthing in them in the House where he was borne, he set up a chimney in the upper roome looking eastward; and in the next room joyning he put out a window next to the street and made it a study: In which he composed for the most part those things which he afterwards published.

His thoughts were strangly distracted, and his mind overwhelm'd with Melancholy by reading a book entit*led A true and faithfull Narration of what passed for many yeares between D*^r *Joh*n *Dee and some spirits* &c. which was published in fol*io* by Dr Meric Casaubon about the beginning of this yeare. f. 35^r

The pictures of Prophets, Apostles, Saints &c. that had been painted on the back-side of the stalls in Merton Coll*ege* Choire in various and antique shapes, about the beginning of the raigne of K*ing* Hen*ry* 7, were daubed over with paint by the command of the usurpers, about 1651, to the sorrow of Curious men that were admirers of antient painting. But that daubing wearing away in two or three yeares, they were all painted over in Oyle=colours this yeare (1659) and the antient pictures quite obliterated. While the workmen were performing this work, several of the Brass-plates, with Inscriptions, on Grave-stones were most sacrilegiously toren up and taken away, either by some of the Paynters, or other workmen then working in the chappell. AW complayn'd of these things to the Fellowes and desired them to look after the Offenders, but, with shame be it spoken, not one of them did resent the matter, or enquire after the sacrilegists, such were their degenerated and poore spirits. However AW had before this time transcrib'd them, which were afterwards printed — See *Hist. et Antiq. Univ. Oxon* lib. 2. p. 91.⁹⁹

Har MS. e

Anno $\left\{\begin{array}{l} \text{Domini 1660} \\ \text{12 Caroli II} \end{array}\right.$ f. 37^r

30 Mar. Fri. Fulk Grevill living at or neare Banbury, of the antient and gentile familie of the Grevills of Warwickshire was condemn'd at Oxford Assize for robbing on the high way, and killing as 'twas said a man —

1 Apr. Sun. AW, his two brothers and mother sealed a Lease of 21 yeares to
John Willgoose Taylor of a Tenement in S. Martins parish, in the
Bocherew — It is an Appertenent of the Flower de Luce —

10 Apr. Tues. He was with Dr Conant Rector of Exeter coll*ege*, and   f. 36^v
Vicechancellour of the Universitie, to obtaine his leave to see the
Universitie Registers and writings, in order to the drawing up a
Discourse of the Antiquitie of the Universitie — He looked upon
him as a yong man and not able to doe such a matter: And AW
took him to be a man that did not understand the nature of such
a question, being either surpriz'd with the suddainness or novelty
of it, or that he did not understand that studie, as really he did not
— So nothing being done they parted.

May 10 Thursday gave to Dr Hen*ry* Savage the Master of Balliol coll*ege*,   f. 37^r
the collection which he made of the lives of all the worthies of that
coll*ege*, from John Leland, Bale and Pits. Also the opinions of several
Authors concerning the Founder and Foundation of that coll*ege*,
and certaine Observations of the name of Balliol which he had
collected from several Histories and chronicles. — These things D^r
Hen*ry* Savage made use of when he was compiling his book called
*Balliofergus: or a Commentarie upon the Foundation, Founders and
Affaires of Balliol Coll* &c. Oxon. 1668. qu*arto*.[100]

14 May &c. Mon. etc. He perused the MSS. in the Archives of Corp*us*
Chr*isti* Coll*ege* and found several matters there material for his
use —

24 May. Thur. There was a most excellent Musick-lecture of the practick
part in the public school of that facultie, where AW performed a
part on the Violin. There were also Voices, and by the direction of
Edw*ard* Low Organist of Chr*ist* Church, who was then the Deputy
Professor for Dr Wilson, all things were carried very well and
gave great content to the most numerous Auditory. This meeting
was to congratulate his Majesties safe arrival to his Kingdomes.
The School was exceeding full, and the Gallery at the end of

the School was full of the female sex. After all was concluded,
Mr Low and some of the performers, besides others that did not
performe, retired to the Crowne Taverne where they dranke a
Health to the King, the two Dukes, Monke &c.[101] Of the number
of performers that were there present were Sylv*anus* Taylour of
All*souls* coll*ege*. Chr*istopher* Harrison of Queens coll*ege*, Franc*is*
Parry of C*orpus* c*hristi* coll*ege*, AWood &c. besides some Masters of
Musick — There were also with them Will*iam* Levinz of S. Johns
Coll*ege*, Thom*as* Gourney and Jack Glendall of Brasnose, the last of
which Mr Low took with him to make the company sport, he being
a witty and boon companion; Joh*n* Hill Fellow of Alls*ouls* coll*ege*,
Esay Ward of C*hrist* ch*urch*, Hen*ry* Flower of Wadham Coll*ege*, &c.
These were not performers only the last. There were others but
their names I have forgot.[102]

f. 37^v

29 May. Tues. The day of restoration of K*ing* Ch*arles* 2 observed in all or
most places in England, particularly at Oxon, which did exceed
any place of its bigness. Many from all parts flocked to London to
see his entrie, but AW was not there, but at Oxon, where the jollity
of the day continued till next morning. The world of England was
perfectly mad. They were freed from the chaines of Darkness and
confusion, which the Presbyterians and Phanaticks had brought
upon them; yet some of them seeing then what mischief they had
done tackd about to participate of the universal joy and at length
clos'd with the Royal Partie.

8 June. Fri. AW began to peruse the Manuscripts in Ball*iol* Coll*ege* Libr*ary*
and afterwards at leisure times he perused the Manuscripts in other
college Libraries.

18 June. Mon. The uncle by the mothers side of AW, named Harcourt
Pettie Master of A*rts*, and somtimes of Gloc*ester* hall died at Bister
in Oxfordshire, after he had spent a fair estate left to him by his
Father Rob*ert* Pettie Gent*leman* which estate was the Mannour
of Wiveold or Wyfald between Henley and Reading, and a large
Farme at Cotsford neare Bister before mention'd. He was buried in
Bister church.

June. In the latter end of June the antique Marbles which the great
Selden had left to the University were set up in the wall which
parts the Area lying before the Convocation-house dore and
Canditch. But when the wall was pul'd downe to make roome for
the Theater, the marbles were laid aside for the present: Afterwards
when the Theater was built they were set up on the wall that
encompasses it. Each of them hath the letter S engraven or painted,
to distinguish them from Howards, which have an H. on them.[103]

18 July. Wed. Dr Edward Reynolds late Deane of Christ Church was elected   f. 38^r
Warden of Merton college by vertue of the Kings letters sent
thereunto, dated July 7.

19 July. Thur. At Meysey-Hampton in Glocestershire to visit his Kinsman
Henry Jackson Bachelor of Divinity and Rector of that towne — He
heard from him many stories of his contemporaries in Corpus
christi college.

20 July. Fri. At Fairford neare Meysey-Hampton, where Mr William
Oldsworth the Impropriator did with great curtesie shew him the
beautiful church there, and the most curious paynted windows,
set up in the raigne of King Henry 7. The said church Sr Edmund
Thame K^t (who died 1534) did finish, having been begun by his
father John Thame Esq, who died anno 1500. It may compare with
any country church in England for its admirable structure. It is
built cathedral wise and hath a stately Tower standing in the midst
of it, adorn'd with Pinacles, and sculptures of mens Faces and
Armes. The church is also adorn'd with Pinacles, and hath a fair
roof: and in it is an Organ Loft where hath been a tuneable set
of Organs. The windows consist of several scripture stories, verie
well painted considering the time when done: and the excellency
of them is describd in a copie of verses in a book called *University
Poems*.[104]

30 July. Mon. Dr John Wallis the Keeper of the Universitie Registers,
Muniments, writings, of the said Universitie, did put into the hands

of AWood the Keys of the School-Tower and the Key of the Room
where the said Registers &c. are reposed,[105] to the end that he might
advance his esurient genie in Antiquities, especially in those of the
said Universitie. This was done at the request of Dr Ralph Bathurst
and on purpose to promote his generous designe. Here he layd the
foundation of that book, which was 14 yeares after published, viz.
Hist. et Antiq. Univ. Oxon. He was so exceedingly delighted with the
place and the choice Records therein, and did take so much paynes
for carrying on the work, least the Keys should be taken away from
him, that a great alteration was made in him. About 2 months after
his entrance into the said Tower, his Acquaintance took notice of
the falling away of his body, the fading of his cheeks, the chang
of the redness in them to white, &c. yet he was very cheerfull,
contented and healthfull, and nothing troubled him more than
the intermission of his Labours by eating, drinking, Sleeping, and
somtimes by Company which he could not avoid. Afterwards D^r
Wallis seeing his diligence, he told him that he might carry home
with him such books and writings that he wanted, which he did.

f. 38^v

4 Oct. Thur. He was with Dr Savage of Balliol Coll*ege*, and he told him
that he should peruse his collection which he had made of the said
coll*ege*, within a quarter of an yeare after, when then he should have
finishd them.

8 Oct. Mon. Joh*n* Glendall Master of Arts and Fellow of Brasn*ose* Coll*ege*
died, and was buried at the upper end of S. Maries Chancell in
Oxon — He was a Ministers son of Cheshire, had been the witty
Terræ-filius of the Universitie in 1655, at which time the Acts
were kept in S. Maries church. His company was often desired by
ingenious men and therefore thrown out at a reckoning.[106] He was a
great Mimick, and acted well in several playes which the scholars
before acted by stealth, either in the stone house behind and
southward from Pembroke Coll*ege*, or in Kettle hall, or at Halywell
Mill, or in the Refectory at Glocester hall. AW was well acquainted
with him and delighted in his company.

1660/61. 11 Feb. Mon. Charnell Pettie Esq*uire* somtimes High Sherriff of
Oxfordsh*ire* and kinsman to AW died at Stoke-Lyne neare Bister
in the House of his Grandson Ralph Holt Esq*uire* He was buried in
the church there.

14 Feb. Thur. D^r E*dward* Reynolds resign'd his Wardenship of Merton
Coll*ege*, having been lately promoted to the See of Norwich.

5 Mar. Tues. The Fellowes of Merton coll*ege* proceeded to the election of   f. 39^r
a new Warden,[107] according to a citation that had before been stuck
up, but they supposing, not without good ground, that Dr Tho*mas*
Jones one of their society would act foul play in the election,
(having been encouraged so to doe by Dr Tho*mas* Barlow Provost
of Queens coll*ege* viz. that he should name Dr Tho*mas* Clayton
a Stranger and so make a Devolution) the Fellowes proposed to
Mr Alex*ander* Fisher the Subwarden that they might exclude him
from Voting for that time, and assigne another Fellow in his place,
according as the statutes of the college enabled him in that point.
But Mr Fisher being of a timorous spirit, and looking upon it as an
Innovation, denied their request, so that Dr. Jones remaining one
of the 7 electors, Mr Joseph Harvey and Mr Nath*aniel* Sterry two
of the said seaven did desert them out of discontent, and the two
next Fellowes were called up into their places. So that the said 7
Fellowes going to election in the Public Hall, all the said 7 seniors
except Jones, did unanimously name three persons according to
Statute viz Sr Rich*ard* Browne somtimes Fellow, now one of the
clerks of the Kings Privie Councill, M^r A*lexander* Fisher and D^r
Rich*ard* Lydall a physitian, somtimes Fellow; but Jones named
Sr Rich*ard* Browne, Dr Tho*mas* Clayton the Kings Professor of
Physick in the University, somtimes Fellow of Pembr*oke* Coll*ege*, and
D^r. Priaulx somtimes Fellow of Merton. This being done and the
election devolv'd to Dr Juxon Archbishop of Canterbury who is the
Visitor or Patron of the Coll*ege*, Clayton and Jones immediatly went
to London to act in their business, and by their Friends endeavours
to get the said Archb*ishop* to confirme Clayton. Dr Barlow by these
his under-hand and false doings gained the ill will of the society of

Merton College, who stuck not to say, and that with concernment
that he was a most false, busie and pragmatical person.

18 Mar. Mon. Dr Wallis sent for AW to com to him, then in the Muniment-   f. 39^v
Room in the school Tower. He desir'd him to give his assisting
hand to the drawing up of some Things that he was then about,
against his going to London to prosecute the business then in being
against the citizens of Oxôn. AW was there five dayes in assisting
D^r. Wallis and wrot about 7 or 8 sheets, concerning the Brewers,
Inholders, Bakers, Alehouses-Taverns, Malsters &c. viz of the
Incorporating them, and of other matters concerning them. — The
Universitie gave content to Mr Wood for his labour.[108]

$$\text{Anno} \begin{cases} \text{Domini 1661} \\ \text{13 Caroli II} \end{cases}$$ f. 40^r

26 Mar. Tues. Dr Clayton obtained his Instruments in Parchment from
Archb*ishop* Juxon to be Warden of Merton coll*ege* — This was
done by the perpetual sollicitations of S^r Ch*arles* Cotterell, which
was troublesome to the Archbishop, even so much, that he was in
a manner forc't to it for quietness sake. The next day Sr Charles
procured his brother in law Dr Clayton to have the honour of
Knighthood confer'd upon him.

30 Mar. Sat. Sr Tho*mas* Clayton comming to Oxon, in a stage=coach, some
of his Neighbours of S. Aldates parish went on horsback to meet
him, as —— Kirby Clerk of the Parish, Tho*mas* Haselwood his
Barber, —— his shoemaker, Turner the cook of Pembroke coll*ege*,
Will Collier the Butler of the same Coll*ege*, —— Wilcocks a Barber
living in S. Michaels Parish, Anth*ony* Haselwood a Book-seller of
S. Maries Parish, and other rabble, besides 4 or 5 Scholars of his
Kindred. These I say meeting him about Shotover, Sr Thomas,
either ashamed of their company, or for some other reason best
knowne to himself, desired them to disperse, and not to accompany
him by his Coach-side; which they did accordingly and afterwards
came scatteredly into Oxon a quarter of an hour before the Coach
came in.

31 Mar. Sunday, there was a Sacrament and Ordination of Ministers made
in the cath*edral* ch*urch* of Ch*ri*st ch*urch* by Dr Rob*er*t Skinner
Bishop of Oxon: Savil Bradley[109] M.A. Fellow of New Coll*ege*
(and afterwards Fellow of that of Magd*alen* Coll*ege*) was one of
the persons that was to have holy Orders confer'd on him; but he
having been used to eat Breakfasts and drink mornings Draughts,
being not able to hold out with Fasting, was troubled so much with
wind in his stomach, that he fell in a sowne and disturb'd for a time
the ceremony. At length some cordial being procur'd it set him up
againe; yet he could hardly keep himself from a second sowning.

Further also Dr Barton Holyday Archdeacon of Oxon being
there as an Assistant to the Bishop and to give the sacrament,
it so hapned just before he was to give it, that the Canopy over   f. 40^v
the communion Table (which had been put up there when the
choire was wainscoted about 1633) fell downe upon the vessells
and spilt the wine and tumbled the Bread about. This was a great
Disturbance to the ceremony and many wondred at it. Afterwards
when all things were put in order, Dr Holyday took the Bole
of wine in his hand and going downe the steps to administer it
fell down and hurt his face. So Dr Thom*as* Lamplugh of <u>Qu*eens*</u>
Coll*ege*, who was there, was faine to officiat in his place — All
these Accidents hapning together, did cause much discourse in the
Universitie and City; and the Phanaticks being ready to catch at any
thing that seemed evill made a foule story of it, as if it had been a
judgment that had befallen the loyal clergy.

1 Apr. Munday in the morn*ing* Sr Tho*mas* Clayton sent his man to the
Bible-Clerks of Merton coll*ege*, to tell them that their Master would
speak with them: whereupon the clerks immediatly went to M^r
Fisher the Sub-Warden, and asked him what they had best to doe,
whether to go to him or not. He told them he would not bid them
goe or not goe. So they went to Sr Thomas, who told them that
they were to returne to their coll*ege* and warne all the Fellowes
thereof to meet him in the public hall of Merton Coll*ege*, between
9 and 10 of the clock that morning. Accordingly they return'd and

did their Errand: whereupon when it drew towards nine of the clock, the Fellowes commanded the Butler to go out of the Buttery and to deliver up the Key to them. Which being done, the juniors who were at Breakfast in Hall were put out, and the dores thereof were barred up within side. Afterwards they went into the Buttery, bolted the Dore thereof within and then they conveyed themselves thro the cellar dore next to the Treasury-vault, locked it, and one of them put the Key into his pocket. The Fellowes by this time expecting the comming of Sr Tho*mas* Clayton, they retired to the Chamber of Mr Rob*ert* Cripps which is over the common gate, to the end that they might see towards Corpus Christi Coll*ege* when Sr Thomas came. The Bachelaur Fellows also retired to the Chamber of Georg Roberts one of their number, over that of Mr Cripps, for the same purpose.

f. 42^r

About 10 of the clock in the morning came Sr Tho*mas* Clayton with the Vicechancellour[110] and his Beadles, D^r R*obert* Skinner Bishop of Oxon, Dr Mich*ael* Woodward Warden of New College, Dr Tho*mas* Yates Principal of Brasnose coll*ege*, Dr Walt*er* Blandford Warden of Wadham coll*ege*, D^r Jo*hn* Fell Deane of Ch*rist* church, Dr Rich*ard* Allestrie and D^r Jo*hn* Dolben Canons, Mr Joh*n* Houghton Sen*ior* Fellow of Brasn*ose* coll*ege*, and many others. All which (some of whome were of the number of visitors or commissioners appointed by the King to visit the Universitie, an*no* 1660.) met the said Dr Clayton in the Lodgings of Dr Yate at Brasnose and came thence by Oriel coll*ege* to Merton.

f. 41^v

At their appearance neare Corp*us* Ch*risti* College Gate, the Fellowes and Bachelaurs came down from the aforesaid chambers, and ranked themselves in the Gatehouse next to the street. The Fellowes names were these viz Rog*er* Brent, Edm*und* Dickenson, Joseph Harvey, Pet*er* Nicolls, Rob*ert* Cripps, Nath*aniel* Sterry, Hen*ry* Hurst and Rob*ert* Whitehall. The Bachelaur-Fellowes were these, viz Georg Roberts, Edw*ard* Jones, Rich*ard* Franklin, Jam*es* Workman, Rob*ert* Huntingdon, Edw*ard* Turner and John Powell. All these had not long stood in the Gatehouse but Sr Tho*mas* Clayton and his company came in at the Wicket (for the common

f. 42^r

78

Gates were not set open) and going straight forward towards the
Hall (he putting off his hat to the Fellows as he passed by) D^r
Edm*und* Dickenson one of the Fellowes went after him, pluckt him
by the Sleeve and said *Sr Thomas the Gatehouse is the usual place of
Reception.* When he heard this he beckoned to the Vicechancellour
and Bishop and told them *they were to be received at the Gate.*
Upon this they returned back and all stood in the gatehouse, and
when they were all placed Sr Thomas asked where Mr Fisher
the Subwarden was? Mr Brent the Senior Fellow answer'd *S^r M^r
Subwarden keeps*[111] *his Chamber, and is in his usual course of physick
so that he hath appointed me at this time his Deputy.* Then Sr Thomas
replyed that *he came for admission and possession of the Wardenship of
Merton Coll.* Mr Brent thereupon asked him *where was his Instrument
or Authority for it?* Then Sr Thomas calling his man, produced
two black boxes, and in them two Instruments, both with the
Archbishops Seale to them, and putting them into the hands of M^r
John Holloway a Covetuous civilian and public Notary, (father to
Rich*ard* Holloway a Counsellour and afterwards in the time of K*ing*
Jam*es* 2 a Judge) he read them both uncover'd with a loud voice
before the Company and many others from other colleges that by   f. 42^v
this time were gathered together to see the effect of the matter,
being all exceeding wrath against the unreasonable proceedings and
against Clayton, by snatching the bread out of other folkes mouths.

After the Instruments were read Mr Brent desir'd them before
they went any farther to read a paper which he had in his hand,
containing a protestation in the name of all the Fellowes, under a
public Notaries hand against the admission of Sr Tho*mas* Clayton
to the Wardenship of Merton Coll*ege.*

After Mr Brent had read the paper, Mr Holloway asked him
where was their Inhibition? (meaning an Inhibition from some
court to stop Sr Thomas's proceedings) at which Mr Brent made a
stop, and looking wistly upon the Fellowes, they all replyed *they
needed no Inhibition, till they found Greiviance, and that the public
Notaries hand was sufficient for that time.* Then replyed Holloway
your protestation is invalid and worth nothing, and therefore they

would proceed. Then Holloway according to the Forme required of them Admission *primo, secundo, tertio;* which the Fellowes did all coragiously denie, and so immediatly withdrew themselves and went to their chambers.

After this Sr Thomas asked *where the clerks were?* the clerks thereupon appeared. He bad them call Dr Tho*mas* Jones. Dr Jones was thereupon called and came forthwith to him in the Gatehouse. After some whispering passed between them, they drew down to the Wardens Lodgings and finding the Dores fast shut, Holloway read the Instruments againe bare-headed at the Dore or Gate leading into the said Lodgings. Which being done Sr Thomas asked Dr Jones *where the Keys of the Lodgings were?* he said *the subwarden had them.* Then Sr Thomas desired Samuel Clerk the Superior Beadle of Law, to go to the Subwarden and demand of him the Keys: Mr Clerk thereupon asked him *whether he should goe in the Vicechancellours name or in his name?* Sr Thomas replyed *in the Archbishops and Kings Commissioners names.* Clerk thereupon went and soon after brought this Answer, that *there were two Keyes of the Wardens Lodgings, one that belonged to the Warden, which he* (the Subwarden) *had, the other to the senior Deane, which Dr Jones had lately, but when he went up to London they took it from him, which is now layd up in the Exchecquer: As for the Key which he hath, he saith he will not deliver it up but to the Warden when he is admitted.*

After Sr Thomas had received this Answer, he sent for Mr Brent the Deputy-Subwarden, and then Holloway asked him againe *primo, secundo, tertio* for possession, but Mr Brent denied it. Then Holloway bid Sr Thomas lay his hand upon the Latch of the dore leading into the Wardens Lodgings, which he did. Afterwards Dr Jones whisperd Sr Thomas in the Eare, and then they went to the coll*ege* chappell. In the way Dr *Dickenson,* who had more than once protested against what had been done at the Wardens dore, drew up to Sr *Thomas,* and told him that *what he and other fellowes had done at that time, was not in contempt of him or his person, but to save their Oaths and not break the Statutes* &c. but his words were heard with scorne by Sr Thomas, and so Dickenson left him.

f. 43^r

Sr Thomas being entred with all his company (except Fell, Dolbin and Allestrie, who ran home to prayers as soon as the Instruments were read at the Gate) into the chappell thro the south dore, the said Instruments were read againe neare the Wardens seat. Which being done Jones took Sr Thomas by the hand and lifted him up into the Wardens seat, and said that he as one of the senior fellows did install him, or give him possession as Warden, or words to that effect. Afterwards rising from his seat Jones took him by the hand and repeated the Induction or admission, as Holloway read it verbatim to him. After this was done they all went out of the chappell, the same way as they came in, and so retir'd to their respective homes.

The Key of the Chappell they got thus. Robert Hanham Under-   f. 43^v
Butler and Grome of Merton Coll*ege*, having been employed by the Society to carry letters to London to hinder Sr Thomas from comming in Warden of Merton College, did, that night on which Sr Thomas came from London, go to his House in S. Aldates Parish, opposite to the Bull inn, and humbly desired of him forgiveness for what he had done: which Sr Thomas easily granting, Hanham laid downe before him the Key of the College Stable: Whereupon Dr Jones who was then there consulting with Sr Thomas what was to be done on Munday morn*ing* following, when he was to crave admission, took it up, and told Sr Thomas privately that *that Key would open the Chappel dore in case he should be denied entrance therein*. Whereupon Dr Jones kept it, and made use of it when the warden Sr Thomas went to take possession of his place, as before tis told you.

Afterwards the Fellows used all the Endeavours they could to hinder his admission and comming in among them, but all, it seems was in vaine. The next Munday following, Sr Thomas sent word to the college, that he would come in by force. Whereupon the Fellows meeting together, caused all the college gates to be shut both forward and backward, and so they kept them a fortnight or 3 weeks, and caused some of the Bachelaurs to keep possession of the Wardens Lodgings. At length the Appeale of the Fellows being stopt, and seeing that no justice could be done for them, nor have right nor Law for their money, they concluded, by the continual intercessions of *timorous Fisher*, to admit him.

3 May. Fri. Friday, Sr Thomas, with the Vicechancellour, some of the Kings Commissioners, and certaine Heads of colleges, came a little before 10 of the clock in the morning, and the college gates being set wide open, and the Fellowes in the gatehouse, Mr Fisher the subwarden did there formally according to the manner and statutes admit him: which being done they all went to the Wardens Lodgings and gave him possession: which being done also, they went up into the   f. 44^r dining Rome, and there had a short banquet at the college charg. Which being all done by 3 quarters past ten, the Fellows went to the Letany.

After Sr Thomas was admitted at the publick gate, he spake a speech according to the custome: the effect of which is registred. But whatsoever was acted in this matter, which is at larg here set downe, is not, nor would he suffer any thing of it to be, registred; which is the reason that it is here committed to memory by AW, who was present throut all the transactions of the said affaire, and wrot all the particulars downe, immediatly after they were acted.

While these things were in doing, all the University and City were much concern'd at them as several people elswhere were. All seniors that had known what Tho*mas* Clayton had been, did look upon him as the most impudent Fellow in nature to adventure upon such a place, (the Wardenship of Merton coll*ege*) that had been held by eminent persons. They knew him well to have been a most impudent and rude Fellow. They knew him to have been the very Lol-poop[112] of the University, the common subject of every Lampoon that was made in the said University, and a fellow of little or no religion, only for Forme-sake. They knew also that he had been a most lascivious person, a great Haunter of womens company and a common Fornicator. Also that he had sided with the times after the grand Rebellion broke out in 1642, by taking the Covenant, submitting to the Visitors in 1648, by taking the Engagement, and

afterwards the Oaths to be true and faithfull to Prince Oliver
and Prince Richard, otherwise he could never have kept his
Professorship of Phisick in the Universitie, as he did, from 1647
to his Majesties (K*ing* Ch*arles* 2) restoration and after. In fine all
people were strangly surpris'd and amased to behold such unworthy
things done after his Majesties restoration, when then they thought
that nothing but justice should have taken place, and Royallists
prefer'd. But as I have told you before, Dr Juxon Archb*ishop* of   f. 44^v
Canterbury being overpres'd by S^r Ch*arles* Cotterel, and weary of
his solicitations in behalf of Clayton, he sealed the Instruments,
without any more adoe for quietness sake, he himself being a very
quiet man, tho he knew well what Clayton had been. The fellows
of Merton Coll*ege* did usually say in the hearing of AW, that as the
College was dissolv'd in the time of the grand rebellion, so 'twas no
matter to them if it was dissolv'd againe, rather than Tom Clayton
should be warden thereof.

Now lets proceed: all these things being done: I think it fit at
this time that wee should take into consideration the author of all
this mischief, (Tho*mas* Jones) and then what mischief befell the
College in having a stranger so unreasonably thrust upon them.

Dr Tho*mas* Jones therefore being thought the fittest Instrument
for Clayton to compass his Designes, and especially for this reason
that he was ambitious, discontented, covetuous and destitute of
preferment, Clayton told him that if he would dissent from the
Fellowes, and name him with the rest to be Warden, he would
endeavour by all meanes imaginable to requite him for it, either by
gratuity, preferment or other wayes. This was seconded by Th*omas*
Barlow of Queens, who had first began to be tampering with him
and draw him on in this piece of Roguery. He (Clayton) told Jones
that he could easily preferr him thro the endeavours of his brother
in law Sr Charles Cotterel Master of the Ceremonies: and if that
took no effect, he would after some yeares resigne his wardenship,
and by Friends get him to succeed him.

With these pitiful Promises, Invitations to his House, Dinners,
Treats, fair words, flatteries and I know not what, *Jones* promised

to be faithfull to him in his knavery, and so he was as 'tis before told you. But when Clayton was setled in his place, and Jones fully saw that he neglected him, and made him only a shoing-horne (for the truth is Clayton was false, mealie mouth'd and poore spirited) and that also the Fellows and others of the junior party did dispise him and look'd upon him as an errant Knave, he in great discontent retir'd, kept his chamber, and never came into the company of any person in the Coll*ege*. or out of the coll*ege* f. 45^r so that soon after being possest with a deep Melancholy, which his strength and reason could not weare away, without charg to himself; he fell as 'twere downe right mad, not raving, but idle and frantick, as it appeares by these passages. (1) By his walking on the Mount in the College Garden very betimes in the morning at which time he fancied Birds to flutter about his head, and therefore he would be waving his armes and hat to keep them off. (2) By going oftentimes very unseasonably to the Wardens Lodgings, and there court and embrace one M^{ris} —— Wood, asking her at the same time, whether the Lord Chancellour (Hyde) was not then behind the Hangings. (3) By going once, if not twice betimes in the morning to the chamber of Mr Pet*er* Nicolls one of the fellows, to get him to go with him to take possession of the Wardens Lodgings, fancying himself to be Warden. (4) By walking often in the Wardens Gallery supposing himself to be Warden &c. with many other ridiculous matters, not now to be named; which shew that the man wanted sleep, and that he was blinded with ambition and Covetuousness.

At length upon some perswasion, he went to London an*no* 1662–3. or thereabouts, and by the favour of some people (of whom Arnold a Civilian and College Tenant was one) he got a Chamber in Doctors Commons, endeavouring to get practice there among the Civilians. But at length being found to be craz'd had little or no employment. Afterwards taking a Lodging in Great Woodstreet in that city, remained there in great Discontent till the great plague raged, and then by the just hand of God being overtaken by that Disease he was cut off from the living in the latter end of Sept*ember*

or beginning of Octob*er* an*no* 1665, being a just reward for a knave
and a rogue.

Now for the mischief that befel Mert*on* Coll*ege* by having a
married Stranger thrust upon them, will appeare by that which
followes: but before I proceed to the particulars I must tell you
that Clayton being fully possest at his first comming in Warden
that the Fellowes were all his Enimies, and that they endeavour'd   f. 45^v
to conceale the College-Treasure from him, and not let him know
the worth of his place, as it was often buz'd into his Head by his
Flatterers (among whome D^r Th*omas* Barlow must not be forgotten,
Dr Jones also, and another of inferior note named John Haselwood
a proud, starch'd, formal and sycophantizing Clisterpipe, who was
the Apothecary to Clayton when he practiced physick) he took all
occasions imaginable to lay out money, spend and imbezile, and
this forsooth was done upon the information of those persons, that
whatsoever the Warden disburses for his owne use, the College must
defray.

First therefore he and his family, most of them women-kind
(which before were look'd upon, if resident in the College, a
scandall and an abomination thereunto) being no sooner setled,
but a great Dislike was taken by the Lady Clayton to the Wardens
standing Goods, namely Chaires, Stooles, Tables, chimney-
Furniture, the furniture belonging to the Kitchin, Scullery &c. all
which was well liked by Dr Goddard, Brent, Savile &c. These I say
being dislik'd by that proud woman because forsooth the said goods
were out of Fashion, must be all chang'd and alterd to the great
expence of the College.

Secondly the Wardens Garden must be alterd, new Trees
planted, Arbours made, Rootes of choice flowers bought &c.[113] All
which tho unnecessary, yet the poore coll*ege* must pay for them,
and all this to please a woman. Not content with these matters,
there must be a new Summer-House built at the south-end of the
Wardens Garden, wherein her Ladyship and her Gossips may take
their pleasure, and any Eves-Dropper of the family may harken
what any of the Fellows should accidentally talk of in the passage to

their owne Garden. And tho the Warden (Clayton) told the Society, that it would not cost the College above 20^li, yet when it was finish'd there was an 100^li paid for it by the Bursar, wanting some few shillings. This work was thought unnecessary by many persons, because it joyned almost to the Long Gallery, the larg Bay-window whereof at its south end, affords a farr better prospect, than that of the Summer-House.

Thirdly, by enlarging his Expences in the Stable, much more   f. 46^r
than any of his predecessors. For tho Sr Nath*aniel* Brent did keep four Coach-Horses, yet he was often absent. But S^ir Thomas tho he be often absent, yet two of his Coach-Horses (besides Saddle-Nags) were alwaies in the Stable. Farther also, whereas the former Wardens would take but ten or twelve load of Hay out of Halywell Meads (which belong to the coll*ege*, and are in the Tenure of a Tenant) yet this doughty Knight did take up 34 load at least. And tho he used it not half, yet at the yeares end, he did, like a Curr-Mudgin, sell it and put the money in his purse.

Fourthly by burdning his Accompts with frivolous Expences to pleasure his proud Lady, as (1) for a key to the Lock of the Ladies Seat in S. Maries church, to which she would commonly resort (2) for shoes and other things for the Foot-Boy.

Fiftly by burning in one yeare threescore pounds worth of the choicest Billet that could be had, not only in all his Roomes, but in the Kitchin among his servants; without any regard had to cole, which usually, (to save charges) is burnt in kitchins, and somtimes also in Parlours.

Sixtly by encroaching upon, and taking away the rooms belonging to the Fellows. One Instance take for all. Mr Fisher quitted his Lodgings (viz an upper chamber with 3 studies, and a lower chamber with as many, in the great quadrangle) in July an*no* 1665, upon notice that the King and queen would shortly come to Oxon, there to take up their winter-quarters till towards the Spring. When the K*ing* and qu*een* came, which was about Michaelmas following, M^ris Franc*es* Stuart one of the Maids of honour (afterwards Duchess of Richmond) took possession of

86

those Lodgings, and there continued till Febr*uary* following; at
which time the queen who lodged in the Wardens Lodgings, went
to Westminster, and M^ris Stuart with her, and then Mr Fishers
Lodgings laid empty for some time. At length the Warden finding
that the lower chambers of the said Lodgings, were convenient
for him, because they joyned on the south side to his Parlour and
therefore they would make a dainty retiring room, or at least
an Inner Parlour, he did by egregious Flattery with some of the
Fellowes, particularly with Mr Sterry by inviting him and them
often to his Lodgings, did get their consents so farr, as when it
was proposed at a meeting of the society, to have the said rooms
granted for his use, it was done conditionally that the lower
chamber joyning to the Bay-Tree, in the first quadrangle which did
belong to the warden, may henceforth be allowed to that Fellow
which should hereafter come into that chamber over those lower
Rooms that were allow'd for the wardens use. This being granted,
the warden broke a dore thro the wall that parts his Parlour from
the said lower Romes and makes them fit for use, at his owne, and
not at the College, charge; and they yet remaine for the wardens
use: whereby the best Lodgings in the College, which usually
belonged to the senior fellow, were severed and spoyld: and all
this to please a proud and silly woman. But afterwards when *Sterry*
saw that he was made a shoing-horne to serve the wardens turne,
for afterwards Clayton disus'd his company and never invited him
to his Lodgings as formerly (only at Christmas, when the whole
society used to dine there) he became his Enimy, repented of what
he had done, before the society, and blamed his owne weakness
much, to be so imposed upon, as he had been, by the most false and
perfidious warden.

f. 46^v

Seventhly by his going to law with the city of Oxon concerning
certaine liberties in Halywell neare the said Citie, (the mannour
of which belongeth to Merton coll*ege*) an*no* 1666. For the doing of
which, tho, with much adoe, he got the consent of the Fellowes,
yet going inconsideratly on, and not taking the Counsell of Old
Charles Holloway Serjeant at Law the college was cast and much

endamaged. And AW doth well remember that the citizens insulted
so much when they overcame the Coll*ege*, in their sute which was
tried in Westminster hall, that in their returne from London, the
Mayor, or chief Officers of the city did ride into Oxon triumphantly
thro Halywell, to take, as it were, possession of the Liberties
that they had obtained therein. And one —— Chilmead, as he
remembers, who had been one of the Bel-men of the City, but
then living as an Under-Tenant in Halywell, did in their Passage
present them with wine and Ale, while the Parish Bells rang for joy,   f. 47ʳ
occasion'd, as twas supposed, by the said Chilmead.

In all these unreasonable proceedings, Joseph Harvey one of the
Fellowes did constantly oppose the warden, and had there been
more Harveys (for he was a man of a high and undaunted spirit,)
they would have curb'd his proceedings so much, that they would
have made him weary of the place; but most of them (the Fellowes)
being sneaking and obnoxious, they did run rather with the temper
of the warden, than stand against him, meerly to keep themselves in
and enjoy their comfortable importances.

And now by this time the college was ran exceedingly into
debt, and how to pay it the Society knew not. At length, upon
consultation, the Society address'd themselves to their Patron
the Archbishop of Canterbury (Sheldon) an*no* 1671, before whom
they made it plainly to appeare, that, by the Wardens meanes, the
Coll*ege* was run into debt, and that by comparing his Accompts,
with the Accompts of those of Sʳ Nath*aniel* Brent he had spent a
thousand pound more than the said Sʳ Nathaniel, for the yeares
behind, since he had been Warden. &c. The warden Sʳ Thomas
is therefore chid and reprehended by the Archbishop; which was
all the remedy that they could get, and an order was then made
that the college should pay the debt and not the Warden; which
was then look'd upon as a most unreasonable thing. But there was
falsness in the matter, for he that had for 7 yeares spoken against
the Warden and his proceedings and was an Enimy to him, E*dmund*
D*ickenson*,[114] the Warden did by his usual Flatteries gain him for a
time, collogu'd together, and work'd their ends so much that they

found meanes that the college should pay the Debt: which being done he slighted him.

In 1667 twas expected there should be an Election of Fellowes, but upon pretence that the college was in debt, there was no Election made till 1672 so the publick suffer'd, and all people than said that *Merton coll. made but an inconsiderable Figure in the Universitie* &c

Notwithstanding all these things yet the Warden by the motion of his Lady, did put the College to unnecessary charges, and very frivolous Expences, among which were a very larg Looking=Glass, for her to see her ugly face, and body to the middle, and perhaps lower, which was bought in Hillary Terme 1674, and cost, as the Bursar told me, above 10^{li}. A bedsteed and Bedding worth 40^{li} must also be bought, because the former Bedstede and Bedding was too short for him (he being a tall man) so perhaps when a short warden comes, a short bed must be bought. As his bed was too short so the wicket of the common gate entring into the coll*ege* was too low, therefore that was made higher in 1676 in the month of August. The said Bursar G*eorge* Roberts hath several times told me, that either he the Warden, or his Lady do invent, and sit thinking how to put the college to charge, to please themselves, and no end there is to their unlimited Desire. He told me also that there was no Terrier taken of the Goods he had, which were bought at the college charg; and therefore they did carry many of them, especially the Looking Glass, to their country seat, called the Vach in Chalfont parish neare Wycomb in Buck*inghamshire* which Sr Tho*mas* Clayton had bought of the Duke of York, who had received the said mannour from the King, fallen unto him by the Attainder of Georg Fleetwood Esq*uire* one that sate in judgment on K*ing* <u>Cha</u>rles I.

f. 47^v

29 June. Sat. AW was at Sandford neare Oxon, in the House of John Powell Gent*leman*, which was a House and Preceptory somtimes belonging to the Knights Templars. He took a note of some Armes in a Bay-window in a low Room there — Thence he went to Littlemore and neare it he found an antient House called Mincherie, or

f. 48^r

Minchionrea, that is the Place of Nunns, founded there of Old time. But nothing of the Chappel or Church is there standing.[115]

20 Aug. Tues. He was at Thame, continued there one or more nights, transcribd all the Monumentall Inscriptions in the church, Armes in the windowes, and the Armes in the windowes of the Free-schoole.

Sept. With D[r] John Fell Deane of Christ church to have a sight of the leiger books of S. Frideswides Priory and Einsham Abbey. His answer was that he would acquaint the Treasurer D[r] John Dolbin, which he did. — Afterwards AW went to D[r] Dolbin, who told him he would propose the matter at the next Chapter. But the matter being defer'd from time to time, nothing was done in it this yeare.

2 Oct. Wed. His fatherly acquaintance D[r] Barton Holyday Archdeacon of Oxon,[116] died at Eifley, of an Ague, or of the new Epidemical Disease which now raged.

5 Oct. Sat. Saturday, buried in the Cathedral of Christ church.

1661/2. 10 Jan. Fri. AW had an Issue made in his left Legg under his knee, by the advice of Richard Lower a Physitian of Christ church.
— This he kept open several years after. And tho it did his stomach good, yet by his continual standing at his study, and much walking withall, too much of the Humour issued out, which alwaies after made his left Legg and Thigh cold, especially in the winter-time. And he now thinks that when Age comes upon him it will turne to the dead Palsie and be his Death.

f. 48[v]

10 Mar. Mon. His Kinswoman Ellen Pettie the widdow of Charnel Pettie Esquire died at Stoke-Lyne aged 85 or more, and was buried by her husband in the church there.

21 Mar. Fri. He received his first Letters from William Somner the Antiquary of Canterbury, with a Copie of the Foundation-charter of Canterbury College in Oxon.[117]

$$\text{Anno} \left\{ \begin{array}{l} \text{Domini 1662} \\ \text{13 Caroli II} \end{array} \right.$$

Mar.   ult. Charles Duke of Richmond took to wife Margaret the widdow of Will*iam* Lewes of Glamorganshire and of Blechindon in Oxfordshire Esq*uire* and soon after with her consent, sold her Estate at Blechindon, which her husband had bought as it seems, of S*r* Tho*mas* Coghill, to Arthur Earl of Anglesie. — This Duke was a most rude and debauchd person, kept sordid company, and having employed a little crook'd back taylor of Oxon, named —— Herne, he would often drink with him, quarrel and the Taylor being too hard for him, would get him downe and bite his eare —

4 June.   Wed. Hen*ry* Jackson his Kinsman, Rector of Hampton Meysey died — and next day AW went thither and gave his assisting hand to lay him in his grave. — [118] He was one of the first learned Acquaintance that AW had; and being delighted in his company he did for the 3 last yeares of his life constantly visit every summer, continue with him 4. or 5. dayes and heare his stories with Delight that he would tell him concerning divers learned men of the Universitie and his College (Corp*us* Chr*isti*) that lived and flourished when he was a yong man.

6 June.   Fri. J*ohn* W*arnford* Esq*uire* an intimate Acquaintance with AW, when a junior, died in the flower of his youth; and two dayes after was buried in the church of Highworth in Wilts*hire* He was the eldest son and heir of Edm*und* W*arnford*

      quid species, quid lingua mihi, quid profuit ætas?
      Da Lachrymas Tumulo, qui Legis ista meo.[119]

July.   AW having then and before often considered what want there was of a Register for the Parish wherein he was borne, and wherein he lived, called the Collegiate Parish of S. Joh*n* Baptist Merton; he was resolved to begin one: Wherefore getting the notes of all such

Marriages, Births Christnings and Burialls which M[r] John Wilton
an antient Chaplayn of Merton College, had made before he went
to be Vicar of Great Wolford in Warwickshire, and also taking an   f. 49[v]
Account of all the Fathers and Mothers of the same Parish then
living, what children they had borne therein, christned or buried,
he bought a parchment Register which cost him 7[s] at least, and
remitted them all therein, as also the names of such that had been
taken in the time of Oliver and Richard, by one Matthew Jellyman
that had been appointed by the usurp'd powers to write downe in a
Register the names of such that had been christned and buried in
several parishes in Oxon, of which S. John Baptists parish was one
&c. This Register which AW began, he doth continue to this day
and will do the like till the time of his death.[120]

10 Sept. Wed. At Abendon in Berkshire with John Curteyne purposely to
see the manner of the visitation then held by the Diocesan, D[r]
Humphrey Henchman Bishop of Salisbury. He then saw the Ruins
of the most antient and stately Abbey that once stood there; but
those Ruins are since gone to Ruin: — A great Scandal it is that
that most noble structure should now have little or no memory of it
left.

11 Oct. Sat. With D[r] Michael Woodward Warden of New College to see the
Registers and some Records of that House — He put me off for
the present with some notes of his owne concerning the wardens
thereof, Benefactors, Bishops &c.

10 Nov. Mon. His Kinsman John Taverner of Soundess in the parish of
Nettlebed, was made choice of by his Majestie to be High-sherriff
of Oxfordshire &c.

1662/3. 11 Feb. Wed. He was with his cozen Taverner at the Swan-Inn in
Oxon, where he was a witness that M[r] Abraham Davis should let
his House in Grandpool in S. Aldates Parish during the time of
Assize then approaching, and in the time of Assize in the summer
following, for 6[li] a time; but if M[r] Taverner should die before

summer Assize then should he have only 6^{li}, for the Lent Assize. He was also then a witness to other things, agreed upon between them &c.

6 Mar. Fri. Jo*hn* Taverner made his first Entry into Oxon, to conduct   f. 50^r
thereunto Justice Rob*ert* Hyde.

9 Mar. Mon. Given to his cozen Taverner the High Sherriff and M^{ris} Mary Harris his Daughter upon their departure from Oxôn each of them a book fairly bound, containing the works of his brother Edw*ard* Wood, deceased.

$$\text{Anno} \left\{ \begin{array}{l} \text{Domini 1663} \\ \text{14 Caroli II} \end{array} \right.$$

23 Ap. Thur. He began a course of Chimistry under the noted Chimist and Rosicrucian Peter Sthael of Strasburgh in Royal Prussia, and concluded in the latter end of May following — The club consisted of 10 at least, whereof Franc*is* Turner of New Coll*ege* was one, (since Bishop of Ely) Benjam*in* Woodroff of Ch*rist* Church another, (since Canon of Ch*rist* ch*urch*) and Joh*n* Lock of the same house, afterwards a noted writer — This Joh*n* Lock was a man of a turbulent Spirit, clamorous and never contented. The club wrote and took notes from the mouth of their Master, who sate at the upper end of a Table, but the said Jo*hn* Lock scornd to do it; so that while every man besides, of the Club, were writing, he would be prating and troblesome — This *Peter* Sthael who was a Lutheran and a great Hater of women, was a very useful man, had his Lodging in University Coll*ege*, in a chamber at the west End of the Old Chappel — He was brought to Oxon, by the honorable Mr Rob*ert* Boyle, an*no* 1659, and began to take to him Scholars in the House of Joh*n* Cross next, on the *west* side, to University Coll*ege*, where he began but with three Scholars; of which number Joseph Williamson of Queens Coll*ege* was one, afterwards a Knight and one of the Secretaries of State under K*ing* Ch*arles* 2. After he had taken in another Class of six there, he translated himself to the

House of Arth*ur* Tylliard an Apothecary, the next dore to that of
Joh*n* Cross, saving one, which is a Taverne: where he continued
teaching till the latter end of 1662. The chiefest of his Scholars
there were Dr Joh*n* Wallis, Mr Christopher Wren, afterwards
a Knight and an eminent Vertuoso, Mr Thom*as* Millington of
Alls*ouls* coll*ege*, afterwards an eminent Physitian and a Knight,
Nath*aniel* Crew of Linc*oln* coll*ege*, afterwards Bishop of Durham;
Tho*mas* Branker of Exeter coll*ege*, a noted Mathematician, Dr Ralph
Bathurst of Trin*ity* coll*ege*, a Physitian, afterwards President of his
college and Deane of Wells; Dr Hen*ry* Yerbury and Dr Tho*mas*
Janes, both of Magd*alen* College; Rich*ard* Lower a Physitian of
C*hrist* ch*urch*; Rich*ard* Griffith M.A. fellow of University Coll*ege*,
afterwards D^r of Phys*ics* and Fellow of the Coll*ege* of Physitians,
and severall others.

About the beginning of the yeare 1663 Mr Sthael removed his
School or Elaboratory to a Drapers house called Joh*n* Bowell,
afterwards Mayor of the citie of Oxon, situat and being in the
Parish of Allsaints, commonly called Allhallowes. He built his
Elaboratory in an old Hall or Refectory in the Backside, (for the
House it self had been an antient Hostle) wherein AW and his
Fellowes were instructed. In the yeare following Mr Sthael was
called away to London and became Operator to the Royal Society,
and continuing there till 1670, he return'd to Oxon in Nov*ember* and
had several Classes successively, but the names of them I know not;
and afterwards going to London againe, died there about 1675 and
was buried in the church of S. Clements Danes within the Libertie
of Westminster.

30 May. Sat. The chimical Club concluded, and AW paid Mr Sthael 30
shill*ings*, having in the beginning of the class, given 30 shillings
before hand. AW got some knowledge and experience; but his mind
still hung after Antiquities and Musick.

June.   Sr Charles Sedley B^t, somtimes of Wadham coll*ege*, Charles Lord
Buckhurst (afterwards Earl of Middlesex) Sr Thom*as* Ogle &c.
were at a Cooks house at the signe of the cock in Bow-street neare

Covent-Garden within the Libertie of Westminster; and being all inflam'd with strong Liquors, they went into the Balcony joyning to their chamber-window, and putting downe their Breeches, they excrementized in the Street. Which being done Sedley stripped himself naked, and with Eloquence preached Blasphemy to the People. Whereupon a Riot being raised, the people became very clamourous, and would have forced the Dore, next to the Street, open, but being hindred, the preacher and his company were pelted into their Rome or chamber, and the windows belonging thereunto were broken.

This Frollick being soon spread abroad, especially by the fanatical party, who aggravated it to the Utmost by making it the most scandalous thing in nature, and nothing more reproachful to Religion than that, the said company were summoned to the Court of Justice in Westminster hall, where being indicted of a Riot before Sr Rob*ert* Hyde Lord Ch*ief* Justice of the Common Pleas, were all fined, and Sr Char*les* Sedley being fined 500^{li}, he made answer that he thought he was the first man that paid for shiting. Sr Rob*ert* Hyde asked him whether he ever read the book called The Compleat Gentleman &c. to which Sr Charles made Answer, that *set aside his Lordship he had read more books than himself* &c.[121] The day of payment being appointed Sr Charles desired Mr Hen*ry* Killigrew and another Gent*leman* to apply themselves to his Majestie, to get it off, but instead of that, they begd the said sum of his Majestie, and would not abate Sr Charles, two pence of the money. Afterwards Sr Charles taking up and growing very serious, he was chosen a Recruiter for that Long Parliament which began 8. May 1661. and was dissolved in the latter end of 1678. This Memoir is here set downe because AW had some acquaintance with S^r Ch*arles* Sedley; and afterwards some acquaintance with Charles Lord Buckhurst, when he was Earl of Middlesex; at which time he would come with Fleetwood Shepheard to Great Rowlright in Oxfordshire, and thence 3 miles beyond, to Weston in the parish of Long-Compton to visit Mr Sheldon; where he found AW, and discoursed very seriously with him.

f. 51^v

15 June. Mon. About the 15 of June Arthur Crew of Magot Mill near
Highworth in Wilt*shire* Gent*leman* died. — AW had been
acquainted with this Gentleman about 6 yeares before (he living
then in Halywell neare Oxon) because of his great skill and
knowledge in Heraldry and matters relating to English families.
This M[r] Crew was very deaf, and therefore living a retir'd and
studious life, did collect and write much. After he had left Halywell
he retired to Magot-Mill, where, having but little comfort of his
wife, he soon after died, leaving behind him a yong Heire, who
valuing not his fathers labours, because of his Ignorance, put most
of his papers, as I have heard to infimous uses.[122]

27 July. Mon. Thom*as* Baltzar one of the Violins in the Kings service,
mention'd before under the yeare 1658 was buried in the Cloyster
belonging to S. Peters church in Westminster, see before, under
the said yeare. This person being much admired by all lovers of
musick, his company was therefore desired: and company, especially
Musical Company, delighting in drinking, made him drink more
than ordinary which brought him to his grave.

1663/4. 1 Mar. Tues. A controversie having been on foot for some time
between D[r] Tho*mas* Barlow and D[r] Tho*mas* Lamplugh concerning
the Archdeaconry of Oxford, after the death of D[r] Holyday, it was
decided on the first day of March by the Judges of Assize sitting in
Oxon, for D[r] Barlow, the acquaintance of AW.

f. 52[r]

Anno $\begin{cases} \text{Domini 1664} \\ \text{15 Caroli II} \end{cases}$

13 Apr. Wed. A meeting of the Warden and Fellowes of Merton Coll*ege*
where the renewing of the leases belonging to the Family,
concerning the Housing (Portionists hall and its appurtenances)
against Merton Coll*ege*, as also of the Flowr de luce with its
appurtenances was by them proposed. — They set a Fine of 70[li],
and the lease was but 13 yeares expired.

21 Apr. Thur. The said Sum of Money was paid into the hand of D^r
Dickenson the Bursar, and the leases were seald, the Fees of which
came to 7^{li}-9^s — [123]

Rog*er* Brent and Edw*ard* Turner, one a poore, and the other a
busy and sneaking Fellow shewd themselves Back-friends in this
Matter, to Mary Wood widdow, Robert, Anthony and Christop*her*
Wood her Sons.

28 Apr. Thur. Will*iam* Ayliff LL. Bac. somtimes Fellow of New Coll*ege*, and
a founders kinsman there, now Vicar of Amersden neare to Bister in
Oxfordshire, and lately schoolmaster of Thame School (but began
to teach there after AW had left that school) leaped naked out of his
window belonging to the Vicaridge of Amersden, and broke several
parts of his body; and died soon after. — He had married a yong   f. 52^v
rich widdow, lived high, and had severall children by her, but shee
dying in the prime of her yeares, and leving him and the children
little or nothing of her estate, and her joynture going away with her
life, he grew exceedingly discontented thereupon and made away
with himself.

29 Apr. Fri. From Apr. 29 to May 27 AW assisted D^r Jo*hn* Wallis in
digesting and ordering the Evidences, Writings and Books
belonging to the University, which are reposed in the Muniment
Room in the School-Tower.

13 June. Mon. Dr Tho*mas* Barlow installed Archdeacon of Oxon in the
cathedrall of Ch*rist* church.

6 Sept. Tues. At North-More with Mr Pet*er* Nicolls where we were
entertained by M^r —— Twyford. Thence wee went to Bampton
where wee lodged one night in the House of Mr Tho*mas* Cook one
of the Vicars. The next morning very early I went to the castle
neare the Church there and took the Ruins thereof and so return'd
to Oxon.

14 Sept. Wed. Upon the taking up of a thick marble stone lying in the
middle of the choire of Beverley in Yorkshire, neare the entrance

97

into the choire, was found under it a Vault of squared free-stone, five foot in length, two foot in breadth at the head, and one foot and a half at the foot. In this vault was discovered a sheet of lead, four foot in length, containing the dust of St John of Beverley, as also six Beades, three of which were Cornelian, the other crumbled to Dust. There were also in it 3 great brass pins and 4 iron Nayles. Upon this sheet of lead was fixed a plate of lead, whereon was this following inscription, a copy of which was sent to AW.

> Anno ab incarnatione Domini MCLXXXVIII combusta fuit hec ecclesia in mense Sept, in sequenti Nocte post Festum Sancti Matthei Apostoli: et in anno MCXCVII
> VI Id. Martii facta fuit Inquisitio Reliquiarum Beati Johannis in hoc loco, et inventa sunt hec ossa in orientali parte Sepulchri; et hic recondita, et pulvis cemento mixtus ibidem inventus et reconditus.[124]

A Box of lead about 7 Inches in length, six Inches broad and five in height, did lay athwart the Plate of lead. In this Box were divers Pieces of bones mixt with Dust, yeilding a sweet smell.

f. 53^r

16 Dec. Fri. A blazing starr seen by several people in Oxon, and AW saw it in few nights after on Botley Causey about 6 at night in his returne from Cumnore — In the next yeare followed a great plague in England, prodigious Births, great Inundations and Frosts, warr with the Dutch, sudden Deaths, particularly in Oxon &c.

31 Dec. Sat. AW, and his mother, and his eldest brother and his wife went to the Lodgings of Dr Ralph Bathurst President of Trinity College, to welcome him to Oxon, who had then very lately brought to Oxon his new married wife, Mary, the widdow of Dr *John* Palmer late Warden of Alls*ouls* Coll*ege* which Mary was of kin to the mother of AW. They had before sent in Sack, Claret, Cake and Sugar to welcome the said married couple. Dr Bathurst was then about 46 yeares of age, so there was need of a wife —

1664/5. 2 Jan. Mon. Thom*as* Henant M.A. vicar of Thame, in whose House AW sojourned when he went to school there, died — He was buried in the Chancel there, and was descended from the Henants of Henant in the Arbour in Herefordshire.

30 Jan.   Mon. M^ris Kath*erine* Fisher the wife of Thom*as* Rowney of Oxon an Attorney, and Godmother to AW, died in her husbands House in S. Giles Parish. Buried in the Chancell of S. Thomas parish church, Oxon, at which time AW was one that held up the Pall.

13 Feb.   Mon. AW having now spent some years in perusing the Registers and Muniments in the School Tower, by the leave only of Dr Wallis; it was now the desire of the said Doctor, for his owne security, that I should gaine the leave of the Vicechancellour Dr Rob*ert* Say of Oriel Coll*ege*. Whereupon AW did repaire to him on the 13 of Febr*uary* and desired his leave, which was afterwards granted.

18 Mar.   Mon. Dr Wallis and AW repaired to the Vicechancellour, and there AW did take an Oath before them in the presence of Mr Thom*as* Hyde a Publick Notary, to be true and faithfull in the Trust put on AW, and not to imbezile or purloyne any of the said Registers or Muniments.

$$\text{Anno} \left\{ \begin{array}{l} \text{Domini } 1665 \\ \text{16 Caroli II} \end{array} \right.$$

f. 53^v

27 Mar.   Tues. Another Comet in N*orth* E*ast* was seen at Oxon, with the Tayle towards S*outh* E*ast*.

May   ult. He began to peruse the Evidences of Oriel Coll*ege*, in their Treasury, where the society left him to himself, and lent him the Key — He continued there till the 5 of June. And at that time perused some of the Registers of that coll*ege*.

11 June   Sun. He began to peruse the Evidences of Linc*oln* Coll*ege*. — The Rector and Fellows put the keys of the Tower in his hands, and perused them in the Chamber of Mr Hen*ry* Foulis joyning to the said Tower. Robert Clerke a fellow, conceited and impertinent pretended to direct him and instruct him — So whispering Foulis

99

in the eare, wee got him to be removed. AW continued there at least 4 dayes, and the Rector and Fellows had so good opinion of him, that they intrusted him with a long bag of Money in the said Treasurie or Tower, which AWood saw their laying.[125]

22 June Thur. He began to peruse the Evidences of Universitie College — Mr William Shippen one of the Fellows and lately proctor of the Universitie, did attend him. They took the Evidences and Rolls out of the Tower into an upper Chamber adjoyning, and there continued till the 29 day.

July. In the month of July he perused the Evidences belonging to divers churches in Oxon, as S. Michael, on the 5. and 6. S. Peter in the East on the 7. and 8. St Martin on the 21 and 22, St Aldate 28. 29. &c.

24 Aug. Thur. He began to peruse the Evidences of Exeter College — These are well ordered, and methodically digested, and are reposed in a lower Rome neare to the Gatehouse looking Northwards — They were taken out of the said Roome and carried to the Lodgings of the Rector of that college called Dr Joseph Maynard, and in his dining Roome AW perused them in 4 or 5 dayes; in which time the said Doctor was exceeding civil to him. This D^r was an old standard, had much of a true English Temper in him, was void of Dissimulation and sneaking politicks, and at leisure times he would entertaine AW with old stories relating to the Universitie and the learned men of his time. He also then perused some of the registers.

29 Aug. Tues. He began to peruse the catalogue of Fellowes of Exeter college,   f. 54^r which is reposed in the Library there, and soon after transcribd it all for his owne use.

21 Sept. Thur. He began to peruse the Evidences of Balliol College — They were taken out of the Treasury there, which is a kind of a Vestry joyning on the *South* Side to the *East* End of the Chappell — The Evidences were taken thence by Dr Savage the Master of that college and conveyed to his Lodgings, where AW perused them

in the space of 3 or 4 days — The old Accompts of that college wherein their Fellowes are either weekly or quarterly mention'd, are lost. So AW was much put to a push to find when learned men had been of that College.

25 Sept. Mon. The King came from Salisburie to Oxôn, to avoid the plague raging throughout the Nation, and took up his Quarters in Christ church.

26 Sept. Tues. The Queen came for the same purpose, and took up her Quarters in Merton college.

1665/6. 27 Jan. Sat. The King left Oxon, in order to goe to Westminster.

3 Feb. Sat. AW was with D*r* Say the Vicechancellour, to have his leave to go up into the Galleries in Bodlies Library, where the Manuscripts are reposed, to the end that he might have a full perusal of them, without troubling the second Keeper, or Porter of the said Library to fetch every book that he wants, which was granted. A little before this grant AW told M*r* Thomas Hyde the chief Keeper of the said Library, what he intended to doe and that he should goe with him to be a witness of the Vicechancellours leave. Whereupon the time being appointed to goe, which was in the afternoon of the same day, he (M*r* Hyde) did goe in the morning before, to the Vicechancellour, and desired him not to grant M*r* Wood leave, unless he would promise him to give him his helping hand to the Making of a Catalogue of the Manuscripts in Bodlies Library. So tho there was underhand-Dealing in this Matter, yet M*r* Wood did then partly promise to do it, yet M*r* Hyde seeing afterwards how he (M*r* Wood) was involv'd in a public work, he never urged him to it a second time.

16 Feb. Fri. The Queen left Oxon, and went after the King to Westminster.
 About that time AW began to peruse the Manuscripts in the Public Library and took great paynes in plucking downe every book.[126]

Anno $\left\{\begin{array}{l}\text{Domini 1666} \\ \text{17 Caroli II}\end{array}\right.$

11 Apr. Wed. He began to peruse the Evidences of All*souls* Coll*ege* which
were brought from the Tower over the Gate into the Lodgings of
Dʳ Th*omas* James Warden of the said coll*ege*. They were put in
good Method, as Exeter College Evidences were, and therefore it
saved him much Trouble — He also perused certaine Registers of
that House, which he was permitted to carry home with him for a
time. — Dʳ Th*omas* Millington was not then at home, otherwise (as
he had told AW, afterwards) he should never have seen them. AW
asked him the reason why; he answerd that as the publication of the
Monasticons had bred a great deal of trouble, and had caused suits
in Westminster hall, so would the publication of *Hist. et Antiq. Univ.
Oxon*, which AW was about to publish; but it hath not as yet.[127]

4 May. Fri. It was allowed by the Society of Merton Coll*ege* that AW might
peruse the Evidences in their Treasury, in the Presence of Mʳ Pet*er*
Nicolls one of their number.

31 May, &c. Certain Registers belong to Magd*alen* Coll*ege* were by AW
perus'd.

2 June. Sat. He began to peruse some of the evidences belonging to the
said coll*ege* — They were taken out of the Treasury for his use, and
put into the Exchequer where he perus'd them and kept the Key in
his pocket till he had finish'd them — They were Evidences that
mostly belonged to Sᵗ John Baptists Hospitall, which was annex'd by
the Founder to his Coll*ege*.

25 June. Mon. Perused the Evidences of Queens Coll*ege*, and afterwards
a Leiger, or Transcript of all the Evidences by the favour of Dʳ
Barlow: All done in the dining roome belonging to his Lodgings.

30 June. Sat. Dʳ Hen*ry* Deane of New coll*ege* and AW, waited on the
Warden of that House, with a Desire to see the Evidences of that
House — His answer was that he would aske the consent of the

Fellowes — All their Evidences are transcrib'd into several Folios of Parchment or Velum.

30 July. Mon. The Warden of New College with the consent of the Fellowes lent AW the first Leiger-book, containing Evidences relating to the scite of the college, their tenements in the City of Oxon, and Lands in Oxfordshire — The leave was granted 28. July, and AW perused it in his owne Study.

Aug.   AW repaired to Dr Rich*ard* Baylie president of S. John's Coll*ege*, to   f. 55^r
do him the favour to let him peruse the Evidences of his Coll*ege*, as other societies had done — He refer'd him to Mr Joseph Taylour a lame Fellow of that house, who had drawne up a short and trite account of the Founder, Foundation, Presidents and Benefactors thereof, which he lent to him, and he transcrib'd it. But this contenting him not, Dr Pet*er* Mews who shortly after succeeded Dr Baylie in Presidentship, did freely give him Leave to peruse the Evidences.

   About the same time he perused the Evidences of Brasnose and other colleges.

   Dec. In the beginning of Dec*ember* he was taken with an Ague: whereupon taking physick and blooding, his body was pluck'd downe, and much time was lost before he could recover himself, and be in a posture to study.

1666/7. 28 Feb. Thur. Marie Wood widdow, the mother of AWood, died in her house against Merton Coll*ege* aged 65 or more.[128]

1 Mar.   Fri. Buried by the Remaines of her husband in Merton College Church.

18 Mar. Mon. Paid to the collectors of the Pole-Money, of the parish of S. Joh*n* Bapt*ist* wherein he lived, 1^{li} as a gentleman, and 1^s for his Head, towards the carrying on the warr between the English and the Dutch at sea. This is set downe here, because it was the first Tax that AW ever paid. He paid others afterwards, especially in the raigne of K*ing* Will*iam* 3.

Anno $\left\{ \begin{array}{l} \text{Domini 1667} \\ \text{18 Caroli II} \end{array} \right.$

2 Apr.   Tues. The bones of Tho*mas* Wood father to AW, were taken up and
laid close to those of his wife.

2.3 May. Thur., Fri. Perused the Evidences of S Marie Magd*alen* church
in the north Suburb of Oxon, reposed in a vestrie joyning to the
church there.

13 June. Thur. He received letters of Commendation from Dr Thomas
Barlow Prov*ost* of Queens coll*ege*, to Will*iam* Dugdale Esq*uire*
Norroy K*ing* of Armes, to introduce him into the acquaintance
of the said person, and consequently into the library of S^r. Joh*n*
Cotton at Westminster

14 June. Fri. He went to London in the Stage-Coach[129] — His Companions
were all Scholars, among whome was Obadiah Walker the
senior Fellow of University Coll*ege*. They all lodg'd that night at
Beconsfield, and then AW became acquainted with the said M^r
Walker, and so continued his acquaintance til death parted them.

16 June. Sun. Early in the Morn*ing* being Sunday AW went to the Middle
Temple and found out Mr Dugdale in the apartment belonging
to Elias Ashmole. He gave him Dr Barlows Letters, and after he
had read them, which were to introduce him into the Cottonian
Library, he expressed great Civility to him — He then appointed
him to call on him the next morning and he should have letters
from him to Sr Joh*n* Cotton.

17 June. Mon. Accordingly he went and found him in the said Apartment
(where he lodged) and discoursed with him concerning various
matters of Antiquity — He then gave him his letter to Sr Joh*n*
Cotton, wherein was inclosed that of Dr Tho*mas* Barlow; so posting
forthwith to Westminster, he found Sr Joh*n* Cotton in his house,
joyning almost to Westminster hall — He was then practicing on
his Lute with his Instructor, and when he had done, he came out

to him in the Hall, and receiv'd him kindly, invited him to Dinner, and directed him to Mr Rich*ard* Pearson who kept the Key of his Library — Here was another Trouble, for the said Mr Pearson being a Lodger in the House of Rob*ert* Scot a Bookseller living in Little Britaine he was forced to walke thither, and much adoe there was to find him, but find him at last he did, and by his appointment he met him the next day at Sr John Cottons house, where he lent him two MSS.; which being run over and perused in half a day, yet before he could get two more (for no more were to be at a time lent out) it would be a whole day (perhaps two) before AW could find out the said Mr Pearson to let him have more. This was very troblesome and how to help it he could not tell. At length an antient Gentleman named Mr Withrington, who was an old servant, and House-Keeper when Sr John and his family went into the Country, seeing to what Trouble AW was put to, advis'd him for the future to take his opportunities to come in the Long Vacation to study, for then Sr John being absent for 3 or more months together, he did usually leave the Key of his library in his hands. Afterwards he took his Advice, and went to London in the Long Vacations, and then Mr Withrington being constantly in the House, he would conduct AW into the very next roome joyning to the library, where he would bring to him what books he pleased, which he pointed at in the Catalogue. So that spending there 9 houres in a day constantly for a fortnight or more together, he at length did effect his business.

21 June. Fri. This Mr Pearson[130] (who was a learned man and yonger brother to Dr John Pearson Bishop of Chester) being seldome to be found, AW went with letters of Commendation from Dr Rob*ert* Say Provost of Oriel Coll (which he brought with him from Oxon) to the Lodgings of Mr Will*iam* Prinn in Lincolns Inne, chief Keeper of the Records in the Tower of London, to the end that he would introduce him among the Records there for the carrying on of a publick work. — Mr Prynne received him with old fashion Complements, such as were used in the raigne of K*ing* Jam*es* I and told him he should see what he desird, and seem'd to be glad that

f. 56^r

such a yong man as he (AW) was (for so he cal'd him) should have inclinations towards venerable Antiquity &c. He told him then that if he would call upon him the next morning at 8 of the clock, he would conduct him to the Tower, for he had business then to do there, being about to print another book.[131]

f. 56ᵛ

22 June. Sat. AW went precisely at the time appointed, and found Mʳ Prynne in his black Taffaty-cloak, edg'd with black lace at the bottom — They went to the Tower directly thro the city, then lying in Ruins (occasion'd by the grand conflagration that hapned in 1666) but by his meeting with several Citizens and prating with them, it was about 10 of the clock before they could come to the same place. He there shew'd AW a place where he should sit and write, shew'd him the Reportorium[132] and spoke to Jennings the Reacher of the Records, that he should let him have any record that he should point at in the said Repertorium. After that he conducted AW into the White Tower, where he was strangely surprized, to see such a vast number of Charters and Rolls, that were there reposed &c. He found Mʳ Dugdale in the Office where he was to sit, who was running over a course of Rolls in order to the drawing up and finishing either his 3ᵈ volume of *Monasticon Anglicanum*, or his *Baronage*:[133] And so long as AW stayd in London, which were but a few Dayes, he spent them there in his company, and at 12 of the clock every day they dined together at a cooks house within the Tower, and somtimes had Jennings (a boon Blade) among them.

The same day at night, AW sent Letters by the Post to Dʳ Thomas Barlow, to let him know what he had done at London, and to give him thanks for the fatherly favours he did unto him.

29 June. Sat. He returned to Oxôn — It was the first time that AW was at London, and the truth is his time being short, he only took measures, what to doe at his next going to that place.

18 July. Thur. He began to peruse the Evidences, rent-rolls &c. in Christ church Treasury, over the Cloyster there; and continued so doing, all the remaining part of July, all August, and part of Sept. For

there was work enough for a curious and critical Antiquary that
would hold him tugg for a whole yeare. f. 57^r

There are a great many Evidences which belonged to S^t
Frideswydes Priory, but no Rent-rolls of their Lands and Tenements
— There are many Evidences and Rent rolls that belonged to
Osney Abbey, and innumerable broken writings and Rolls which
belonged to the Priories and Nunneries that were dissolv'd by the
meanes of Card*inal* Wolsey towards the erection of his College in
Oxôn. But this the Reader must know that the said college being
not setled by Law when the Cardinal fell, all the lands which
were appointed for the said coll*ege*, came into the Kings hands. So
that between the Cardinals fall, and the settlement of the College
by the King, which was 3 years at least, most of the Lands of the
said dissolv'd Priories and Nunneries, being sold to, or beg'd of
the King by, hungry courtiers, who had only the Kings grant for
them, without the antient Evidences belonging to them; those
Evidences remained still in Cardinal, now ch*rist* ch*urch*, Coll*ege*.
And because the members thereof have not the Lands, which
those Evidences concern, they take no care of the Evidences, but
lay them in a By-place expos'd to weather, and thereby are much
perished and become not legible. From these Evidences did AW
furnish Sr Will*iam* Dugdale with many things, which he inserted
in his third vol*ume* of *Monasticon Anglicanum*, viz. with those four
Evidences in p. 11, concerning Wallingford: with eleven others in p.
13. 14. 15, concerning Littlemore Nunnery within the Precincts of
Sandford in Oxfordshire, which by a mistake Sr William hath added
to Sandford in Berks*hire*: with 4 copies in p. 30. 31. concerning
Horkesley a Cell to the Abbey of Tefford: with a copie in p. 77.b.
concerning Otteham Priory: with the Charter concerning the
Hospital of Ginges in Essex, otherwise called Gynge-Montegney,
and with many others which he thought not fit to be published.

John Willis yonger brother to Dr Thom*as* Willis the famous
Physitian, was then chapter-clerk of Ch*rist* church; and he then
designing to make a repertorie of Records belonging to the said
church, made choice of that time to do it, to the end that he

might have the Assistance of AW, which he freely imparted, and demonstrated to him from several evidences what encroachments that church had suffered in many places in Oxon, on their Lands and Tenements, which formerly belonged to St Frideswyde and Osney.

31 Aug. Sat. John Aubrey of Easton-Piers in the parish of Kington S. Michael in Wiltsh*ire*, was in Oxon, with Edw*ard* Forest a Book-seller living against Alls*ouls* coll*ege*, to buy books — He then saw lying on the stall *Notitia Academiæ Oxoniensis*, and asking who the Author of that book was, he answer'd the Report was that one Mr Anth*ony* Wood of Merton Coll*ege*, was the Author, but was not. Whereupon Mr Aubrey, a pretender to Antiquities, having been contemporary to AWoods elder brother in Trin*ity* Coll*ege*, and well acquainted with him, he thought that he might be as well acquainted with AW himself. Whereupon repairing to his Lodgings, and telling him who he was, he got into his acquaintance, talk'd to him about his studies and offer'd him what assistance he could make, in order to the completion of the work that he was in hand with. — Mr Aubrey was then in a sparkish Garb, came to Towne with his Man and two Horses, spent high and flung out AW at all recknings:[134] But his Estate of 700^li per an*num*, being afterwards sold, and he reserving nothing of it to himself, liv'd afterwards in a very sorry condition, and at length made shift to rub out by hanging on Edm*und* Wyld Esq*uire*, living in Blomesbury neare London, on James Earle of Abendon whose first wife was related to him, and on Sr Joh*n* Aubrey his kinsman living somtimes in Glamorganshire, and somtimes at Borstall near Brill in Buck*inghamshire*. He was a shiftless person, roving and magotie-headed, and somtimes little better than crased. And being exceedingly credulous, would stuff his many letters sent to AW with fooliries, and misinformations, which somtimes would guid him into the paths of errour.

Sept. Perus'd the Evidences of S. Joh*n* Baptists coll*ege*, by the favour of Dr Mews the President, who treated AW, with more freeness and libertie, than any other Head of a House — The Keys of the Tower over the Gate were freely put into his hand, and he perused the Evidences partly in the Tower and partly in a chamber on the south side of it, which then belonged to Edw*ard* Bernard one of the Proctors of the University, for thro his chamber was the passage up to the Tower — There are many Evidences belonging to Walton mannor, and the mannour of S. Giles, both in the north Suburb of Oxon: which Evidences had belonged to Osney, Godstow &c. as having been formerly Lords of those mannours.

1667/8. Mar. Whereas in the month of May 1667 AW had leave given to him by the Parishioners of S. Marie Magdalen Parish to peruse their Evidences reposed in their church, he did then find among them a Register of paper containing (1) Marriages from 1574 to 1591, (2) Christnings from 1577 to 1591. (3) Burialls from 1574 to 1591, which Register being worn, torn and hardly legible, AW did transcribe on Dutch paper, and caused it to be bound with a past-board cover and velum over it. Which Register, with the old he delivered to the Parishners, 24 Mar*ch*, the old to be laid up in the Chest, the transcript to be kept in the Clarks hands &c.

Anno $\left\{ \begin{array}{l} \text{Domini 1668} \\ \text{19 Caroli II} \end{array} \right.$ f. 58^v

16 May. Sat. Matthew Hutton M. A. Fellow of Brasn*ose* College and AW went to Borstall neare Brill in Bucks, the habitation of Lady Penelope Dinham, being quite altered since AW was there in 1646; for whereas then it was a Garrison, with high Bulworks about it, deep Trenches and Pallosadoes, now it had pleasant Gardens about it and several sets of Trees well growne. The Errand of AW there was to see the Leiger of the family, first for the satisfying of himself as to matters to be extracted thence for his book, about to be published, and secondly to extract thence what he could find for the 3^d Vol*ume* of *Monasticon Anglicanum*; which were the copies of some charters that are printed in the said 3^d Vol*ume* p. 18, concerning the Hermitage of Muswell in the parish of Piddington

neare Borstall. This Leiger-book written in Parchment containes
the Evidences and other Matters concerning the lands pertaining
to the Lords of Borstall lying at Borstall, and in Buck*ingham*shire,
and Oxfordshire, and was made and written by the care of Edm*und*
Rede Esq*uire*, Lord of the Mannor of Borstall, temp*ore* H*enry* 6. In
the beginning of this book is represented in colours the Mannour
House of Borstall, with a Moat round it, and the Lord of the
Mannour (Johannes filius Nigelli) issuing out of his house to meet
a certain King and his retinew. And at some distance from the
House the Lord kneels downe to the King and presents him with a
Boares head on the top of a sword or speare. This, as the Tradition
of the family goeth, is an Allusion to the custome of the Mannour
(Borstall) to present the King with a Boares head, because the said
Mannour was in antient time, when twas wooddy, a *stall* or Den for
wild *Boares*.

Between 9 and 10 of the clock at night, being an hour or two   f. 59^r
after supper, there was seen by them, M*atthew* H*utton*, AW and
those of the family, of Borstall, a Draco volans fall from the sky. It
made the place so light for a time, that a man might see to read.
It seemed to AW to be as long as Allsaints Steeple in Oxôn, being
long and narrow: And when it came to the lower Region it vanished
into Sparkles, and, as some say, gave a Report. Great Raines and
inundations followed &c.

18 May. Mon. M*atthew* Hutton and AW walked from Borstall to see some
Churches, and what of Matter of Antiquity wee could find in them,
and about 12 of the clock they arrived at Notley in the parish
of Long-Crendon in Bucks, to see the ruins of the Abbey there,
originally built for Black Canons. Mr Norris Lenton the owner of it
(from the family of the Lord Norris) was an antient Bachelaur, and
had formerly been a great Traveller, and being a person of good
breeding and a scholar he received them with great Curtesie. They
met there Capt*ain* —— Sanders of Hadnam, and after Dinner they
viewed the Ruins which shew'd that it had been a stately place, and
therefore the spectacle was more sad &c. In one of the windows of a

lower Roome were the Armes of Stafford Duke of Buck*inghamshire*
— When AW went to school at Thame he usually retired to this
place to gather Nuts having been then great plenty, and more in
antient time which caused it to be called Nutley that is the place of
Nuts.

21 May. Thur. Received from Dr Savage Master of Balliol coll*ege* his book
lately printed, entit*led Balliofergus* &c.[135] in requitall for what AW
had done in order to its composition. — In the said book p. 28 he
calls AW *his friend.*

30 May. Sat. He went to the house of Sr George Croke Lord of Water-stoke
neare to Thame in Oxfordshire, where he found a great Diversion
in perusing and taking the Armes and monuments in the church,
and in the mannour house belonging to the said Sr George. AW
lodged by the appointment of the said Sr George in an antient
Rome called the Kings Rome, because K*ing* H*enry* 6 had lodged
therein, and 'twas as he remembers at the end of the Dining-
Rome. The mannour of Waterstoke, Sr George Croke a Judg had   f. 59^v
purchased of the Caves or Danvers, and having an only son who
was a sot or fool, or both, would not leave Waterstoke to him, but to
the son of his brother (a clergy man) named Sr Georg Croke before
mentiond, somtimes Fellow of <u>All</u>*souls* coll*ege* and afterwards High
Sherriff of Oxfordshire; but after the death of his wife (who was an
Onslow of Surrey) he ran into Debt, retired to London, followed
women and ruin'd himself. Some yeares after his death (which
hapned in 1680) the heir and Executor, or those that were intrusted
with the Estate, sold Waterstock to —— Ashurst a Trader of
London, who pulling downe all the old House, built this that stands
of Brick, an*no* 1695.

July.   Tho*mas* Gore of Alderton in Wiltsh*ire* Esq*uire* having published
about the beginning of this yeare a catalogue of Authors that had
written of Heraldry, he sent AW a printed copie of it, with a desire
that he would add more Authors to them: Whereupon interleaving
the Book, he added to it as much as came to half that book that was

printed this yeare: Which being done he sent them away in the beginning of July this yeare, and afterwards more as they came to his hands — See more in October 1674.[136]

Aug.   Received a letter from Cornwall that the body of a Giant of 10 foot long was there lately found in digging or plowing — Dr Rich*ard* Trevour had also a letter thence, or else from Devonshire, that attested the like matter.

1 Sept.   Tues. AW went to Coopers hill in the Parish of Brockworth, 4 miles distant (towards Oxon) from the city of Glocester, in the company of his Acquaintance Tim*othy* Nourse M.A. and Fellow of University Coll*ege*. — This Coopers hill is a Lone-house own'd by their Acquaintance John Theyer Gent*leman*, who had then a very fair Library of MSS., repos'd in a Roome which he had built to   f. 60^r retaine them — The next day Mr Nourse went forward to see some of his Relations, and AW set himself to peruse the MSS., which the said Mr Theyer had been neare 40 yeares in gathering, and did catalogue many of them.[137]

4 Sept.   Fri. Mr Nourse returning to us the day before, wee went this day to Glocester, where wee saw the cathedral and monuments therein, and several parts of the city; afterwards wee went to the Taverne with one or two of the choire, drank a glass of wine and had a song, and so when 'twas neare dark wee return'd to Coopers hill.

7 Sept.   Mon. Returned to Oxon, brought a MS or two with him and others were sent after him by a Carrier to peruse; which afterwards he returned.

12. 13 Sept. Sat., Sun. Took Physick and blooded to prevent the comming on of an Ague.

10 Dec.   Thur. His Acquaintance Rob*ert* Dormer of Rowsham in Oxfordshire Esq*uire,* did take to wife M^{ris} Anne Cotterel one of the Daughters of Sr Charles Cotterel Master of the ceremonies — This Rob*ert* Dormer, when he was a yong man lived very high in London, in the time of Oliver, and he and Sr Will*iam* Sedley Elder Brother to

Sr Charles, did strive who should out-vie each other in Gallantry
and in splendid Coaches, but afterwards marrying Catherine the
daughter of Mountague Earl of Lindsey, which was his first wife he
took up and grew rich.

30 Dec. Wed. Went with Franc*is* Dryer (an outlander, borne at Breme)
now a sojournour in Oxon for the sake of the Library, to Sr Georg
Crokes house at Waterstoke, to keep part of the Christmas, and
continued there till the 2 of Jan*uary*.

1668/9. 18, 19 Mar. Thurs., Fri. Sr Edw*ard* Bysshe Clarenceaux King of
Armes was at the Crowne Inn neare Carfax in Oxon, in order
to visit part of the county of Oxon, being part of the Province
belonging to Clarenceux — AW was with him several times,
eate and drank with him, and had several discourses with him
concerning Armes and Armory, which he understood well, but he   f. 60^v
found him nice and supercilious. Few Gentlemen appeared because
at that time there was a Horse-Race at Brackley. Such that came
to him, he entred if they pleased, If they did not enter, he was
indifferent, so the Visitation was a trite thing. Many look'd on this
matter, as a Trick to get Money. A little before his Departure he
gave AW a dash of his Office viz. he entred 3 or more Descents
of his family, a copie of which he hath lying by him. Afterwards
Sr Edward having a coach and four horses with him, he went to
Banbury. There were only with him old —— Wither a Herald
Painter of London and his clerk (Gregorie) the former of which
trick'd the coates, the other entred them in the book of Visitation.
He the said Sr Edw*ard* Bysshe was in Oxon againe in 1675 to make
an end of his Visitation but AW was then absent.

$$\text{Anno} \begin{cases} \text{Domini 1669} \\ \text{20 Caroli II} \end{cases}$$ f. 61^r

15 Apr. Thur. By Virtue of a Ticket some dayes before put into the hands
of AW, he went to the Guildhall of Oxon to participate of a Feast
there kept for the Natives of Oxon.

They all met at 9 of the clock in the Morn*ing* in the said Hall,
and marched thence very orderly (in number about 440) downe
the high street, with a minister before them, had a sermon in the
church of S. Pet*ers* in the East, preached by Rob*ert* Field M. A.
of Trin*ity* Coll*ege*, borne in Grope Lane in S*t* Maries parish, and
retiring to the Hall againe, had a noble Entertainment; which
done there was a Collection made to bind out two or more Boyes
Apprentices. This was the first time that the Natives of Oxon had a
Feast, being begun and put forward by —— Paynton the Townclerk
a Native of Oxôn. This was done in imitation of Berkshire men,
who kept their Feast on Candlemas day going before, Joh*n* Lamb
being then Mayor.

26 Apr. Munday was the first day that the Flying-Coach went from Oxon
to London in one Day — AW went in the same Coach, having
then a Boot on each side. Among the six men that went M*r* Rich*ard*
Holloway a counsellour of Oxôn (afterwards a Judge) was one.
They then, according to the Vicechancellours Order stuck up in
all public places, entred into the Coach at the Tavern Dore against
<u>All</u>*souls* coll*ege* precisely at 6 of the clock in the morning, and at
7 at night they were all set downe in their inn at London — The
occasion of AWoods going to London was to carry on his studies in
the Cottonian Library and elswhere.

3 May. Mon. Cosmo de Medicis Prince of Tuscany entertaind by the
Members of the Universitie of Oxon.

7 May. Fri. AW return'd from London, and soon after collected from his
friends the particulars of the Princes entertainment.[138]

21 May. Fri. D*r* Rich*ard* Pearson of Cambridge, and M*r* Tho*mas* Hyde the
chief Library-Keeper gave a visit to AW — AW entertain'd them at
the Taverne against <u>All</u>*souls* coll*ege* — see before, in the yeare 1667.

26 June. Sat. AW was dismist from his usual and constant Diet, which for
many yeares he had taken in the House where he was borne, and

f. 61*v*

then lived, by the rudeness and barbarity of a brutish woman, of
which she afterwards repented, when too late — AW was put to his
shifts, a great deale of Trouble, and knew not what to doe because
his Dismiss was suddaine, whereas there should have been a months
warning at least. He was asham'd to go to a publick house because
he was a senior Master, and because his Relations lived in Oxôn,
and to go to Merton coll*ege* (which he had left, as to his Diet, for
several yeares before) he was much resolv'd in himself against it. He
had a name in the Buttery-book there and took bread and beere,
when he could go no where else for meat. By his much fasting,
and drinking more than usually the whole course of his Body was
chang'd. Weaknesses came into several of his joynts, especially
in the Leggs, and great noises in his eares: And in the next yeare
he found a Deafness, first in his right, and afterwards in his left,
eare, which continued more or less till Death. This Disaster, AW
look'd upon as the first and greatest Misery of his Life. It made him
exceeding Melancholy and more retir'd; was also at great charg in
taking physick and slops to drive the noises out of his ears, and D^r
Joh*n* Lamphire took a great deal of paines about them, but in vaine.
— You will heare more hereafter what Trouble and charge AW was
put to, to obtaine his hearing.[139]

6 July. Tues. Elias Ashmole Esq*uire* came to Oxôn to spend some time
there, and to see the Solemnity of the great Act approaching. He
lodged in the Greyhound Inn without the East-Gate of Oxon, and
then he very kindly sent for AW to come to him, purposely to
deliver Commendations to him from his Father in Law Will*iam*
Dugdale Norroy K*ing* of Armes. He continued in Oxôn 7 or 8
Dayes and AW attended him every day in seeing many curiosities,
as the painting in Allsou*ls* Coll*ege* Chappel, the paynting in
Magd*alen* Coll*ege* Chappell, and the paynting in the Theater. They
were often in the Physick Garden with Jacob Bobart the Keeper,
(an old acquaintance of Mr Ashmole) who shewd them many choice
plants, Herbs, Grafts, and other Curiosities to Mr Ashmoles great   f. 62^r
content.

9 July. Fri. The Dedication of the Theater for a learned use — After which followed a very great and splendid Act.[140]

24 Aug. Tues. AW went to London in the Flying-coach, having before been nominated by the Proctors one of the 12 Masters of Arts to attend the Solemnity of the Installation of James Duke of Ormonde to the Chancellourship of the Universitie of Oxon.

25 Aug. Wed. AW went about 8 of the clock in the morning by Whitehall towards Sr John Cottons house neare Westminster hall, to borrow some Manuscripts from his Library to carry on the grand work of the *Hist. and Antiq. of the Univ. of Oxon* — He met neare Whitehall Gate with Dr Joh*n* Fell, Dr Rich*ard* Allestrie, Dr Thomas Yate &c. comming from prayers, as it seems at Whitehall, who told him that at 12 of the clock of the said Day, he was to meet the Oxford scholars then in London to dine with his Grace the Archb*ishop* of Canterbury (Sheldon) at Lambeth. They told him then that if he met by chance with any Oxford Doctors or Masters between that time and 12 of the clock he should tell them of it, which he did. Afterwards he borrowed certaine MSS., and at 12 of the Clock he passed over the water to Lambeth with Dr Yate, Proctor Alsop and others. When they came there the Archb*ishop* was at the Councill Table at Whitehall with the King and did not returne till one of the clock. In the meane time the Doctors and Masters entertaind themselves with pictures and other rarities in the Gallery and had divers Discourses. At length the Archb*ishop* came among them with Dr Fell, and at their first entrie into the Gallery AW being next to the Dore Dr Fell said to the Archbishop — *If it please your Grace here is a Master of Arts* (pointing to AW) *that you must take notice of. He hath done the Universitie a great deal of honour by a Book that he hath written.* Whereupon the Archb*ishop* comming towards him AW kneeled downe and he bless'd him, and laying his hand upon his shoulder when he was risen spoke very kindly to him, and told him that *he was glad that there was such a person in the Universitie that*   f. 62^v *had a generous mind to do such a work.* He bid him to proceed in his

Studies, that *he should be encourag'd and want nothing that was equal to his Deserts.*

Afterwards they all went downe into the common Hall, where were divers Bishops and persons of Qualitie, and others that thrust in, besides the Oxford Scholars that dined there. There was a high Table went cross the upper end of the Hall, and Tables on each side, as in College Halls. Sr Leolin Jenkins being then there, he laid his hands on AW, and made him sit at the high Table (wheras he should have sit at one of the side Tables with his contemporaries) between him and John Cook an under-secretarie to the Lord Arlington one of the Chief Secretaries of State. He was then exceedingly caress'd by all learned and good men. &c.

26 Aug. Thur. James Duke of Ormonde was install'd Chancellour of the Universitie at Worcester house in the Strand neare London. After which, followed a most noble Banquet — AW was there and complemented by many &c.

29 Aug. Sun. With Mr Hugh Cressey at Somerset house — He discoursed with him, but found not his expectation satisfied — He was then one of the chaplaines to Queen Catherine.

Thence he was conducted by William Rogers of Lincoln's Inn to Mr Davenport commonly called Sancta Clara who also had an apartment in the same house. He was then or had been lately confessor to Queen Catherine. He found him a complaisant man, very free and discoursive. Which made him when he went afterwards to London to visit him often.[141]

5 Sept. Mon. With Mr Cressey againe, and discoursed of divers matters relating to antiquities &c.

7 Oct. Sun. John Curteyne M. A. somtimes Fellow of Lincoln College was buried in the church at Borough in Lincolnshire — He had been Physitian to AW after Richard Lower went to London to practice physick, which was in 1666.

22 Oct. Fri. The Delegacy for printing of Books met between 8 and 9 in the morn*ing* in Anthony Halls house behind and northward of the schooles, at which were present Dr Pet*er* Mews the Vicechancellour,   f. 63^r Dr Joh*n* Fell, Dr Tho*mas* Yate, D^r Th*omas* Barlow, Obad*iah* Walker, Alsop proctor &c. They sent for AW to come unto them, and told him that whereas he had taken a great deal of paines in writing the *Hist. and Antiq. of the Universitie of Oxôn,* they would for his paines give him an 100^{li} for his copie, conditionally that he would suffer the book to be translated into Latine for the honour of the University in forreigne countries, and that he would take more paines in recovering transcripts of original charters which he cites in his book, as also *verba ipsa,* the words themselves of old MS. Authors &c. to be put in Italic character, and thereby add to the authority of the book. These proposalls, tho they were suddain to the author yet he granted them their Desires. They it seems had before been informed of the worth of the book by Mr Obad*iah* Walker and Mr Will*iam* Stone the Principal of New inn, who some time before had been at the Lodging of AW to see and peruse the Book.[142]

Nov.   AW took a compleat catalogue of all the MSS. in Dr Tho*mas* Barlows Library in Queens coll*ege.* — They were then in number at least 76. besides Bundells of writings concerning Differences between the Universitie and citie of Oxon, concerning Hedington in Oxfordshire, found among the papers of Mr Joh*n* Hearne a Lawyer, besides divers papers and bundells that had belonged to Dr Usher Primate of Ireland, and the copie of divers modern sermons preached by eminent Divines of the ch*urch* of England.

24 Dec. Fri. His Acquaintance and deare Friend Henry Foulis[143] Bac*helor* of Div*inity* and Subrector of Lincolne coll*ege* died between 4 and 5 of the clock in the Afternoone — He left behind him a larg studie of Books; which being afterwards to be sold AW did for the most part make a Catalogue of them, at the desire of Tho*mas* Law and Joh*n* à Court Masters of Arts and fellows of the said Coll*ege.*

1669/70. Jan. Upon the desire of Dr Bathurst President of Trinity college,
AW did communicate to him part of the *Hist. and Antiquities of
the Universitie of Oxôn*; but he being a most false person, did shew
several parts of it to other persons, particularly to Anth*ony* Etterick
somtimes a commoner of Trin*ity* coll*ege*, who accidentally came
to give him a visit, who finding a passage therein which reflected,
as he thought, on the credit of Dr Joh*n* Bidgood a Physitian of the
city of Exeter; he did forthwith acquaint him by letters — et hinc
Lachrymæ &c. Severall complaining letters he sent to Dr Bathurst
to have that passage expurg'd, wherein the Author was very slightly
mentiond &c. see *Ath. et Fasti Oxon.* vol. 2. p 806.[144] He the said
Dr. Bathurst did also shew to Dr Joh*n* Wallis the memoire of his
Election to the Custodie of the Archives under the yeare 1657, as
Dr Wallis did afterwards intimate to the Author; but when the Hist.
or Annalls of the said university were printed that memoire was
omitted, because the Annalls reached no farther than the latter
end of 1648. — When the author also communicated to the said D^r
Bathurst his second book of the said Historie he dashed out many
things relating to Trin*ity* Coll*ege*, and somthing of the Epitaph of
Dr Rob*ert* Harris there: which Epitaph Dr Bathurst had made, but
afterwards was asham'd of it.

    Now was AW put to a great deal of trouble to unravel his
Histori, and make it fit for a Latin Translation (1) He was to take
several journeys to London and elswhere to recover the copies of
Charters, Bulls and other matters, from the Tower and Sr Joh*n*
Cottons Library (2) He was to runn over all his English copie,
to direct the Translator where, and what space to leave for the
said charters &c. and whatsoever was to be represented in Italick
Character; which done, he was to enter them into the Translation,
with his owne hand (3) He was also to put all the Quotations and
marginal Notes with his owne hand. (4) He was to correct every
sheet as it came from the press, and if the Translator did omit any,
he was to supply it.

    He was also according to the desire of the Delegacy to write
while the Translation was in doing the lives of all the writers that

he could obtaine, to be put in the respective Colleges and Halls, wherein they had been bred; which accordingly he did, before the Historie and Annalls were workd off. But this was not all; for, for the completion of this work he was forced to send very many letters abroad, to his great charge,[145] for a Notitia of some of them. He also did, before the Annals, (beginning Will*iam* the conquerour) went to the press, write the History, of the Black, Grey, Austin, White, Trinitarian, Crouched and Penitentiarian, Fryers, amounting to about 10 sheets when printed, which were not in the English copie when it was sold to the Universitie. And this he did because he knew full well, that the enumeration and characters of those many learned Fryers mention'd in the History of those orders, would make very much for the honour of the University of Oxon in forreign parts. — His life day and night was in a continual Agitation.

f. 64ʳ

Sr Pet*er* Leycester of Cheshire having written a book containing the Antiquities of some part of Cheshire,[146] he sent the copie by his son of Brasn*ose* coll*ege* to be put into the hands of Mr James Hamer fellow of that House: Mr Hamer being acquainted with AW, he sent him, Feb. 13, a note to tell him that he had such a Book, signifying that it was the desire of the Author that some of Oxford, who were knowing in Antiquities, might peruse it, and correct or add to it as they thought fit. And AW being willing to see it, it was sent to him, so that he taking some pains about it, he soon after returnd the Book to Mr Hamer, with a loose paper containing some corrections and additions.

Anno { Domini 1670
       { 21 Caroli II

f. 64ᵛ

29 Mar. Tues. Received of Dr Mew the Vicech*ancellor* an 100^{li} for the copie of *Hist. et Antiq. Univ. Oxôn*; which he afterwards put into the hand of his brother Christopher.

27 Apr. Wed. AW went to London to carry on the work relating to the Lat*in* Edit*ion* of *Hist. et Antiq. Univ. Oxon.*

1 May. Sun. Dined with Mr Ashmole at his House in Sheer-lane neare Temple Barr and John Davis of Kidwelly was there — After dinner he conducted AW to his Lodgings in the Middle Temple where he shewd him all his rarities, viz antient Coines, Medalls, pictures, old MSS. &c. which took them up neare two hours time.

6 May. Fri. Din'd with Fran*ciscus* à S. Clara in his apartment in Somerset house. It was Friday, and they had a good Fish-Dinner and whitewine: Will*iam* Rogers was with him, there was hearty welcome and good Discourse and Freedome; and when AW went away S. Clara gave him his works in two folios,[147] printed at Doway in Latine —

11 May. Wed. Return'd to Oxon, and soon after he received from the Carrier the said two volumes: see in Octob*er.*

26 May. Thur. At the Feast at the Guildhall for the Natives of Oxon: Mr Ben*jamin* Woodroff of Ch*rist* ch*urch*, preached at S. Peters church in the East, as having been borne in a house opposite to the Theater in Canditch.

July. Nich*olas* Lloyd M. A. fellow of Wadham a deare and intimate Acquaintance of AW, published his Geographical Dictionary:[148] And because AW had communicated his *Hist. et Antiq. Oxon* in MS for his approbation; he therefore, being exceedingly taken with the performance, did give this character of it and its author in the said Dictionary in verbo Oxon, p 593, col. 2 running thus —

> Propediem vero, favente Deo visurus est librum vero aureolum, plurimo labore nec minore judicio consignatum, in quo Oxonia,   f. 65^r sive celeberrimæ Universitatis Oxoniensis Historia ex intima Antiquitate luculentur illustratur. Autore Antonio Wood collegii Mertonensis in eadem Universitate Artium Magistro. Cujus laudes, integerimam erga me Amicitiam et singularem in hisce studiis Industriam et scientiam depredicabo.
> *Dum Thymo pascentur Oves dum rore cicadæ* — [149]

Note that this Geographical Dictionary was published 4 yeares
before *Hist. et antiq. Oxon* became extant.

11 Aug. Thur. Dr Fell having provided a Bach*elor* of Arts of his college
(Ch*rist* Ch*urch*) Rich*ard* Peers, to translate the *Hist. and Antiq. of
the Univ. of Oxon* into Latine he sent to the Author for some of the
English copie. The Author brought it, and Dr Fell putting it into
Peers's hands he did then begin to translate — But so it was that he
being to seek for a version that would please the Doctor, it was a
long time before he could hit it, and the Doctor took much paines
to instruct him, and would correct what he had done so much, that
the Translator would be forced to write his copie over twice, before
it could go to the press. At length having obtained the knack of a
right version to please the Doctor, he went forward with the work,
yet all the proofs that came from the press went thro the Doctors
hands, which he would correct, alter, or dash out or put in what
he pleased, which created a great Trouble to the Composer and
Author; but there was no help. He was a great man and carried all
things at his pleasure so much that many lookd upon the copie as
spoyl'd and vitiated by him. Peers was a sullen, dogged, clownish
and perverse Fellow, and when he saw the Author concerned at the
altering of his copie, he would alter it the more and studie to put
things in that might vex him and yet please his Deane Dr Fell &c.[150]

20 Sept. Tues. With Dr Barlow in his Lodgings in Queens coll*ege* where   f. 65^v
complaining to him of wearing out his eyes with reading old
Manuscripts written in a smal hand, he did therefore give to
him (AW) a larg magnifying glass, which cost as he told him,
40 shillings. He found it very serviceable to him afterwards, and
it help'd him out at many a dead Lift, in perusing obliterated
Manuscripts &c.

24 Sept. Sat. John Wood a Scot, Philosophie Professor of the Universitie of
Edenburgh and Mich*ael* Geddes M. A. one of the first 4 Scotchmen
that did participate in the Exhibition of Dr Joh*n* Warner Bishop
of Rochester were in Oxford. Afterwards AW, had them to the
Taverne against All*souls* coll*ege*, and there liberally treated them

with wine. At the same time Mr John Wood gave to AW a book by
him lately published entit*led*—[151]

Oct. In the beginning of Octob*er* AW received from Franc*iscus* a S Clara
his Scholastical and Historical works: which tho printed at Doway
an*no* 1665 yet he found a place therein to put a supplement into the
remaining part of the copies that were left behind. The supplement
is thus entit*led Supplementum Historiæ Provinciæ Angliæ* &c. printed
at Doway 1671 fol*io*. Towards the making of which Supplement
AW lent to him a MS. then in his hands, entit*led De primo Adventu
Fratrum Minorum in Anglia, et Eorum Gestis*, written by Thom*as*
Eccleston a Minorite or Franciscan Fryer living in the raigne of
Henry III.[152]

26 Oct. Wed. At a meeting of the Delegates for printing in the House
behind and northward of the schooles, it was agreed upon by them
that subscribers be admitted to come in at what proportion they
think fit to the printing of the *Hist. and Antiq. of the University*,
written by M^r A Wood, and accordingly receive the proportion of   f. 66^r
the Books, or advantages to be received by them. There were then
present Dr Mews the Vicechancellour, Dr Yate, Dr Edw*ard* Pocock,
D^r Jo*hn* Fell and M^r Ob*adiah* Walker. But this project comming to
nothing, or else that it was dislik'd Dr Fell undertook to print it at
his owne charge.

12 Nov. Sat. Received from Tho*mas* Blount of the Inner Temple Esq*uire*
a book of his writing and publishing entit*led A Law Dictionary,
interpreting such difficult and obscure words, as are found either
in our Common or statute, antient or modern, laws* &c. printed in
folio.[153] This book he gave AW, because he had in his great reading
collected some old words for his use, which were remitted therein.
Afterwards sending to him more, they were remitted into the
second edition of that Book.

19, 20 Dec. Mon., Tues. William Henry Nassau Prince of Aurang and
Nassau, was entertain'd by the University of Oxon — AW hath a
larg Account of this entertainment elsewhere.[154]

1670/1. 5 Jan. Thur. —— Goodson Tenant to AW at the Flowr de Luce died
— His son[155]

19 Jan.   Thur. D[r] Herb*ert* Pelham senior Fellow of Magd*alen* Coll*ege* and
the Acquaintance of AW died in Magd*alen* Coll*ege* — He had
been for several years a constant companion with him at a certaine
club;[156] and from him had received several Informations concerning
the learned men of his time, especially those of his coll*ege*. — He
was at least 74 yeares of Age when he died.

21 Feb.   Tues. A conference or Delegacy held in the Lodgings of D[r] Joh*n*
Lamphire Principal of Hart hall, where were present D[r] Joh*n*
Fell, D[r] Joh*n* Lamphire and S[r] Samp*son* White Justices of the
peace; Georg Napier Gent*leman* Chief Tenant to Merton coll*ege*
in Halywell, Rob*ert* Whitehall Subwarden of Mert*on* coll*ege*, and
Anth*ony* Wood of the said Coll*ege* Masters of Arts. This conference
was in order for a course to be taken, that the Towne Ditch on the
east side of New coll*ege* wall, be drayn'd, that buildings may be
erected on it, and that the owners of the said buildings repaire the
way lying before their dores, viz, that way between the said Ditch
and Magd*alen* coll*ege* wall, that incloses the grove.

Anno $\left\{ \begin{array}{l} \text{Domini 1671} \\ \text{22 Caroli II} \end{array} \right.$ f. 66[v]

1 June.   Thur. Whereas the Parishioners of S Peter in the East had for some
yeares intruded in their time of Procession on Holy Thursdayes
on the Limits of S. John Baptist Parish de Merton, by taking in
the East Part of S. Albans hall, AW complained of it to some of
the senior Fellowes of Merton Coll*ege*. Whereupon they desired
him the said AW to go with the Sub-Warden M[r] R*obert* Whitehall
on Holy-Thursday this yeare to prohibit them in comming into
S. Albans hall; which they accordingly did while they were
making their Cross on the Kitchin dore; but were run downe by
clamours. Yet afterwards by the perswasion of AW, the Subwarden
and Fellowes of Mert*on* coll*ege* took order that on the Following

Holy-Thursdayes S. Alban hall Gates should be kept lock'd till the Procession was over.

7, 8, July. Fri., Sat. Mr John Huddleston a Benedictin Monke, a preserver of his Majesty King Charles 2 in his flight from Worcester fight anno 1651 and Thomas Vincent alias Vincent Sadler another Benedictin Monk were in Oxon, to see, as it seems, the solemnity of the Act. Their Lodging was in Allsaints parish in the Back-side Housing called Amsterdam — Mr Timothy Nourse of University College, being acquainted with them, he conducted AW to their company: where he heard Mr Huddleston (who in 1651 had been Chaplayn to a Roman Catholic Gentleman called Mr Thomas Whitgrave living at Moseley in Staffordshire) tell all the particulars that passed between his Majestie and him during his stay there, with very great delight — AW desir'd him then, for posterity sake that he would committ to writing what he knew of that affaire; which he promised me he would. — This is the same Mr Huddleston who gave the extreame unction to King Charles 2 when he lay on his death bed. You may see many things of this Mr Huddleston in a book entitled Boscobel.[157]

20, 21 July. Thur., Fri. Ralph Sheldon of Beoly in Worcestershire and of   f. 67^r
Weston neare Long-Compton in Warwickshire Esquire being lately at London in the company of Mr Serenus alias Hugh Cressey an Acquaintance of AW, it fell out that among other Discourses between them, the said Serenus Cressey talking of AW and his worke in the press, commended Mr Sheldon to his Acquaintance; and that he might have access to him he sent by him to AW a book entitled Tabula Votiva &c.[158] written by Father John Reed a Benedictine to be delivered to him by the said Mr Sheldon. Soon after Mr Sheldon came to Oxôn. (July 20) and the next day, July 21, in the Morning he went to the chamber of Roger Sheldon in Christ Church, and desir'd him to go with him to find out AW. They therefore came to his Lodging about 10 in the Morning of that day and enquir'd for him, but being not at home (for he was at the public Library) they went to Merton College and enquired there,

but non est inventus.[159] About a quarter of an hour after they came
againe and left word that when AW came home they (the servants)
should tell him, that one M[r] Sheldon was to enquire after him, that
he had a mind to be acquainted with him, and that he should find
him at the Miter Inn &c. About XI of the clock AW returnd home
and receiving the errand from the servants, he put himself in Order
and went to him at the *Miter*, where he found with him S[r] Littleton
Osbaldeston and S[r] Tho. Penyston with him. Upon notice given
that AW was there, he came out of his chamber, talk'd kindly with
him at the stair-head, told him he had been lately at London with
M[r] Cressey, who remembred his service to him, and had sent to
him a book, but it being put up into his cloak-Bagg he could not let
him have it at that time till he came home, and then he would send
it by the carrier, which he did. M[r] Sheldon then told AW that he   f. 67[v]
had a great love for the study of Antiquity, and that if he had any
occasion for a Cut, or Cuts to put into his book, he would freely
give him one or more

    This was the beginning of the Acquaintance between M[r]
Sheldon and AW. And seeing that he sought after him and desired
his Acquaintance, he could not in civilitie denie him. &c. Now M[r]
Sheldon being a zealous Papist, and AW afterwards being often in
his company, must be esteem'd a Papist also, as he was by many
sniveling Saints, who make it a most horrible thing to be seen in
the company of any one of them.

29 July. Sat. Sent many additions to Thomas Gore Esquire, to be put in the
    next Edition of his Catalogue of Heraldry books — see in Oct. 1674.

17 Aug. Thur. Thomas Hallum M. A. fellow of Balliol college and an
    Acquaintance of AW died — buried in the chancell of S. Cross of
    Halywell, neare the graves of the Napiers related to his mother.

22 Aug. Tues. At Oxford Feast at the Guildhall — William Browne Bachelor
    of Divinity and Fellow of Magdalen College preached at S Maries
    — Three poore Boyes were bound Apprentices with Moneys then
    collected.

23 Oct. Mon. Alex*ander* Fisher senior Fellow of Mert*on* Coll*ege* and a
Fatherly Acquaintance of AW died suddenly in his new house in
Halywell — About half an yeare before he was taken suddenly with
an apoplectical Fit, but recovering, he set workmen on work to pave
Mert*on* Coll*ege* Chap*el* with black and white Marble at his owne
Charge.

3 Nov. Fri. Received from Mr Ralph Sheldon a book entit*led The Rule*   f. 68^r
of Faith, translated by his uncle Mr Edw*ard* Sheldon with several
others to put into the hands of Oxford Booksellers.[160]

27 Nov. Mon. A book entit*led Animadversions upon Sr Rich. Bakers Chronicle
and continuation*, was first of all published at *Oxon*, in 8°, having
been printed there — The book was written by Tho*mas* Blount of
the Inner Temple Esq*uire* and 'twas sent to AW to have it printed
there, and to be by him corrected — In the ninth page of it are
these words — 'Note likewise that the Foundations of the colleges
of the Universities, especially of Oxford, are for the most part
mistaken, either in point of time or names of the Founders, which
I attempted not alwaies to rectifie, both in that it exceeded my
skill, and chiefly because the Historie of that Universitie, as I am
inform'd is now in the Press, which will cleare those Mistakes
with much certainty and satisfaction, being performed by the
hand of that faithfull and most industrious searcher of Antiquities
Mr *Anthony Wood* of *Merton* College' &c.[161] There was more that
followed of AW, but AW scor'd it out —

1671/2. Jan. The said *Animadversions*, were called in and silenc'd in the
beginning of Jan*uary* by Dr Mews the Vicechancellour, because
therein p. 30 'tis said that the word *Conventicle* was first taken up in
the time of Wickliff.[162]

9 Feb. Fri. AW went to London and the next day he was kindly received
by Sr Liolin Jenkyns in his Apartment in Exeter house in the
Strand, within the city of Westm*inster*: For his Lodgings in Doctors
Commons which had been burnt in Sept*ember* 1666, were not then
rebuilt.

11 Feb. Sunday Sr Leol*ine* Jenkyns took with him in the morn*ing* over the
Water to Lambeth AWood, and after prayers he conducted him up
to the dining Rome where Archb*ishop* Sheldon received him and
gave him his blessing. There then dined among the Company Joh*n*
Echard the Author of *The Contempt of the Clergy*,[163] who sate at the   f. 68^v
lower end of the Table between the Archbishops two chaplayns
Sam*uel* Parker and Tho*mas* Thomkins, being the first time that
the said *Echard* was introduced into the said Archbishops company.
After Dinner the Archbishop went into his withdrawing Roome,
and *Echard* with the chaplaynes and *Ralph Snow* to their Lodgings
to drink and smoak. S^r L̲eoline Jenkyns took then AW by the hand
and conducted him into the withdrawing Roome to the Archbishop;
at which time desiring him to produce the 12 printed sheets of his
book, (which he had carried with him from Oxon by the advice of
Dr Fell) he thereupon put them into the hands of Sr Leolin, and S^r
Leolin into the hands of the Archbishop; who spending some time
upon them, liked well the character and paper, and gave AW great
encouragement to proceed in his studies. After the returne of AW
to Exeter house, Sr Leolin, who came after, told him that he would
warrant him an ample Reward if he would present a fair copie
bound to the Archb*ishop* when the book was finish'd &c. but this
came to nothing, because Dr Fell who printed the book at his owne
charg took so much libertie of putting in and out what he pleased,
that the Author was so far from dedicating or presenting the book
to any one, that he would scarce owne it.

16 Feb. Fri. Returned to Oxon — This journey was taken to Lond*on* by
AW. purposely to peruse the Will=office then in or near Exeter-
house, in order to write the lives and characters of certaine eminent
writers to be put into his book of *Hist. et Antiq. Univ. Oxon.* — S^r
Leol*ine* Jenkyns was Judge of the Prerog*ative*[164] and had the cheif
authority over the said office —

$$\text{Anno} \begin{cases} \text{Domini 1672} \\ \text{23 Caroli II} \end{cases}$$ f. 69^r

16 May. Thur. Will*iam* Cox M.A. somtimes Fellow of Brasnose coll*ege*, now Vicar of Emildon in com*itatus* Northumbr*ia* and Kinsman to AW, died there at Emildon.

June.   With Dr John Fell in his Lodgings in Ch*rist* ch*urch* — Wee were then looking over and correcting the story of Joh*n* Wycleve in *Hist. et Antiq. Univ. Oxon*, before it was to be wrought off from the press — He then told me that 'Jo*hn* Wycleve was a grand Dissembler, a man of little Conscience, and what he did as to Religion, was more out of vaine Glory, and to obtaine unto him a Name, than out of honestie' &c. or to that Effect.

6 July. Sat. Received from Elias Ashmole Esq*uire* his book entit*led The Institutions, Lawes and Ceremonies of the noble Order of the Garter.* For which he sent him a letter of Thanks for the present, and afterwards his *Hist. et Antiq. Univ. Oxôn* when finisht.[165]

With Dr. Barlow in his Lodgings at Queens Coll*ege* — and among several Discourses AW told him what a certaine Person of this Universitie, (not naming the man) had lately said of Joh*n* Wycleve — Whereupon he presently made answer that it was Dr Fell.   *Tan MS. ends*

PLATE 4   Rough sketch by Wood, probably of himself and, perhaps, his genie. Wood 602, lower flyleaf. For the transcription, see *LAW*, 6268.

Antonius à Wood.
Oxon. Antiquarius.
A.D. 1677.

PLATE 5   Wood's portrait done by Mr Rose in 1677.
Watercolour drawing, now in the Bodleian Library.

WOOD'S LIFE
AFTER 1672

A NTHONY À WOOD ended his *Secretum Antonii* at the entry of 6 July 1672. After that date, the major triumphs and crises of his life might be condensed into: the publication of his *Historia* in 1674; his difficulties during the anti-Catholic persecutions; research for and publication of the *Athenæ* in 1691–92 and his trial for defamation; his three written defences of himself and the preparation of volume III of the *Athenæ* and the *Secretum*; and his final illness and death in 1695.

The publication of the *Historia* in 1674

The *Historia* owed its inspiration to the great Dean of Christ Church, John Fell, who saw that Wood was capable of writing a history of the university and prodded him to do so. But Wood wrote it in his own way; that is, as he later wrote, he 'never conceal'd an Ungrateful Truth, nor flourish'd over a Weak Place'. The less flattering details, either about institutions or members, infuriated some readers. Even before the volumes were published, Ralph Bathurst, the President of Trinity College, before this time a friend, made the point that, as Wood put it, 'I never spoke well of any man'. It was an accusation that Wood was to hear again and again until the end of his life. Others tried to control Wood's selection of what or whom to include. Henry Wilkinson, a moderate Principal of Magdalen Hall, told Wood to omit the controversial Thomas Hobbes, the Arian John Biddle and the Catholic Franciscus à Sancta Clara (Christopher Davenport). Wood ignored the advice. He had to deal with Catholics because all Oxford scholars were Catholic before the reformation of Henry VIII in the late 1530s, and there were a number of prominent Catholic scholars who were associated with the University in the seventeenth century. The inclusion of these people did not bother John Fell, who had a sense of history, but it vexed many who thought that Wood was a closet Catholic. Wood faced such suspicions at a dinner at Bathurst's home in 1674:

> 6. Feb*ruary* at night. I was at the Vicech*ancellor* Dr Bathurst. He was very civil to me. But she [Mrs Mary Bathurst] said not one word, neither dranke to me, because shee thinks I am a papist, but shee is mistaken. Mrs Betty her daughter followes her.... People avoid my company and shun, every one tells me I receive not the sacr*ament*.[1]

Another problem for Wood was that Dean Fell had himself financed the project and arranged for the University Press at the Sheldonian Theatre to publish it. In return he made certain that it conformed to his scholarly standards and be well documented. This made the *Historia* all the better, but it caused grief for Wood because he had to travel to London five times to verify sources. Fell also insisted that the work be translated into Latin by his appointed translators, and then he himself edited the text. Wood had complained of this in his *Secretum* on 11 February 1672, and a year later the two were not on good terms with one another. Wood wished to include details of this problem in his *Secretum* and in the entry of 17 March 1673 in a commonplace manuscript he wrote:

> Dr Fells mangling Hist*oria* et Antiq*uitates* Ox*oniensis*. Alm*anac* in the beginning — Something of it to be brought in here.[2]

On the same day he wrote in his almanac diary about a meeting which began badly and went downhill:

> Dr Fell Deane of X$^{tch.}$ sent for me. I could not come but wrot a note to this effect.
>
> S^r I desire if yo*u* please to meet me at D^r [Thomas] Yates at any time this day, or if yo*u* please I shall come with Dr Yates to your lodging. I forsee stormes a comming, and tis fit I should prevent them &c.
>
> After this he sent for me to dine with him, I told the man, that I was to go to Magd*alen* Coll*ege* to the presid*ent* but I would meet him at Dr Yates lodg*ing* at one of the clock.

At one I came, and there he was. He set upon me after a verie foul rate, all which I scarse remember, but the most part was this. How came[3] that he sent for me so many times and I did not come, I told him I was busy at Mag*dalen* Coll*ege*. He told me I was a verey uncivill fellow and then plucked out of his pocket the aforesaid note, that I should meet him forsooth and I not come to his lodgings — I told [him] I did not care and would not come or run the Chapter through uncivill people (I meant grinning in Peckwaters Inn which he understood well enough) [He told me] that I was also uncivill and did not come when he sent for me, I asked what he had to doe to send for me — he said nothing. I told him if the vicechanc*ellor* sent for me I would come or if the head of my coll*ege* sent for me I would come, but I was not bound to come at his command — My cheif desire was at that time that I might have security given that I write a preface wherin I might apologize and excuse my self for what the Translator hath [altered]. Further also that I wrot the book that it might be a way to, facili*ta*te preferment for me but now forseeing that it might be a ruine I might have liberty to write a pref*ace*. —

All this he denied and said I should, but then the Translator should another, so that if I write Truth that Rogue must contradict me —

He commanded my Copie, to be delivered, I denied it unless they would satisfie me for what I had done — and then [he] told me that they would have it of me, or else turne me out of Towne, I told them they should not I was a native and borne there to an estate and I would not etc —

[He said] that I kept drunken Company and they had infused matters into my head against them — I sc*or*nd his words[.] I told him twas false — he meant [Nathaniel] Greenwood.[4]

The most notorious changes by Fell concerned Wood's entry on Thomas Hobbes. Even though Hobbes was no favourite of Wood, he included a number of details about Hobbes's reputation, friends and influence, which Fell blotted out. To get back at Fell for this particular offence, Wood told John Aubrey of the censorship, knowing that Aubrey would go directly to his friend Hobbes with the information. And Aubrey did so. Hobbes was outraged and wrote a letter of protest, and on 25 April Wood received a copy. Hobbes then had it printed so that it would appear in Oxford before the *Historia* would be published. On 11 July Wood wrote in his commonplace manuscript that it was posted 'in all coffey houses at Ox*ford* Fell stormes — '. What Fell did not know was that Wood planned to insert the letter in copies of the *Historia* at the press. When Fell learned of this, he quickly took advantage of a printing situation which Wood described in a later account, 'the last sheet of paper being then in the presse, and one leafe thereof being left vacant, the deane supplied it with his answer'.[5]

In spite of all these problems, Wood could now rest for a time:

S[r]. James day. [25 July] at 3. in the afternoone W*illiam* Br*iscoe* and I in Witham meed under a haycock. Deus nobis haec otia fecit [God gave us this respite]...

27 July. My book published at Oxon.

Wood then began work on an English version, not to be censured by anyone, and vented his rage in his diary. He wrote on the day the book was published:

Full of base things put in by D[r] Fell — to please his partial humor — and undo the author. The author wrot it for preferment but he cared not for it nor took notice of it — Vide Alm*anac* 1673 in the beginning —

With the extensive help of Dean Fell, who overlooked Wood's petulance, the book made a grand impression. Fell arranged that it be presented to the king, distributed to various European universities, and offered to all visiting dignitaries over the next several years.[6]

No matter how successful Wood's book was on one level, it stirred up jealousy on the part of some Oxford academics. Several months after the publication Wood was invited to the lodgings of Gilbert Ironside, the Warden of Wadham College, for dinner. Though Ironside was on a committee that had only a few days earlier approved a payment of £50 for Wood's work on the *Historia*, Ironside showed a less generous spirit during the meal:

29 Oct. I supd with the warden of Wadham at his lodgings, M[r] [Nicholas] Lloyd being with me. He desird M[r] Lloyd to bring me

with him. He gave me roast meat and beat me with the spit. He told me that my book was full of contumelies, falsities, contradictions and full of frivoulous stuff — viz what need was there of saying that Dr Wilkins was married, or that he was promoted to the Bishoprick of Chester by Commendation to the K*ing* of the Duke of Bucks [George Villiers] or that D^r [Thomas] Sprat was chapl*ain* to the Duke of Buks etc. That every sniveling fellow should undertake to write of secret matters of state, (meaning that I should forsooth take notice of Buckinghams commendation of Wilkins) —

He also said that if he had been vicechancellour, he would instead of buying and printing the book, have caused it to be burnt — He had the book there and read it scornfully.

After wee had supd and all took away and servants gone, Mr Warden drunk to Mr Lloyd and told him that he should pledge him in claret, but the bottle being set on the side table, I made an offer to fetch it, wherupon he said twas clownish rude and uncivill to doe so. That Scholars were generally clownes — But who was more clowne I or the warden, he for abusing me and my book in his lodgings, or I for my humilitie — A fool, puppie, child.

Memorandum my cheif intent was to give the warden thanks for his speaking for me to allow me 50^{li} for my book.[7]

Wood's difficulties during the Anti-Catholic persecutions

After the publication of the *Historia*, Wood turned more of his attention to the biographies of persons associated with the University, eventually to be called the *Athenæ Oxonienses* and *Fasti*. One of the advantages of his research and fame as an antiquarian was that they led to friendships with Catholic authors, mainly Oxford alumni, in London. Through the intercession of one of these, Serenus Cressy, Wood met the wealthy Ralph Sheldon, 'a zealous papist', at the Mitre Inn in Oxford on 21 July 1671. The two, both active antiquarians with collections of manuscripts and books, shared their knowledge during the remainder of the decade.[8] On 7 August 1674 Wood went to Weston, Sheldon's magnificent country home, for a month's stay. This was the first of sixteen such visits from

1674 until Sheldon's death in July 1684. They generally lasted for a month, though five lasted for three months or more, and were a pleasure for Wood. He was generously paid for cataloguing Sheldon's extensive library of books and manuscripts; enjoyed the company of the constant stream of visitors at Weston, many of whom were antiquarians; and ate well. Most importantly, Sheldon promised £100 to help finance the publication of the *Athenæ*.[9]

The stays were not without problems. Sheldon and most of his visitors were Catholics, and during Lent of 1676 Wood noted in his diary: 'kept a Lent, which I never did before. not eat a bit of flesh from Shrove Tuesday till Easter day'. There was also some pressure to participate in Catholic rituals. On 27 February 1678, Wood wrote in his diary that 'Mr. Tat. of Salf. sollicited me much in Mr. [Richard] Reeves his name.' Reeves was a Benedictine friend of Wood. On two occasions when Wood stayed for over three months, Sheldon, possibly to dissuade Wood from making Weston his permanent residence, feigned departures to other locations and sent Wood home to Oxford. Sheldon, however, returned to Weston after three and eight days, details which Wood recorded in his almanac diary.[10] The visits were more sporadic after the summer of 1681 when the cataloguing was completed. A constant irritation for Sheldon was that Wood was pressuring him to make good on his promise to give £100 for the *Athenæ*, but during the virulent anti-Catholic campaigns of the late 1670s, Sheldon was trying to maintain his estates and avoided the payment during his lifetime. When Sheldon died on 24 June 1684, the heir, Ralph Sheldon of Steeple Barton, asked Wood 'to take order about the funerall', and Wood arranged sumptuous decorations for the body lying in state at Weston, an elaborate procession from Weston to Beoley, and a second ceremony and burial at Beoley church. The only provision in Sheldon's will was for £40 to Wood to oversee a transfer of Sheldon's books and heraldry manuscripts to the College of Arms. The funeral, along with the transfer of Sheldon materials from Weston to the College of Arms, occupied Wood for a month. Throughout the decade, Wood constantly reminded the new heir of the promised £100, and in time the second Ralph paid half of the promised sum to Wood, £50. In all, Wood received £80 specifically for the publication, from both Sheldons. No matter how strained the relationships with the family had been, Wood

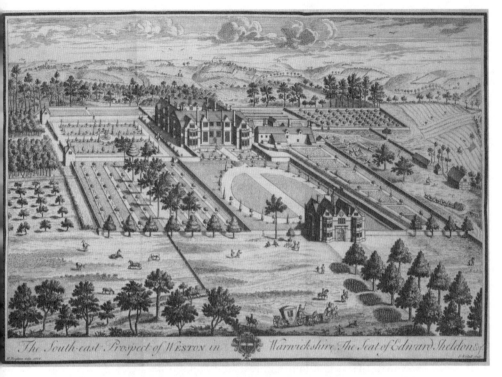

PLATE 6   Southeast prospect of Weston, *Henry Beighton delineavit 1716,*
E. Kirkall sculpsit, in W. Dugdale, *Antiquities of Warwickshire,* 2nd edn
(1730), i. 583. Weston House was built in 1588 and demolished *c.* 1826.

continued to journey to Weston until 1695, making seven more visits after
Sheldon's funeral.[11]

Wood was interested in theological books only in so far as they provided biographical and bibliographical information. He avoided theology
or theological discussions. By October 1678, however, the anti-Catholic
movement became frenzied, fuelled by pamphlets and accusations of
treason by the likes of Titus Oates and the half-mad Israel Tonge.
Anyone could get caught in the Protestant inquisition. Wood's Catholic
benefactor, Ralph Sheldon, was for a time 'clapt up in prison', and Wood
himself got into trouble for his research in pre-Reformation, that is
Catholic, sources. In 1679 the parliamentarian Harbottle Grimstone,

as fearful as anyone of Catholics, listed Wood's *Historia* among 'popish books' printed at the Sheldonian Theatre in Oxford:

> Apr*il* ult*ima*. M*r* [Obadiah] Walker told me that more than a fortnight since S*r* Harbottle Grimstone made a speech in the Parliam*ent* house and therin took occasion to mention the printing of popish books at the Theater in Oxon. among which were the Life of K*ing* Alf*red* and the Hist*ory* of Ox*ford* wherin are many unseemly things of the reformation said, ([he was] informed so by Gilb*ert* Burnet).[12]

On his return to Oxford from a visit to Weston in November 1678, Wood learned how dangerous it was to be on good terms with a Catholic:

> 28 I returned from M*r* Sheldons
>
> 28. 29. No*vember*. D*r* [John] Wallis took away all writings and reg*iste*rs that I have had in my keeping 18 yeares — for feare that they should be seised on. He supposing that I might be in the plot because M*r* Sheldon was lately clapt up in prison —
> A man that is studious and reserved is popishly affected.[13]

The situation soon became even more dangerous. On 1 December:

> about 1. of the clock in the afternoone D*r* [John] Nicholas Vicechanc*ellor* with a Bedell and his two men taking my lodgings in their way to S*t* Maries ch*urch* he the said D*r* Nicholas came up into my chamber and there told me in my eare that he had lately received command from above to enquire after all such under his government that are supposed to be popishly addicted, and to search their chambers and studies for any papers or writings relating to the plot. — Hereupon I told him verie freely that I should submit to his will — That being done, he told me that I was the person that kept correspondence between M*r* Sheldons family and the Miter Inn in Oxôn. — I told him that that could not be for I onlie frequented that Inn when my horse came for or with me to it — after which saying no more — he desired me that I would walk into my studie and so I did and he after me, and looked upon what papers he pleased but found nothing — afterwards he desired

to know where my letters lay[.] Wherfore I had him into another study and shewd him divers letters from Mr Ralf Sheldon (with others:) the last of which was dated about the last of July 1678. All which he perused but could find nothing but great expressions of love and kindness in Mr Sheldons letters: Afterwards he told me that I must receive the oath of alleigiance, I answered him I would if he would appoint a time — wherfore he told me that next morn*ing* at 10. of the clock he should be at leisure — ... He studies to be active and shew himself zealous in his office and sorry he seemd to be because he could find nothing that could not please the parliam*ent*. — he would have hanged me.[14]

Two months later, in February 1679, the Warden of Merton, Thomas Clayton, an old enemy, found his chance to make Wood feel discomfort. The Vice-chancellor had sent to all college heads to report back to him any person who might be a Catholic recusant, 'or so reputed'. Clayton was the single college head who had determined that a member of his college was suspicious and he answered the Vice-chancellor: 'there is only Mr Anthony Wood who hath been suspected to be Popishly affected'. Nicholas did not follow up on Clayton's response because the plot promulgated by Tongue and Oates was losing the centre stage and the Parliament had been discontinued in the preceding month. A few years later, during the reign of the Catholic King James VI (1685–1688), Wood remained on the sidelines, observing the shifts made by various people from the Church of England to the Catholic, and after December 1688, back again to the Church of England, when James left for France. One such who received his attention was John Dryden and Wood quoted a scurrilous poem directed against the shape-shifter:

> On all Religions Present and on Past,
> Long hast thou Rayld and Chose the Worst at last.
> Tis like thy selfe, tis what thou didst before,
> Rayld against all Women, and then married a Whore,

Made on John Driden Poet Laureat, who turn'd Papist in May or June 1686.
    Return'd to his old opinion when the Pr*ince* of Orange came to be King.[15]

Research for and publication of the *Athenæ* in
1691–92 and Wood's trial for defamation

During the late 1670s and all through the 1680s Wood worked intensely on his record of all Oxford writers and bishops from 1500 to the present day. He made eight more journeys after 1674 to London for research; wrote thousands of letters of inquiry for more facts about his subjects; and visited nearby churches for information. No trip outside of Oxford was unrelated to his research. He was always recording, describing, and even making drawings of churches, coats of arms and tombs. When he became hard of hearing after 1670, he twice went to Bath for a cure. He recorded the ordeal in 1676:

> 23. June I went to the Bath for the recovery of my hearing, remained in the house of John Bedford neare to the Cross bath till 14. July and on St Swithins day I was at Oxon, I received at the drie pump in the Kings bath nine thousand 2 hundred and odd pumps on my head in about a fourtnights time — but I found no present remedy. My Journey, horses and servant cost me 14 or 15 pound.[16]

He did not give up hope and two years later, in 1678, made a more leisurely trip, combining research with the cure:

> [28 May] From Besills Lee I went through pleasant woods to Fyfeild, situated upon a sandy ground, and hath formerlie been well wooded.... Going hence towards Farington, wee have Buckland on the right, and Pusay (two villages) on the left hand: In the church of the first I found these matters [coats of arms and monuments]....
> In Pusay church ... In the church yard a brass fixd to the side of a raised monument ... These Puseys are of ancient extraction and hold their lands from their ancestors by the Horne as given unto them in antient time by King Canutus the Dane — The picture of this horne with the inscription on it, Elias Ashmole Windsore Herald took in his visitation of Berkshire anno 1664.... From Pusay I returned into my old way and left Wadley on the left hand.... Thence I went to Faryngdon, of which place heare what [John] Leland saith in 2. volume Itinerary p. 21 ... In the church I observed these things [the monuments].... From Faryngdon I rode towards

S[t] Johns bridge of which let Leland speake and go forward — ...
From S. Johns bridge to Leechlade, about half a mile — ...

At this place of Leechlade John Rouse the Warwic Antiquary
tells us that in most antient time was a Studium for Leeches or
Physitians as Creeklade was for Greecians, but our Historiola
of Oxon. which is a preface to the statutes of the Universitie
mentioneth no such thing. The Chronicle called Bromptons
Chronicle saith that the Latines setled a Latin schoole there and
that it was from them called Latinelade and since Leechlade, but
these things being dubious or rather vanities I shall let them passe
— See Historia et antiquitates Oxoniæ liber i in initio.

From Leechlade I rode to Fayrford ... Going into the church I
saw a raised tombe of blew marble built between the Chancell and
north isle adjoyning.... This church may compare with any country
church in England — it is built cross wayes, hath a stately tower in
the middle and a tunable ring of bells in the middle — ... On the
29. May 1678 I went to Cirencester from Fairford, and in the verie
fair church there with a steple, and 8 bells therin I found these
following inscriptions on grave stones = .[17]

If Wood's stay in Bath achieved nothing for his hearing, the return
journey was worthwhile:

The 28 June 1678 I went from Bathe to Malmsburie in Wiltshire
once famous for a rich and well endowed Abbey = The ruins of
the church wherof do shew that it hath been a verie statelie and
proud fabrick = ... When I entred into the church I had a strang
veneration came upon me to see the ruins of such a majestick and
gigantick pile, with windowes over windowes, and walkes over
walks in the walls, statelie pillars, curious carved work every where
= but as for monuments I found not one antient but that of King
Ethelstan a Saxon King (son of Edward the Elder) who died anno
940 which is more than an 100 and 20 yeares before the Norman
Conquest....

From Malmsbury I went to Cricklade, a little mercat towne
— wherin are two churches[,] the biggest hath a steeple and within
side of it are the Universitie Armes of Oxon — supposed by some
but I beleive false that the Universitie of Oxon was at that place
— Tis an wholsome seat and prettie places about it — thence

to Latton a little village within 2. mile of it — where the Lattin
tongue was professed.

S. Pet*er's* day I returned to Ox*ford* from the Bath, where I had
been from the 30. of May but rec*eive*d no benefit. it cost me about
8^li.18

A typical journey during the early 1680s was to Spelsbury church,
sixteen miles northwest of Oxford, Wood covered manuscript pages, half
pages and slips with details. He was interested in this church because
John Wilmot, 2nd Earl of Rochester, was buried there. Wilmot had
attended Wadham College and received an M.A. in 1661 at the age
of fourteen. Some of the information given below Wood shared with
William Dugdale:

Spellesbury ... In the north Isle of this church is a great vault....
In the said vault lyeth buried Henry Lord Wilmot, with this
inscription on his coffyn graven on a brass plate.

Henricus Wilmot Baro de Adderbury, Vicecomes de Athlone,
Comes Roffensis, serenis*simo* R*egi* Carolo 2do è Conciliis
Sanctioribus, cui apud Vigorniam periclitandi socius aderat
fidissimus et ferè unicus, dein ad Imperatorem Germ*anium*
Legatus Extraordinarius. Ob*it* 19. Febr*uari* an*no* dom*ini* 1657[8].
ætatis 45 [Baron Henry Wilmot of Adderbury, Viscount of
Athlone, Earl of Rochester, member of the privy councell and a
most faithful ally at the side of his highness King Charles II at
Worcester and then an envoy at the German court. He died on 19
February 1658 at the age of 45].

I sent this to Sr Will*iam* Dugd*ale* to be printed in his 2^d impress*ion*
of Baronagium ...

In this vault also lyes buried Joh*n* E*arl* of Rochester son
and heir to the said Hen*ry* who died in the Rangers Lodge at
Wodstock parke 26. Jul*y* 1680. æt*atis* 33 at two of the clock in the
morn*ing.* — His mother named —— [Anne Lee] was widdow of S^r
—— [Francis Henry] Lee of Dichley.

This Joh*n* made a great noise in the world for his noted and
professed Atheisme, his Lampoones and other frivolous stuffe, and a
greater noise after his death for his penitent departure — as may be
seen in the sermon preached at his funerall by Mr Rob*ert* Parsons

somtimes of Universitie Coll*ege* and in the life of and conferences
had with him, by Dr Gilb*ert* Burnet, printed at Lond*on* in 8° 1681.

I have been credibly enformed by knowing men that this J*ohn*
E*arl* of Roff*ensis* was begotten by Sr Alan Apsley, K^t ...

In the church yard some 6 yards distant from the church dore
lyes an antient monument of stone, wherin, (without question) is
a corps intombed as yet: It had in the memory of man a Canopy
delicately cut in stone over it, but that is broken off, the vestigia of
the supporting pillars are yet extant, but having neither armes nor
inscription left, wee must let it lye in oblivion, as many noble peices
of antiquity doe in thes days where presbytery and phanaticisme
hath ruled, and doth rule at this day — The common tradition of
the people is that it is a tombe of one of the Beachamps, formerly
Lords of this mannour of Spellsbury.

At the end of the Chancell in the ch*urch*yard, is also another
raised altar-mon*ument* and without doubt a body lyes in the ground
under it, but having neither armes nor inscription, I must conclude
with Fidelium animae requiescant in pace [may the souls of the
faithful rest in peace].[19]

As the publication of the *Athenæ* was imminent, there was no one
more feared in Oxford than Wood. Suspicions remained that he was a
closet Catholic, and he was not formally a member of a college and could
not easily be reined in. His aggressive research in the muniments of
colleges and halls and in the archives of the university frightened some
college heads because of the potential scandals that might be uncovered
by an outside investigator. His inquiries about persons who had living
relatives or even of living persons who were subjects to be entered into
the *Athenæ* generated unease. Yet in 1691 Wood was at the peak of his
career. His reputation as an antiquarian scholar was secure, and he must
have thought that the appearance of the *Athenæ* would only increase his
fame. He recorded the events in his diary in June 1691:

18. Thursday Athenæ and Fasti Oxon. were published at Lond*on*.

19. They came in Moores waggon to Oxon.

22 I presented one to the Vicech*ancellor* [Jonathan Edwards] to
whome it is partly dedic*ated* and at the same time I gave him one
for the libr*ary*.[20]

But the situation changed rapidly after the appearance of this first volume. The reception was mixed, especially in Oxford. All of which Wood noted, and responded to, in his diary:

> 25. Jun. at the Kings Head Taverne with M^r [Arthur] Charlet [and] [Thomas] Creech — Charlet shew'd me T*homas* Bennets letter dat*ed* 23. June wherein he tells Mr Charlet that he was told at London by several, that a great deal of ill nature was expressed in my book lately published — So they carried that expression on by telling me that I express a great deal of ill nature in reflecting upon C*hrist* Ch*urch* by saying that the Deane in choosing men of his owne house to read D^r [John] Morris his Lecture had no regard to Alls*ouls* where Dr Morris had his breeding — [William] Camden being denied a fellowship in Alls*ouls* becaus of the popish partie there — That there is bad sense in every page. V*ide* latter end of Allmanac. [They said this] to run down my b*ook.*
>
> Who is ill natur*d* — whether the author who speaks truth, or a company of idle fellowes that sit all day in an Alehouse or Tavern to pick holes in the coates of industrious men, who labour for the honor of the University.
>
> Mr Charlet then told me that the Presid*ent* [Ralph Bathurst] of Trin*ity* Coll*ege* said that I collected it but not writ it, that is in good Language[.]

> Jun. July My book has been the subject of discourse in Oxf*ord* for a month togeather — The Bach*elors* and undergraduats speak generally well of it. Some Heads of houses[,] Bach*elors* of Div*inity* and fellowes are generally against it, study to pick holes in it or at least [to find] popery.
>
> Dr Bathurst complaines that there is bad sense in very many places.
>
> [Michael] Harding of Trin*ity* [College that there is] a great deal of popery and that I speak favourably of the papists —
>
> Ball*iol* Coll*ege* say — I call Parson [Anthony] Hodges a Cuckold — because his wife was dishonest to him. — That they are careless of their M*anuscript*s, because D^r [Thomas] James took some away — so he did from Merton —
>
> All fellowes of houses and ministers that sneer and ministers say — strong and mighty to drink [that is, Wood himself.]

Dr Morgan told me in the Proscholium 13. July that he had
not seen my book, but heard that I spoke of and favoured popery
— and spoke not well of Tho*mas* Cranmer in Will*iam* Warham
— but he did not know that twas in Ital*ic* char*acter,* that I said that
father [Robert] Grebby who was lecturer of Carfax, doubted the
immortality of the soul of man.

13. July. At the tavern with Mr Charlet, D^r [Salisbury] Cade —
[Walter] Fifeild — [Roger] Almond — where Mr Charlet shewd me
a letter received from London last night (from Ja*mes* Harrington)
that my book was better received at London than at Oxon. — that
the bookseller Bennet was well contented with it.

15 at night at the upper gates of Trin*ity* College M^r Ch*arlet* told me
that M^r [Michael] Harding had a lecture for me for several passages
in my book — he passed by soon after and said not one word
— Ead*em* noct*e* at Mr Joyners M^r [Thomas] Creech told me that I
said S —— entered into the holy order of the Carthusians.

July 19. Sunday at Mr Charlets chamber — Mr Hinton told me of
the stone pulpit of S. Maries, vide notes at Card*inal* Morton in
margin[.] He told me *William* Bischop being then there that D^r
[Roger] Mander Master of Ball*iol* College said that it was not (my
book) fit to wipe ones arse with.

25. Jul. Mr Charlet told me that the Master of Ball*iol* College [R.
Mander] should say that 'twas no matter, or that the book deserves
to be burnt in every Coll*ege* Quadrangle[.] False.
    In the latter end of this month Mr Charlet asked —— [William]
Richards somtimes Chapl*ain* of Alls*ouls* College, now Arch*deacon*
of Berks*hire* whether he would subscribe to Athenæ Oxon — He
made answer that he would rather subscribe to have it burnt — The
words as ugly as his face.

17. Nov. Mr Charl*et* and —— at the K*ing*'s H*ead* Tav*ern* — where
his endeavours were to run me and my book downe because he will
not take off 16. copies.[21]

The publication of volume II a year later, in July 1692, gave his critics
more fodder. Wood recorded the details in his diary:

Jul. 18. Munday — Athenæ Oxonienses 2ᵈ. volume published at London — came downe to Oxon by John Bartlets waggon 19. July.

20. at night Dʳ Charlet at Dʳ [Thomas] Sykes dore — told me that Dʳ Wallis was angry, and would complaine and have satisfaction — for what said of him in my 2ᵈ. volume.

21. at night met Mʳ [James] Harris of Jesus College beyond Hinxsey steps between 8. and 9 at night — told me that I had set all Oxford in a flame.

23. met him again towards Wolvercote — He told me of the *scurrulous* answer made by Dʳ Fell to Hobbes his epistle to me — *vide* Hobbes — somthing of Dʳ Yate — in creations 1660 —

24 with Sʳ [James] Bisse at the Fleur de Luce who told me that Dʳ Charlet should tell the booksellers that they make haste with selling the books least they be burnt — that many know me not, and think it impossible that one man can doe such a work — All people endeavour to pick out such things that are bad from it, mention nothing good — and say I abuse all people and speak well of none — false — Wallis is much talked of and he resents it and out of a poor spirit, sends by way of revenge, for [Liber] Matriculae P. in my custody — Fellowes of houses and such in orders doe very uncharitable pick what they can from it, as they did from the first volume and send there reports flying, as in other matters they possess people with strang things — that because I have no place to lose I speak the more freely / they govern Oxford.

Every one tells me I speake freely of Dʳ Wallis and against him —

John Wallis, the Savilian Professor of Geometry and Keeper of the Archives, no doubt resented being called, among other things, a person who 'at any time, can make black white, and white black, for his own ends, and hath a ready knack of sophistical evasion, as the writer of these matters doth know full well'. His order that Wood deliver the *Liber Matriculæ P.* to the University Archives grated on Wood, for he had saved it from destruction in 1686. He told the story in the initial pages of the volume:

Began by Bernard Hore superior Bedell of Law, at the command of the Parliamentarian Visitors. But he having no president or forme how to matriculat (for the former book marked with P.P. was withheld by Mathew Cross, turned out to make room for Hore) he onlie entred the names and conditions or qualities of students, and what they were to pay, which was the cheifest thing he look'd after, there being no such thing entred in P.P.

But when Sam*uel* Clark succeeded, and afterwards had received the former Matric*ula* book from the Executor of D[r] [Gerard] Langbaine then lately Custos Archivorum (which he had received from John Cross, son of Mathew Cross deceased, in Feb. 1655) he then (1660) proceeded according to the forme in PP. viz to set downe the name, fathers name, country, quality, and age.

After M[r] Clerks decease this book came into the hands of D[r] Joh*n* Fell (one of the overseers of his will) an*no* 1669 who taking it to be an ordinary paper book, and not a matricula, because not in a folio, as the book going before this, and that after, are, he threw it aside among other of his paper books. Afterwards when I was drawing up my writers for each Coll*ege* in Hist. et Antiq. Univ. Ox. I made much enquiry after this book. M[ris] Clerk the widdow shee told me she knew nothing of it, and so did several times D[r] Fell, adding that twas verie probably M[ris] Clerk who had taken to her 2[d] husband a cook, had tore it and put the leaves under pies.

At length upon the death of D[r] Fell 1686. (I being then about to make hue and crie after it in the public Gazet) it came into my head to speak to M[r] —— [Henry] Jones parson of Sunningwell (D[r] Fells Nephew and Executor) to make search after it among his papers and paper books. Soon after he doing so accordingly, found it, and verie carefully sent it to me for my use, on the eleventh day of Dec*ember* 1686.

Ita testor Antonius à Wood Historiographus Univ. Oxon.

This book with PP. which I have, I intend to put in the School Tower among the Universities Registers and records, which is the proper place for them, having not as yet (1687) been there.

The next book that follows this, which is in folio, is in Christop*her* Wase's hands the superior Bedell of Law, who is careless of it, and useth it not well. =
    AW.[22]

In late July and August 1692 the criticism continued and Wood wrote the following in his almanac diary:

Some tell me that I speak well of the Nonjurors — Archb*ishop* [William] Sancroft, M*r* [Henry] Dodwell.

M*r* West, bookseller, tells me that the Divins tell him I have many malicious reflections in the book. Nobody shews particulars.

The next day Sunday at night July 31. M*r* [James] Biss told me that the Junior Scholars say it is a most prodigious and elaborate piece — and cannot be the work of one man —

Tho*mas* Cockrill a yong man nephew of Tho*mas* Cockrill a fanatical bookseller at the Three Legs in the Poultry London, in Oxon, with S*r* Biss of Wadham, who told him that on Munday night the 18 of July 1692, the day when the book was published, several Presb*yterians* and Inde*pendents* were at Cockrills house and had Ath*enæ* et Fasti Oxon there in quires, where they decided it to look upon it, Ed*ward* Veale —— Taylor, —— to see what I said of the Presbyterians and independents — And they blamed me much for speaking ill of them, and say that they were civil to me and wonder I should be false to them — but they were not civil to me but were shie and denied me — only Inc*rease* Mather an Independent was civil and I acknowledge it.

D*r* Fran*cis* Bernard a phys*itian* of London told M*r* Th*omas* Bennet Bookseller, that if he was sure that there were but 20 copies remaining of Ath*enæ* Oxon he would not leave his copie for 50*li*.

Aug. 15 M*r* [William] Strachan tells me, people say I am a Jacobite — favour the non jurors — a papist not come to church.

Aug. 18 at D*r* Charlets Lodgings M*r* [Henry] Cruttenden told me — that in New Coll*ege* common chamber, severall of the Fellowes said that I had abused their relations, and that when dark nights come they would beat me — D*r* Wallis will put up an action against me.

— 21 at M*r* Charl*ets* Chamber — He told me all that is good in my book was not of my putting in — that I understood not Greek — if I did I would not speak so well as I have done of D*r* [John] Mill, who understands not Greek also — that if I had been fellow of an house, or had a place I should be turn'd out, — Why? because I speak the truth. [Charlet is] a partial man[,] followes the steps of D*r* Fell.

— 29 Aug. M*r* Biss told me that an Ox*ford* scholar living out of the Univ*ersity* will answer my book — [he had this] from H*arry*

Clem*ents* — Mr Davis of Lond*on* engraver reports Aug*ust* 7. that the
Presbyterians of Lond*on* will raise a Tax (two hundred thousand
pounds) to give to the K*ing* that he will hang me.[23]

Wood should not have been shocked at the response. His two volumes
contained 1,491 lives, and the *Fasti*, far more than a mere record of
academics and their degrees, added hundreds more, some lengthy (that
of William Dugdale came to some 12,000 words). He had not written
hagiographies or glossed over faults of his subjects and, as he later wrote,
he 'aimed at no end but Truth' and 'never conceal'd an Ungrateful Truth,
nor flourish'd over a Weak Place, but in sincerity of Meaning and Expres-
sion has thought an Historian should be a Man of Conscience'. There
was no way that an author in the late seventeenth century with these
principles could escape such negative comments. Yet these were minor
inconveniences for Wood in comparison with what was to come when
the High Steward of the University of Oxford, Henry Hyde, the second
Earl of Clarendon, was made aware of certain statements concerning
his father, the first Earl of Clarendon. On 25 August 1692 Wood heard
that the second Earl had taken offence at something in the *Athenæ* and
asked himself in his diary, in the third person, 'Has he abused the old
Earl of Clarendon'? It was a fair question. The vignette of the Earl in
the *Athenæ* was, if anything, positive. No slander here. Elsewhere in the
Athenæ Wood wrote that the old Earl had been 'accused of divers crimes
in Parl*iament*, which made him withdraw beyond the Seas, he resigned
his Chancellourship of the University' on 7 December 1667. The Earl
had died some eighteen years earlier, in 1674, still in exile in France.
But Wood was soon to learn that his error was to repeat old stories,
two told him by John Aubrey, of the Earl's venality. These appeared in
the vignettes of David Jenkyns and John Glynne in volume two of the
Athenæ. In the first, Wood referred to Jenkyns and his hopes of becoming
a judge: 'After the Restoration of K*ing* Ch*arles* 2. 'twas expected by all
that he should be made one of the Judges in *Westminster* Hall, and so he
might have been, would he have given money to the then Lord Chancellour'. In the second, Wood wrote about Glynne: 'After the restauration of
K*ing* Ch*arles* 2. he was made his eldest Serjeant at Law, by the corrupt
dealing of the then L*ord* Chancellor'. The second Earl of Clarendon,

ever defensive about the reputation of his father, laid the groundwork for a suit against Wood. On 16 November 1692 Wood received a citation to appear in the Vice-chancellor's court to face charges of libel. Wood did everything he could to defend himself, but he was fighting against powerful, wealthy, and angry opponents, and his various attempts to evade the charge, to arrange for a reconciliation with the Earl, or to escape punishment, failed.[24]

It was no surprise that the Earl won the suit. Wood's defence was unconventional — that there was no proof that he wrote the particular words the Earl cited in the *Athenæ*. As the trial approached its conclusion, Wood knew he was beaten and the day before the verdict was handed down, he left Oxford for the home of his friend Ralph Sheldon:

Friday 28 July I went to Weston, and tarried there till Munday 14 of August.

Sat. 29. July Sentence against Mr Wood and his book pronounced in Apody*terium* in the morn*ing* — Late at night were programmaes stuck up and were read and seen on Sunday morn*ing* on S. Maries gate and [the] Schooles — plucked downe in the afternoon —

31. Munday about 10. of the clock in the morn*ing* Skinner the Parator made a fire of two fagots in the Theater-yard and burnt the 2[d] vol*ume* of Athen*æ* Oxon*ienses*. In the Gazet of 3. of Aug*ust* is an account of it, but the scandalous places in the book are not pointed at.[25]

Wood was also banished from the university and fined £40, a year's salary for him. He recorded a rumour about what happened to this money.

6. [January 1694] Th*omas* Wood told me that the Ea*rl* of Clar*endon* and his party will turne my Lords fees into a medall in token of the victory, to be put into the musæum.

Thomas Hearne much later reported what actually was done:

The three Statues in the Nitches of the Gate of the Physick Garden were purchased with the fourty li͡bs that Ant*hony* à Wood was fined

<small>PLATE 7</small>   The entrance to the Physic Garden.
The statues were purchased with Wood's fine.

by the University for words which were judg'd to be reflecting upon
Edw*ard* Hyde Earl of Clarendon: and the Money was laid out to
that End by D^r. [Henry] Aldrich Dean of X^t Ch*urch* & then Vice-
Chancellor.

The judgment against Wood tested him, but he was resilient and
responded as he best knew, with his pen.[26]

Wood's three written defences of himself
and the preparation of volume III of the *Athenæ*

From 11 November 1692, at the beginning of the suit, Wood appealed to
an audience outside the court room by writing three defences of his life
and his publications. The first, a short 'To the Reader' paper, was to be
inserted into the *Athenæ*, though Wood had it printed in late November
1692, four months after the appearance of volume II in July 1692 (he
predated it '5 Jun. 1691' as if it were to appear in volume I). Here Wood
described himself, the author, as

a Person who delights to Converse more with the Dead, than with the Living, and has neither Interest nor Inclination to flatter or disgrace any Man, or any Community of Men of whatever Denomination. He is ... an universal Lover of all Mankind, ...

He fashioned himself as a marginalized outsider, never, like an Oxford academic, frequenting

Common Rooms, at public Fires, in Coffee-houses, Assignations, Clubbs, &c. ... but the author, alas, is so far from frequenting such Company and Topicks, that he is as 'twere Dead to the World, and utterly unknown in Person to the generality of Scholars in Oxon. He is likewise so great an Admirer of a solitary and retired Life, that he frequents no Assemblies of the said University, ... nor holds Communication with any, unless with some, and those very few, of generous and noble Spirits, ... he is but a degree different from an Ascetick, as spending all or most of his time, whether by Day or Night, in Reading, Writing, and Divine Contemplation.

This was nonsense. None of Wood's acquaintances would have recognized him from the portrait. His friends certainly, and most of Oxford, knew him as a gregarious frequenter of inns, bakehouses, and booksellers in Oxford. Wood was desperately trying to generate sympathy in the public arena, but the characterization had more effect on later scholars, who took his words literally, than on any contemporary opponents.[27]

In April 1693, during the trial, Wood published his second defence, *A Vindication of the Historiographer of the University of Oxford*. Though is was supposedly written by 'E.D.', Wood clearly was the author. His purported objective was to respond to the attacks against the *Historia* and *Athenæ* by Gilbert Burnet, the Bishop of Salisbury, but his real purpose was to generate sympathy for himself in this critical time by showing his noble objectives and revealing himself as a modest, unassuming recluse. He began with a quotation of the first sentence of the 'Preface' of the *Athenæ*, by James Harrington, asserting that the author, during his lifetime,

hath only, according to his Abilities, endeavoured to promote the Honour and Glory of that Nation wherein he had been Born, and especially of that University wherein he was Educated.

The last two paragraphs of *A Vindication* are a robust exploitation of the modesty theme. Wood repeats a section that he himself had written earlier in 'To the Reader', part of which is quoted above, and continues with proclaiming his objectivity, 'never Wrote to oblige a Rising Party, or to insinuate into the disposers of Preferment ... aimed at no end but Truth', and so on.[28]

During the post-trial period Wood was engaged in a third defence of his life, to which he gave the title *The Diarie of the Life of Anthony à Wood Historiographer and Antiquarie of the most famous Universitie of Oxford*. It was not, at this time, the most important item on his agenda, but it would take that place during his last days.

Shortly after the formal end of the trial, on 29 July 1693, Wood was working on what he called the third volume of the *Athenæ*, adding more biographies to bring the work up to the present and revising those already published in volumes I and II. In October he had an ominous stomach ailment, but this is the last problem he had with his health for another two years:

> 27. [October] at night taken with a paine in my left side, which
> caused a vomiting all the night and most of the day following
> — too much blood, sharpness and not stone or gravell.

The lack of money was certainly a problem but letters to his various correspondents continued, for example from 21 August 1694 and the beginning of 1695:

> [21 Aug. 1694] Eodem die, to Mr Bateman bookseller about buying my books
>
> Queries for M^r [John] Aubrey — Epistles for M^r [John] Bagford — where he lives
>
> M^r [Robert] Hook for the Christian name of —— Oliver Glass paynter
>
> What is said of father Simons in his Collections
>
> Mr John Gadburie's Almanac for 1693
>
> Thomas Jekyll for an Account of himself and time of burial of Sr William Waller

Dr Walt*er* Charlton who he succeds

John Davies of Kidwelly of S^r Ed*ward* Sherb*urne*

My letters to be returnd

M^r [Henry] Birkhead about Sr Hen*ry* J'anson

where Mr Rob*ert* Boyle lived and died

M^r [Elias] Ashmole's obiit

[early 1695] Qu*eries* to Mr Aubrey

1 Letter to Dr Humph*rey* Hody

2 [John] Nordens Surve*y*

3 Joh*n* Locks works

4 S^r —— Chancey about Georg Ferrers

5 About Dr Walt*er* Charlton

6 G*eorge* Chapmans Epitaph

7 Sr Edw*ard* Sherburne about [George Savile] Marquis Halyfax[29]

Under 'An Act for the Kings most gracious general and free pardon', issued by William and Mary in 1695, Wood sought a pardon through his lawyer, Thomas Wood, for his conviction and received one. This pardon allowed him to enter the university and, very importantly, to read in the Bodleian Library.

> 28 May with the Assessor D^r [George] Gardiner and put him in mind of the Act of Pardon and that I am restored to my gowne, Library, suffraging in Convoca*tion* etc. He told me he wished me no harme —

> 7 [June] I put in the printed Act of Pardon into the hands of the Assessor Dr Gardiner in open court, and told him (in the presence of the Registrary and M^r [John] Smith of St. Johns) that I am restored to the University by vertue of that Act and left it in his hands — He told me that 'twas fit that my Kinsman M^r [Thomas] Wood should have done such a Thing.

> Aug. 2. Dr Rob*ert* Gorges who had been in Ox*ford* 3 weeks before, read part of the 2^d vol*ume* of Athen*æ* and admiring at the industry and curiosity of the Author, then told Dr Charlet that he had rather displease half the University then displease the said Author —

Sept. xi I met with Edm*und* Gibson of Qu*eens* College soon after, who told me he had been at Norwich, and was with Bishop [John] More, who told him that he had read over my book with great Delight and pleasance, and would read it over againe.

All this made him as feisty as ever, and when the Earl of Clarendon came to Oxford in October 1695 Wood was ready for him:

3. with D*r* [Thomas] Turner — to let me know when L*ord* Clar*endon* comes to Towne.

Oct*ober* 9 Wedn*esday* at 8 in the morn*ing* I was with the Earl of Clar*endon* at D*r* Turners Lodgings — and there I began to ripe up all the matter how unworthily he had dealt with me against all law — that no abuse could be made against his father because he was capable of no law to vindicat him, first not in Westm*inster* hall because he had been dead several yeares, and not in any court else where civil or canon, because he had been banished — Whereupon he said that tho he was banished in person, yet they did not banish him in honor. Company came in and stop'd our farther progress.

I told him he had gotten from me more money than I should get againe in 5 or 6 yeares for I earned but 2*d* per diem[.] I told him, I was restored from my banishment by vertue of the late Act of Parliam*ent*. He said not but I was excepted — I told him all matter of Libells was excepted[.] He said not but talked after a rambling way.[30]

Wood's bitterness against the Earl continued until the last month of his life:

Sunday Nov*ember* 10 … The University was at great charge in providing a Banquet for the King — but the King would not eat any thing, but went out — And some rabble and Townsmen that had got in by the connivance of the stairers and some when the K*ing* went in and out — they seyzed upon the Banquet in the face of the whole Universitie, and in spite of their Teeth, all looking on and would not or could not help themselves — And after this the University caused this collation to be put into the Gazett.

This is partly my case — I have spent all my time in providing a Banquet for the honor of the Universitie, which being done

and applauded by the generalitie of the Universitie, come some
barbarous people of the Univer*sitie*, and spoyle that Banquet, burne
in the face of the Universitie[,] undoe the Preparer of the Banquet
in the Universitie, and before and in the face of the Universitie, and
then make publick proclamation of their most excellent dinner.

Had your Excellency [that is, the Earl of Clarendon] been bred
in the Univer*sitie*...[31]

Wood's final illness and death in 1695

There was nothing in Wood's diary or other records before November
1695 to indicate that he was mortally ill. In fact, he would die of a prostate
disorder on 29 November 1695; 'of a Total Suppression of Urine', as
Charlett wrote. On 16 August 1695, only two months before his death,
Wood had walked twenty-three miles to Weston:

> I went to Weston on Friday, on foot: It was a bright moonshinie
> morning. I set out at 12 at night[,] was at Gazingwell hedge,
> alias Cookoldsholt by 5 in the morn*ing*. I went to bed, was up
> at 8. and might have been at Weston by dinner time at 12 had
> not M[r] [William] Bishop of Brailes and his chaplaine come in
> accidentally[.] I tarried there till xi Sept*ember*.[32]

On 9 October Wood was in good health, for he signed an annuity
agreement which would guarantee him £30 a year commencing the
following June, and on 12 October he took a long walk with Thomas
Tanner.

> 9. Wedn*esday* at night the writings past and seal'd betw*een* me and
> M[r] Tho*mas* Rowney concerning the Fleur de Luce — Annuity 30[li]
> per an*num* to commence from 24. June — yet the writings were
> dat*ed* 20. Sept*ember*.
>
> Oct*ober* 12 Sat*urday* with S[r] Tanner of Alls*ouls* Coll*ege* at Binsey
> Chap*el* where in the porch I read and told him the whole story of S.
> Frid*es*wide and the antiquities of that Chap*el* — thence to Godstow
> where I told him the Antiquities of that place — and all matters of
> Lady Edyve and Rosamund — So eat a dish of Fish and then went
> thro part of Wolvercote hamlet.

Wood's physical troubles began on 1 November:

> Early in the morning of the 1 of Nov*ember* I shifted my shirt,
> and after that all my wearing apparell, but by twelve finding an
> alteration in my [body,] I was resolvd to walk it out, so at one of
> the clock I went to Bayworth [the home of Thomas Baskerville],
> and returning exceeding weary, I went to bed at 8 of the clock,
> but bet*ween* 1. and two the next morn*ing* after I had slept four
> houres, I fell to vomiting, and was very uneazie for 3 houres. At
> length drinking a spoonfull or two of cherry brandy it put me into
> a sleep, and sleep I did about 3 or 4. houres. About 10 I rose and
> was hungry, but putting on my clothes without warming, I fell
> to vomiting againe and so continued till 2. or 3. in the afternoon
> — then slept 2 houres and was well, but my urine all the wile was
> as red as blood.
>
> I set these things down to prevent the like for the future — by
> shifting.[33]

Wood made his last diary entry on 12 November, but at about this
time he turned to his *Diarie*, soon to be revised and retitled *Secretum
Antonii*. He died on 29 November. His friends knew he was near death
at least a week earlier. Arthur Charlett visited him on 22 November
and urged him to organize his papers, assign Thomas Tanner, a man
whom Wood could trust, as his literary executor, and prepare a will.
Both Charlett and Tanner were concerned about the future of Wood's
manuscripts and books. They knew that they were valuable but could
hardly have known that they came to almost 7,000 printed items and over
a thousand different manuscripts. He had collected for almost fifty years
from every possible source. He haunted Oxford booksellers; attended
estate sales; picked up single-sheet publications in coffee houses — one
with the owner's note on it, 'The Reader is desired not to take away this
paper'; bought or picked up penny ballads (he had over 500) and other
ephemeral items; and asked for waste sheets at the Oxford printing press.
He wrote on an otherwise unrecorded parliamentary petition 'This I
found in Dr Lowers privy hous 24. May 1675 in Bow Street, Lond*on*', and
on a title page of a similarly unrecorded printed item 'Tobacco wrapt
up in this paper in the beginning of May 1693'. Friends who knew of
his interests gave him books and those whose lives he was writing gave

him copies of their publications. Wood decided at this time to bequeath all his 'Books and Papers' to the Ashmolean Museum, placed next to the manuscripts of his friend William Dugdale. The collections have remained almost completely intact over the centuries; they were transferred to the Bodleian Library in 1860 where, because many are copies not known to exist elsewhere, they are consulted daily by historians and literary scholars.[34]

Two days after Wood's death, Arthur Charlett wrote an account of Wood's death to the Archbishop of Canterbury, Thomas Tenison. He told of his visit to Wood on 22 November 1695 and summarized events until Wood's death.

University College
Dec. 1. 1695

May it please Your Grace.

Having been Absent some days, from this Place, I crave leave now, to give Your Grace an Account, of the Death of our Laborious Antiquary, M*r* Antony a Wood: Having missed him for several days, (more Particularly because he had left several Querys with me, to answer, which I knew he very impatiently desired) upon enquiry, I was surprised to heare, that He lay a dying of a Total Suppression of Urine: Immediately I sent to see him, which was the 22*d*. Nov*r*. His Relations sent me word, there were no *Hopes of his recovery,* being the 11*th* day, but that he apprehended no Danger, was very *froward*, that *they durst not speak to Him* — that therefore they did very much beseech me, to come to Him, being the only Person, they could think on, that probably He would hearken to: I was very sensible of the Difficulty, but having been so long, and Familiarly acquainted, I thought myself obliged to go, without delay: His Relations ventured to leave his Doors unlockt, so I got up into his Room, which he never let me see before: At first sight, Poor Man, he fell into a Fit of Trembling, and disorder of Mind, as great as possible; I spoke all the Comfortable words to him, and complained, that He would not send for me — after He had composed himself, I then began to be plain with him: He was very unwilling, to beleive any thing of it, insisting that He was *very well, and would come to see me at night:* I was forced to debate the Point with him, till at last, upon mentioning a Parallel Case of a Common Acquaintance, with whom I was conversant every day, He yeilded and said, the *Lords will must be done: What would you have me do?* I desired him to loose not a minute, in vain Complaints and Remonstrances, but proceed directly to settle his Papers, that were so *Numerous* and *Confused* — He then askt, *Who he could trust?* I advised him to Mr Tanner of All Souls, for whose Fidelity I could be responsible. His answer was, *he thought so too*, and that He would in this, and all the other particulars follow my advice, promising me immediately to set about his Will and prepare for the Sacrament the next day, (he having otherwise resolved to receave on Christmas day): I was extremely glad to find him in so good a Temper, and having discourst him about several Things, I told him I never expected to see him again, and therefore took my last Farewell, telling him that I should heare constantly by Mr Tanner.

After I came home I repeted, all that I had sayd, in a long letter to Him, being somewhat Jealous of Him, and sent it by Mr Tanner.

He kept his word punctually, and immediately sent to a very good Man, his Confident [Nicholas Martin], to pray with him, appointing his Hours, receaved the Sacrament the next Morning, very devoutly, made his Will, went into his Studdy with his two freinds Mr Bisse and Mr Tanner, to sort that vast multitude of Papers, notes, letters — about two bushells full, he ordered for the Fire, to be lighted, as He was expiring, which was accordingly done, he expressing both his knowledge and approbation of what was done, by throwing out his Hands. He was a very strong lusty man Aged 65 years, he was 22 hours a dying, God Almighty spared him so long, that He had his senses entire, and full time, to settle all his Concerns to his content, having writ the most minute Particulars under His Hand, about his Funeral. He has gave his Books and Papers to the University to be placed next his Freind Sr W. Dugdales MSS., which are very valuable to any of his own Temper. His more private Papers he has ordered not to be opened these seaven years, and has placed them in the Custody of Mr Bisse and Mr Tanner of whose Care I am told, he makes me Overseer. The Continuation of his Athenæ Oxon in two Fol*ios* which he had carried on to the 19th of October last, (Dr Merret and Dudly Loftus being the two last) he gave the day before he dyed, with great Ceremony, to M^r. Tanner for his sole use, without any restrictions.

His behaviour was very well during his Illnesse, was very patient and Quiet, especially towards the latter end, he askt Pardon of

all that he had injured, and desired the Prayers of all the Publick
Congregations. The last night he was very decently buried, all the
Particulars were prescribed by himselfe. He has given great charge
to burne any loose reflecting notes. I beg Your Graces Pardon, for
this long hasty letter, and crave leave to remain

May it please Your Grace
Your Graces
Most obedient and most
Dutifull Servant
Ar*thur* Charlett.
U*niversity* C*ollege*
De*cember* 1. *1695*[35]

Tanner wrote the following letter on 24 November, giving details of
his visit to Wood to Arthur Charlett, who was absent from Oxford after
22 November.

Hon^d Master,
    Yesterday at dinner time Mr Wood sent for me; when I came,
I found M^r [Nicholas] Martin and M^r [James] Bisse of Wadh*am*
with him, who had (with much ado) prevail'd upon him to set
about looking over his Papers, so to work we went, and continued
tumbling and separating some of his MSS. till it was dark. We also
work'd upon him so far as to sign and declare that sheet of Paper,
which he had drawn up the day before, and call'd it his Will; for
fear he should not live till night. He had a very bad night of it last
night, being much troubled with vomiting. This morning we three
were with him again and Mr Martin bringing a form of a Will,
that had been drawn up by Judge [Richard] Holloway, we writt his
Will over again as near as we could in form of Law. He has given to
the University to be reposited in the *Musæum Ashmol.* all his MSS.
not only those of his own Collection but also all others which he
has in his possession, except some few of D^r [Gerard] Langbain's
Miscellanea which he is willing should go to the Publick Library.
He has also given all his Printed Books, and Pamphlets to the said
Musæum which are not there already. This benefaction will not
perhaps be so much valued by the University as it ought to be,
because it comes from Antony Wood; but truly it is a most noble

gift, his Collections of MSS. being invaluable, and his printed books most of them not to be found in Town. And that the University may not be defrauded of this treasure by his Relations, he was willing this Article should be inserted. 'Item, I will and desire that my Books, Pamphlets and Papers both Printed and MSS. be immediately after my decease delivered by my Executrixes into the custody of Dr Arthur Charlett; Mr Bisse of Wadham Coll, and Mr Tanner of All-Souls or any two of them, to be dispos'd by them according to this my last Will and Testament.' So that I could wish you were in Town, for fear any disturbance should be made by his Relations about them: but Mr Bisse and I will endeavour to secure them as well as we can. He has conjur'd us to look over all his MSS. before they are expos'd to the Public View, to see that there are no loose foolish papers in them, that may injure his memory. Merton-College People are mighty officious, sending him notes and paying him visits, either in hopes to suppress any thing that he has writ (as they falsly imagine) to the scandal of their College, or else to prevail with him to give something to their Library. He seems to be very sensible that his time is short, tho' truly he spends his spirits more in setting his Papers in Order, than in providing for another World. He is very charitable, forgiving every body and desiring all to forgive him: he talkt a great while this evening with his sister, with whom he had been so long at variance.

M^r <u>Swall</u> is in Town, he came last night with Mr Bas*il* Kennet

The meeting about M^r [Joseph] Bingham is to morrow morning at nine of the Clock.

I am
Revd Sir
Your most oblig'd
Obedient servant
Thom*as* Tanner./
All. Soul's Coll*ege* Oxon.
Nov*ember* 24. 1695.

Mr Wood in his Will professeth himself a member of the Church of England, and intends to die in the Communion of it./

[Overleaf:] These For the Honored
Dr Arthur Charlett[36]

Wood had others prepare a final copy of his will on the same day and signed it 'Anthny Wood', over which he inserted the missing 'o'. He did not include the pretentious 'à' in his name.

Oxon *Testamentu*m Anthonii Wood Magistri Artium defuncti
Mense Januarii 1695/6

Reg~~d~~ Ex

In the name of God Amen. I Anthony Wood Mast^er of Arts
of the University of Oxford being sick in body but of sound and
perfect memory do this twenty fourth day of November in the year
of our Lord 1695 make and ordain this my last will and Testament,
(revoking all others by me formerly made) in manner and form
following.

Imprimis I commend my soul into the hands of Allmighty God
who first gave it (professing myself to dy in the Communion of the
Church of England) and my body to be buried in Merton Coll*ege*
Church deeper then ordinary under and as close to the Wall, (just
as you enter in at the North on the left hand) as the place will
permitt. And I desire that there may be some litle Monument
erected over my grave.

Item, as touching the distribution of my Worldly estate, I dispose
of it as followeth. First I give and bequeath to Anne and Frances
Wood the daughters of my late Brother Robert Wood all the
interest and share I have in the houses Gardens and Tennis-court
scituate lying and being in the Collegiate Parish of St John Baptist
de Merton to have and to hold to them and their Heirs for ever:
And in case they the abovementioned Anne and Frances Wood
should be willing to sell their share and proportion in the said
Houses Gardens and Tennis-Court, that then they shall be obligd
to allow their Brothers Thomas and Robert the first tender of it
provided that the said Thomas and Robert will give for the same as
much [as] any other person.

Item I give and bequeath the Principle and interest of the two
Bonds (fifty pounds each) past betwixt me and my Brother Robert
Wood to the above mentioned Anne and Frances Wood.

Item I give and bequeath unto the said Anne and Frances Wood
another Bond of one hundred pounds together with all interest
from thence accruing past betwixt me and my Brother Christopher
Wood, (the interest of which was paid to the time of his death.

After his death the interest was paid by his eldest Son and Heir Thomas Wood; and after the death of the said Thomas Wood 'twas paid by his Brother Seymour Wood of London Oyleman, til He left off his Trade.)

Item I give and bequeath unto the abovementioned Anne and Frances Wood all other money plate Jewels Linnen and Cloaths that I dy possess'd of.

Item I give and bequeath unto Mary the Wife of William Hacket Gent*leman* all the Network that I am now possess'd of and which was formerly left me by my Mother Mary Wood.

Item I give and bequeath unto the University of Oxford to be deposited in the Musæum Ashmolæanum all MSS. of my own collection and writing excepting such as are otherwise dispos'd of by me to the Bodlæan Library; also I give and bequeath to the Musæum beforementioned all my other MSS. whatsovever now in my possession.

Item I give to the said University all my printed books pamphlets and papers to be deposited in the Musæum, excepting such as are already in the Musæum.

Item. I do will and desire that all my Books pamphlets and papers both printed and MSS. be immediately after my decease deliver'd by my Executrixes hereafter mentioned into the Custody of Dr Arthur Charlet AND Mr James Biss of Wadham Coll*ege* and Mr Thos Tanner of All-Souls Coll*ege* or any two of them, to be dispos'd of by them according to this my last Will and Testament.

Item I do hereby make ordain constitute and appoint my said Neeces Anne and Frances Wood joynt Execu^{ses} of this my last Will and Testam^t, to whom I give and bequeath all the rest of my goods and chattels whatsoever not herein mentioned. In Witness whereof I have hereunto set my hand and seale the day and Year first above written.

Anthony Wood [*'Anthny' with 'o' added above 'ny'; followed by red wax seal, talbot in field with fess across top*]

Signed sealed and declared in the presence of
Nich^s Martin,
The marke of Jone O Pinnack
The marke D of Jone Crawford

[Below, in court hand:]

Probatû apud Londin &c. vicesimo tertio die mensis Januarij Anno Domini (stilo Angliæ) ~~1696~~ 1695 Coram Domino &c. Juramentis Annæ et ffranciscae Wood Executorium &c. Quibus &c. De bene &c. et vigoro Comissionis Jurati./ [37]

It was important to Wood's contemporaries that he died as a communicant in the Church of England. For this reason Arthur Charlett wrote the following:

Memorandum that M[r]. Antony à Wood told M[r]. [Nicholas] Martin several times before his Sickness, that he intended to receive the Sacrament at his Hands in the Church of Witham the following Christmass.

That during his Sickness he was almost constantly attended by M[r]. Martin, M[r]. [James] Biss etc. who can certifie that he always desired the Church of England Prayers, which he had constantly read to him twice a day for the last week of his Sickness; that he desir'd the Sacrament to be given him by M[r]. Martin; that he himself particularly ordered that it should be inserted in his Will, which was made 3 or four days before his Death; that he died in the Communion of the Church of England, as by Law established: that there was no Papist or reputed Papist that visited him during his last Sickness.[38]

PLATE 8   Wood's monument in Merton College Chapel.
The arms are described in A. Bott, *The Monuments in Merton
College Chapel* (Blackwell, 1964), 93: 'Or a wolf passant sab. ung.
and lang. gu. and a chief of the second', surmounted by a 'crest
— out of a mural coronet gu. a wolf's head sab. collared arg.'

PLATE 9 (*overleaf*)   David Loggan, 'Nova & accuratissima
celeberrimæ universitatis Oxoniensis scenographia',
in *Oxonia Illustrata* (Oxford, 1675), 2 sheets.

Oxoniæ *Prospectus ab Oriente*

Christ Church College Meadow

The River Charwell

Magdalen College Meadow

Magdalen College Water

Magdalen College Grove

The Bowlin Green

The Bowlin Green

Holywell Mill

Holywell

A Bowlin Green

1 Collegium Universitatis
2 Collegium Balliolense
3 Collegium Mertonense
4 Collegium Exoniense
5 Collegium Orielense
6 Collegium Reginale
7 Collegium Novum
8 Collegium Lincolniense
9 Collegium Omnium Animarū
10 Collegium D. Mariæ Magdalena
11 Collegium Enei Nasi
12 Collegium Corporis Christi
13 Collegium Ædis Christi
14 Collegium S. Trinitatis
15 Collegium Divi Ieannis Baptistæ
16 Collegium Iesu
17 Collegium Wadhamense
18 Collegium Pembrochianum
19 Aula S. Albani
20 Aula Cervina
21 Aula S. Edmundi
22 Aula B. Mariæ Virginis
23 Novum Hospitium
24 Aula B. Mariæ Magdalenæ
25 Aula Glocestrensis
26 Schola Publicæ
27 Bibliotheca Publica
28 Theatrum
29 Hortus Botanicus
30 Pædagogchium Ecclesiæ Christi
31 Ecclesia B. Mariæ Virginis

Dav. Loggan Delin et Sculp. cum Privill.

Reverendissimo in Christo
Patri, natalium splendore, vir
tutum meritis, literarum Scien
tiâ, Sacris demum infulis consuma
tissime Illustri, D.no HENRICO COMPTON
Episcopo Oxoniensi; sedes suæ / quæ
tanto Præsule quasi novo fastigio
aucta altius assurgit/ Schnogra
phiam hanc in obsequij debitissi
mi tesseram. D. D. C. Q.
Dav.   Loggan.

The Black Fryers

Broken Hayes

Beaumont

Glocester green

1	Universitie College	27	The Publick Library
2	Baliol College	28	The Theater
3	Merton College	29	The Phisick Garden
4	Exeter College	30	Christ Church Almshous
5	Oriell College	31	S.t Maries Church
6	Queens College	32	Carfax
7	New College	33	Alhallowes
8	Lincoln College	34	S.t Albates
9	Allsoules College	35	S.t Ebbs
10	Magdalen College	36	S.t Peters in the Bayly
11	Brazen-nose College	37	S.t Michaels
12	Corpus Christi College	38	S.t Magdalen
13	Christ Church College	39	S.t Peters in the East
14	Trinitie College	40	S.t Clements
15	S.t Johns College	41	Hollywell
16	Iesus College	42	S.t Giles
17	Wadham College	43	S.t Thomas
18	Pembrook College	44	The Town Hall
19	Alban Hall	45	Bocardo and North gate
20	Hart Hall	46	The East gate
21	Edmond Hall	47	Frier Bacons Study
22	S.t Mary Hall	48	Parrish garden
23	New Inn	49	The Grey Friers
24	Magdalen Hall	50	The Ruins of the
25	Glocester Hall		Fortification
26	The Publick Schools		

TEXTUAL NOTES

T HE COPY TEXT, the Tan manuscript, is a revision of the Har manuscript. This is the first edition to include a record of the additions that Wood made to Tan, some 5,000 words which increase the size by 20 per cent, and of the new readings in Tan. For earlier editions see the Introduction, text at pp. xiii–ix and note 4.

The textual notes do not include the many hundreds of variations between Har and Tan in spelling, abbreviations, or punctuation. When Wood prepared Har for recopying he underscored or lined out many first-person pronouns and frequently added, above these, the third-person replacements. If the changes of point of view made in Tan involve one or two words (and a concomitant change in verb form) they are not normally recorded. Such changes occur hundreds of times as, for example: I > he; I > his son; our > their; my > Mr. Woods; my father > Tho. Wood; to us > to his Brethren. Changes are recorded in the Textual Notes if AW rewrote a phrase or clause to eliminate the first-person perspective; if he changed the number from the singular to the plural, as: 'wee' in Har to 'he' in Tan; or if he changed more than two words as: 'for M^{ris} Wood (mother to AW)] Tan; for my mother Har.' In Tan AW used the first person pronoun some forty times in the 1632–60 portion (not including those in quotations). While most of these first-person pronouns are not the result of his nodding, e.g., 'I think', or 'If I am not mistaken', a number are, and they indicate the unfinished state of the manuscript.

Wood's normal contractions are silently expanded (e.g., y^e = the, w^{ch} = which); and most of Wood's abbreviations are silently expanded by italic letters (e.g., Bapt. to Bapt*ist*, Car. to Car*oli*, Coll. or Coll. to Coll*ege*, or *College*). Already italicized words, as book titles, are not expanded. A few times AW italicized, by underscoring, abbreviations, e.g., <u>Ch</u>. This is expanded in the text as <u>Ch*arles*</u>. Wood underscored words, quotations, and titles to indicate italics to the printer and are in italics here. Wood's use of upper-case and lower-case letters for nouns in Tan is followed. The punctuation in the copy text is followed unless noted in the Textual Notes. Exceptions are AW, M.A., MSS., and &c., which are punctuated haphazardly and are silently regularized. Wood often omitted periods at the ends of paragraphs, and these are silently inserted except when he ended a paragraph with '—', which was his common substitute for a period.

Wood's headings and some dates in the margins before entries are regularized, with the month, abbreviated, and the date inserted into the narrative. The day of the week, abbreviated, is silently added by the editor unless Wood himself wrote it.

Conventions used in the textual notes

] separates lemma from variants.

Ed and **Har**, when bold, indicate emendations made by the editor or readings adopted from Har.

; separates variants to the lemma.

~ indicates the repetition of the word or phrase in the lemma.

^ ^ encloses a word or phrase written above the line.

+ immediately before Har or Tan indicates an addition.

added in margin refers to the preceding printed word(s).

canc = cancelled by lining out, underscoring or subpunction (i.e., ...)

corr = corrected, usually by writing over a letter or a word

om = the omission of a word, or words, in either manuscript, Har or Tan.

Numbers in single brackets following entries below indicate the number of words that AW added to Tan ($+5$), or that occur in Har but not in Tan (-5).

Spelling is retained if it conforms to seventeenth-century practices, e.g., 'sevententh', 'was began', 'he had sit', 'strangely' (strongly), or 'rome' (room).

Entries in the Textual Notes are referenced to the text by folio numbers of the Tan manuscript, e.g., f. 1^r, or f. 1^v, and by the dates before the entries.

f. 1ʳ

Secretum Antonii 2ᵈ. Part] Tan *at top of the f. page, in pencil (not visible on*
Plate 2). For the elaborate title page in Har, see Plate 1.

Anno { Domini ... 8. Caroli I.] **Ed;** An. { Dom.... Reg. 8. Car. I Har–Tan.
All headings are regularized, passim.

1632. 17 Dec.

17 Dec. Mon.,] **Ed;** Dec. 17 Har–Tan *in left margin. AW entered dates of entries,*
the month (abbreviated) and day, in the margins.

within the Universitie] Tan; within the City and Universitie Har. (–2)

morning an*no* 1632:] **Ed;** morn. an. 1632: Har; morning: Tan. (–2)

December. an*no* 6. Jac*obi* I] **Ed;** Dec. an. 6. Jac. I Har; December. 6. Jac. 1
Tan. (–1)

23 Dec.

taken into the] taken into —— the Tan. *There is an ink smudge before* the.

by his second ... 1691.] **Ed;** *om* Har; by his second ... 169 +Tan. (+14)

1633.

of whome shal be mention made under] Tan; of whom I shall make mention
under Har.

f. 1ᵛ

1634. July.

Sec tonii] *at top of f. page, in pencil. That is,* Secretum Antonii. *Remainder is*
illegible, not reproduced here.

before the Judg, Justices] Tan; before the Justices Har. (+1)

and to have them entred into their Books;] +Tan. (+8)

or more Descents of] ~ ^more^ ~ Tan.

Maximilian] Har–Tan. *Blank space until AW later added the first name, in*
pencil.

Fees, and he the Heralds] Tan; Fees, and he, the said Heralds Har. (–1)

It was afterwards to Mʳ A*nthony* Wood when he came to understand those
things a great Trouble to him] Tan; It was a great Trouble to me, when
I came to understand those things, Har. (+5)

had then been] **Ed;** had been Har; had then *om* Tan.

wife (Pettie). And] **Ed;** wife: (Pettie) And Har; wife. (Pettie) And Tan.

his son could never obtaine them from] Tan; I could never learne those
things (which he in all probability knew) from Har. (–6)

Grandfather came] **Har;** ~ *om* Tan. (–1)

1635. 1 Aug.

his son A. Wood] Tan; I Har. (+3)

f. 2ʳ

let to his father] Tan; let to my said father Har. (–1)

1636. 29 Aug.

a little before which time] +Tan. (+5)

mother going to] Tan; mother to Har. (+1)

he saw the K*ing*, Qu*een*, and] Tan; wee saw the King, Qu. and Har.

Ch*urch* Ch*urch* great Quadrangle] Tan; Ch. Ch. great Gate Har.

This was the time ... he was a man] +Tan. (+40)

1636. 30 Aug.
   and by Dr Laud] Tan; and Dr Laud Har. (+1)
1636. 31 Aug.
   See the whole story of this entertainment] Tan; more Har. (+6)
   which Hist*ory* was written by M^r A*nthony* Wood==.] +Tan. (+8)
1637.
   to learne the] Tan; to learne to read the Har. (−2)
   And about that time playing ... came to reason] +Tan. (+82)
1638.
   In the] Tan, *written in different ink over canc words.*
f. 2^v
   Secretum Antonii] Tan. *At top of f. page, in pencil, not reproduced here.*
1639.
   He was in his Bible] Tan; In my Bible Har. (+2)
   into his Accedence] Tan; into the Accedence Har.
1639/40. 8 Mar.
   My yonger Brother] Tan; My yongest brother Har.
   and was buried] Tan; — Buried Har. (+2)
1640.
   neare to the church] Tan; neare the church Har. (+1)
   The name of his Master he hath forgot, but remembers] Tan; What the
      Masters name was unless —— Worley, in truth I cannot tell: sure I am
      Har. (−5)
1641.
   E*ast* part of] +Tan. (+3).
   as he usually conceived] Tan; as I conceive Har. (+1)
   (afterwards Rector ... neare Oxon] +Tan (+8).
   a quiet man.] Tan; a quiet man &c Har. (−1)
1641. Nov.
   intimate] **Har;** intimade Tan.
   23 October 1641] Tan; 21 Octob. 1641 Har, '21' *added later in pencil.*
   was the daughter of] **Har;** was daughter of Tan. (−1)
f. 3^r
   Secret. Ant.] Tan *at top of f. page, in pencil, not reproduced here.*
   neare to Bister] Tan; neare Bister Har. (+1)
1641/2. Mar.
   Rob*ert* Wood continuing at Bloys] Tan; my brother continuing there Har.
      (+1)
   in the Kingdome of France] Tan; in that Kingdome Har. (+2)
   his native place of Oxôn] Tan; his native place Har. (+2)
   Trouble to his Brethren to] Tan; trouble to us to Har (+1)
   what they spoke to him. —] Tan; our minds &c. Har. (+2)
1642.
   the 2^d brother of AWood, named Edward] Tan; my second brother Edw.
      Wood Har. (+2)

Aug.

which was that there] Tan; because there Har. (+2)

were passing] **Har;** passing Tan. (−1)

f. 3ᵛ

the Deputy-Vicechancellour, called] **Ed;** the Deputy Vicechancellour called Har; the Deputy-Vicechancellour called Tan.

the furniture of Armes of every] Tan; them the furniture of every Har. (+2)

then had any] **Ed;** then had Armes Har; then any any Tan.

Mʳ Woods Father had then] Tan; My father had then, as I remember Har. (−2)

and a Musquet] Tan; and musket Har. (+1)

his men-servants (for he had then three at least)] Tan; his three men-servants Har. (+6)

Tho. Burnham] Tan, *in margin, not reproduced here.*

next servant did traine] Tan; next servant of my father ~ Har. (−3)

Thomas Wood the eldest son, then a] **Ed;** my eldest Brother named Tho. Wood a Har; Thomas the eldest son, then a Tan. (−1)

age, from putting on] Tan; age to put on Har.

the Dep*u*ty-Vicechancellour, then Warden of the said coll. —] Tan; the Pro-vicechancellour; Har. (+6)

Mr. Wood remembred well that] Tan; I remember that Har. (+2)

and activitie and gayitie ... scholars] +Tan. (+9)

be one of the Traine] **Har;** be of the Traine Tan. (−1)

not removed from Oxôn,] Tan; not removed, Har. (+2)

23 Oct.

called Keynton-Battle] Tan; called Keynton Fight Har.

parliament was began] Tan; Parliament — Har. (+2)

that the Armies were] Tan; that they were Har. (+1)

Mʳ Woods eldest brother Thomas] Tan; my eldest brother Tho. Wood Har.

written by AWood] +Tan. (+3)

29 Oct.

York, his two sons entred] Tan; York entred Har. (+3).

Nov. f. 4ʳ

Coll*ege* was] Tan; Coll. (wherein I was borne) was taken Har. (−4)

before had new built] Tan; before had built Har. (+1)

the Master of the school there] Tan; our Master Har. (+4)

(among whome AWood was one)] +Tan. (+5)

It was then a] Tan; It was a Har. (+1)

made the scholars] Tan; made us Har. (+1)

1642/3. 19 Jan.

Wood or à Wood before mentiond died, being] Tan; Wood died Jan. 19 being Har. (+3)

about 4 of the clock in the Morning,] Tan; at about 4 in the morn. Har. (+2)

Wood (father to AW)] Tan; Wood my father Har. (+1)

Coll*ege*) in the yeare 1600,] Tan; Coll) in 1600 Har. (+3)

Esq*uire* (uncle to Tho*mas* Wood his second wife.)] Tan; Esq: (my Mothers uncle) Har. (+4)

f. 4ᵛ

the said second wife named Mary] Tan; my said Mother Har. (+3)

yeares old, Tho*mas* Wood] **Ed;** yeares old Tho*mas* Wood Tan; years old, my father Har.

would often take her] Tan; would use to take her Har. (−1)

and was mother to AWood. —] +Tan. (+5)

By and with the money] Tan; By the money Har. (+2)

Tho*mas* Wood had with the said Margaret,] Tan; my father had ~ Margaret Wood Har. (−1)

also the great Inne] Tan; the great Inn Har. (+1)

which I have before mention'd,] Tan; in Oxon, Har. (+3)

In the yeare 1618 the said Tho*mas* Wood] Tan; In 1618 he Har. (+5)

mother to AWood (the same who had been the child in the Cradle before mentiond)] Tan; my mother; Har (+12)

growing richer thereupon,] Tan; growing richer, Har. (+1)

a matter then lately] Tan; a business than lately Har.

lately brought up to] **Har;** lately brought to Tan. (−1)

This Thom*as* Wood was son of Richard Wood] Tan; The name of my fathers father was Richard Har.

goeth in the family:] Tan; is among us, Har. (+1)

who giving him good breeding, he ever after lived in good Fashion] Tan; who breeding him up, he ever lived after in gentile fashion Har. (+1)

to 2000ˡⁱ per An*num*, and] Tan; to above 2000ˡⁱ per An, are Esquires, and Har. (−3)

1643
f. 5ʳ

(lately of Merton)] +Tan. (+3)

did in this or in the] Tan; did this or in the Har. (+1)

and yet went to schoole] Tan; yet went still to school Har.

noise that was this yeare in Oxôn,] Tan; noise then in Oxon, Har. (+3)

his Master, he and his brother lost] Tan; our Master, we lost Har. (+3)

at his christning] **Ed;** at my christning Har; *om* Tan. (−3)

1644. 29 May.

This gave some Terror] Tan; It gave some Terror Har.

should be removed out of] Tan; should be had out of Har.

sent them with an horse and] Tan; sent us with a Horse and Har.

Rich*ard* Sciense] Har–Tan, *in a blank space. AW later added the forename, in pencil.*

of Bricke (1683)] Tan, *in a blank space inside round brackets. AW later added the year, in pencil;* (1683) Har, *added in the margin.* (+2)

and then they were conveyed] Tan; and then were conveyed Har. (+1)

f. 5^v

and his wife Elizabeth] Tan; and by his ~ Har. (−1)

to the mother of A*nthony* and Ch*ristopher* Wood;] Tan; to my Mother Har.
(+5)

their three elder Brothers] Tan; my three elder brothers Har.

founded by John Lord Williams of Thame] **Har;** *om* Tan. (−7)

there to be educated till they] Tan; there to remaine till wee Har. (+1)

fit to be Academians or Apprentices.] Tan; made fit to be Academians Har.
(+1)

Burt Master of A*rts*, somtimes Fellow of] Tan; Burt M.A. late fellow of
Har. (+1)

kinsman to their Mother] Tan; kinsman to my Mother Har.

Wykehams school neare Winchester] Tan; Wykehams Coll. neare ~ Har.

Warden of the Coll*ege* there] Tan; Warden thereof Har. (+3)

handsome. Shee had several] Tan; handsome, who had several Har.

where A*nthony* and Ch*ristopher* Wood were borne, and her] Tan; where I
was borne. Her Har. (+4)

was Anne Price,] **Ed;** was Price, Har–Tan.

Anne Price] Tan, *in margin, not reproduced here.*

having been brought up] Tan; and had been bred up Har. (−1)

under her kinswoman] **Har;** under kinsman Tan. (−1)

the name of the Magpie, in the same parish] Tan; the Mag-pie in. Har.
(+6)

the second Master of the] Tan; Master of the Har. (+2)

the chief Towne in Leycestershire,] +Tan. (+5)

the many sojourners] **Har;** the many *om* Tan. (−1)

the Vicar Mr Henant while AWood] Tan; by my cozen Henant Har. (+2)

the said AWood was] Tan; I was Har. (+2)

hindred, he would be] Tan; hindred should be Har. (+1)

as Mr Henant ... him when he] Tan; as he ... me after I Har. (+1)

AW did partly] Tan; I do partly Har.

alone, was given much] Tan; alone, given much Har. (+1)

thinking and melancholy;] Tan; thinking and to Melancholy; Har. (−1)

that he would walk] Tan; that I should walk Har.

f. 6^r

in his sleep (only with his shirt on)] Tan; (only with my shirt on) in his
sleep Har.

8 Oct.

Oct. 8] Har–Tan, *in margin, not reproduced here.*

On Sunday the 8 of Octob*er*] Tan; On Sunday Oct. 8. Har. (+2)

southward very] southward ~~and~~ very Tan.

all Houses and Stables] Tan; all stables and Houses Har.

those houses that extend] Tan; those that reach Har. (+1)

those Houses in the north] Tan; those in the north Har. (+1)

Lane on the west] Har; ~ on the *one canc word* west Tan.

among which were two which] Tan; ~ two that Har. (+2)

to the Loss of her sons,] Tan; to her sons, Har. (+3)

1645.

While AWood and his brother Christopher] Tan; While I and my brother Har. (+1)

imagine what] **Har;** ~ was Tan.

they suffered] **Ed;** wee suffered Har; they fuffered Tan.

soldiers of Aylesbury] ~ ^of^ ~ Tan; soldiers from Aylesbury Har.

by the Kings from Borstall] Tan; from the Kings at Borstall Har.

and at Wallingford Castle] Tan; and Wallingford castle Har. (+1)

f. 6ᵛ

Munday, an*nus* 1644] Tan; Munday 1644 Har. (+1)

of stout Horsmen] Tan; of stout horse Har.

northward from Thame] Tan; distant from Thame Har.

was Governour of the Garrison] Tan; was then Governour ~ Har. (−1)

too eagerly] **Har;** ~ eager Tan.

overpowr'd with multitudes] Tan; overpowr'd with Multitude Har.

came in to their assistance] Tan; came in Har. (+3)

stout captaine —— Walter] Tan; stout Captaine Walter Har. (+1)

in which encounter the brave] Tan; wherein the brave Har. (+2)

off all his owne men] Tan; off all his men Har. (+1)

and they came] **Ed;** ~ *om* ~ Har–Tan.

And AW and his Fellow-Sojournours] Tan; And wee Har. *In Har AW later added an emendation in the right margin.* (+4)

with some strangers there] Tan; with some strangers with us Har. (−1)

f. 7ʳ

Walters following] **Har;** Walter ~ Tan. (−1)

as was then guessed by AW and those of the family] Tan; as wee then guessed Har. (+7)

and close by the House] Tan; and by our House Har. (+1)

upon a shelving ground] Tan; upon a sheving or shelving ground Har. (−2)

hors'd and at] **Har;** ~ *om* ~ Tan. (−1)

Crafford rode on] Tan; Crafford rid on Har.

and ever or anon he] Tan; and ever and anon he Har.

of the Fag-end of] Tan; of the hinder men of Har.

leading towards Ricot] Tan; tending towards ~ Har.

I think not] Tan; in truth I cannot now tell: But I think they did not Har. (−9)

Gloscow in Scotland] Tan; Glascow in Scotland Har.

f. 7ᵛ

Major generall] Tan; *in margin. See next note.* (+2)

Legatus secundus, Major generall,] **Ed;** *Legatus secundus* Har–Tan.

under Edw*ard* Montague Earl] **Ed;** under the Earl of Har; under Edw. Earl of Tan.

called our Ladies chappel] Tan; called the Ladies Chappel Har.

continuing in its luster till] Tan; continuing till Har. (+3)

This Laurence Crafford seems to be the same person with] Tan; Now whether this Laurence Crafford be the same with Har. (+1)

who I think was Governour of Aylesbury in Buck*inghamshire* for] Tan; whom I take to be Governour of Aylesbury for Har. (+1)

as for Blagg see Mon*umenta* Westmonast*eriensia* p 186] Har *only, added in the margin, here incorporated in a footnote to Blagge.* (−8)

As for Colonel Blagge, ... the said citie.] +Tan. (+125)

after the king was restored] **Ed;** *om* Har; after the *om* restored Tan. (+3)

rewarded with] **Ed;** *om* Har; ~ with with Tan. (+2)

other things] **Ed;** *om* Har; others things Tan. (+2)

the said citie).] **Ed;** *om* Har; the said citie. Tan. (+3)

AW and his Fellow Sojournours were alarum'd] Tan; wee Har. (+6)

Goodman Hen] **Har;** Goodman *om* Tan. (−1)

f. 8^r

there two dayes] ~ two *altered from* to ~ Tan.

having received notice] Tan; having notice Har. (+1)

Bridg as it seems and] Tan; Bridge as I remember, and Har.

so by the Vicaridge House] Tan; so by our House Har. (+1)

a little by north about a stones-cast from the Vicars house] Tan; by north behind our House Har. (+6)

they faced about] **Har;** the faced ~ Tan.

only one common soldier] Tan; no body but one common soldier Har. (−2)

is that Bunce who] Tan; is that Captaine B that Har. (−1)

the Rebellion against K*ing* Ch*arles* 1] Tan; the said Rebellion Har. (+3)

in the Vicaridge house, particularly to AW] Tan; in the vicaridg Har. (+4)

account I can not tell)] Tan; account I cannot yet tell) Har.

400 Horse from Ox*ôn*] Tan; 400 Horse from Oxford Har.

f. 8^v

strongly barricaded at] strongly barricadoed at Har.

Scrope Medcalf] **Ed;** —— Medcalf Har–Tan.

gallantly led up the forlorne hope,] **Har;** *om* Tan. (−6)

the Rebells Guards] Tan; ~ Guard Har.

and maintained his ... off the Guards] **Har;** *om* Tan. (−21)

to his assistance,] **Ed;** to his assistance) Har. *om* Tan. (−3)

execution al the way to] Tan; execution to Har. (+3)

fly out of the Towne] Tan; fly the Towne Har. (+2)

Sollicitor Gen*eral*] **Har;** Sollictor Gen. Tan.

f. 9^r

buried both in one grave] Tan; buried both in the same grave Har. (−1)

and in the Fields] Tan; and fields Har. (+2)

Adjutant-General —— Puide] Tan; Adjutant General Puide Har. (+1)

Puid see Micro-chron. at the end of Quer. Cant an. 1645 in Sept] Har, *in margin. See note 30* (−13)

Provost-General Marshall (or Prov*ost* Marshall General) and their chief Engineer] Tan; Provost Marshall General and their Engineer] Har. (+5)

quartermasters] **Ed;** quatermasters Har–Tan.

Advance-money). Many]. **Ed**; advance-money) many Har; Advance-money)
  Many Tan.

The one was] Tan; The one is Har.

Non Reos Res] Tan, *underscored in red ink.*

the other was] Tan; the other is Har.

Patria poscente paratus] Tan, *underscored in red ink.*

about break of day] Tan; by break of day Har.

were quarter'd neare the] Tan; laid near the Har. (+1)

and in the Vicars house (where AW] Tan; and those in the Vicars house
  wherein I Har. (−1)

f. 9ᵛ

run into the] **Har;** run run into the Tan.

Parliament Soldiers (Troopers) that] Tan; parliam. Troopers that Har. (+1)

into the garden I think] Tan; in the garden I think Har.

(for they had separated ... went to Oxôn)] +Tan. (+11)

ran into the Vicars House] Tan; ran into our house Har. (+1)

Rebels who had] ~ ^who^ had Tan.

who had lock'd themselves up] Tan; were lock'd up Har. (+2)

up in the church] **Har;** up in the church) Tan.

were beholding out of the c*h*ur*ch* windows] Tan; and ~ of the windowes
  Har. (+1)

day before (Saturday) some] Tan; day before some Har. (+1)

of the said Rebels] Tan; of the Parl. Troopers Har.

in the said House] Tan; in our house Har. (+1)

in Thame Park I think,] +Tan. (+5)

entred into the House.] Tan; entred the House Har. (+1)

so it was that none of the said Rebels] Tan; it seems that none of our
  Troopers Har. (+3)

eat the said pasties] Tan; eat them Har. (+2)

were sojournours in the said House.] Tan; that lived in the said house Har.

As for the beforemention'd ... of the Rebels.] +Tan. (+60)

Besides these, were other] Tan; Besides these here set downe wee had other
  Har. (−4)

yet much to the schoolboyes, who were interrupted thereby] +Tan. (+9)

Road neare Thame] Tan; (eastward from the Towne) Har. (−1)

f. 10ʳ

to lay in wait] Tan; to lay wait Har. (+1)

persons thereabouts that] Tan; persons that Har. (+1)

part with the Rebells] Tan; part with the parliament Har.

the school-boyes that lived in the House] Tan; us that were sojournours
  Har. (+3)

Some of them, AW found] Tan; Some I found Har. (+2)

in them, as by] Tan; in them by the Har. (+1)

they proposed to the Boys:] Tan; they ask'd us, Har. (+2)

the Relations of AW] Tan; some of my Relations Har.

Soldiers or Rebells, than to the Cavaliers] Tan; soldiers, than to those of the King Har.

and factious Families in the said countie] Tan; families in the same countie Har. (+2)

took him] **Har;** took *om* Tan. (−1)

as indeed he was] +Tan. (+4)

1646. 10 June.

Wednesday Jun. 10, the] **Ed;** Jun 10 *in margin and* Wednesday the Har; Jun. 10 *in margin and* Wednesday Jun. 10, the Tan. (+2)

The schoolboys were] Tan; Wee were Har. (+1)

(4 miles distant)] +Tan. (+3)

They, and particularly AW, had] Tan; Wee had Har. (+3)

that not one of them] Tan; that none of us Har. (+1)

f. 10ᵛ

as AW remembred he] Tan; as I remember I Har.

occasion laid flat on] Tan; occasion or other layd flat upon Har. (−2)

ground on his belly to] Tan; ground to Har. (+3)

or some such thing] Tan; ~ matter Har.

24 June.

chiefest Hold the] Tan; chiefest that the Har.

with them about Oxford] Tan; with them about Oxon Har.

for the doing of which] Tan; for which Har. (+3)

of Sept*ember* following his] Tan; of Sept, my (+1)

the Vicar and the Master, and their wives] Tan; and our Relations the Vicar and his wife, and our Master Burt and his wife Har. (−8)

great kindness was] Tan; great kindness there was Har. (+1)

by them towards AW ... they were soon after] Tan; towards us. My said Brother then told me and my brother Christopher that shortly after wee were Har. (+4)

that their mother] Tan; that my mother Har.

seemed very sorry at] Tan; seemed sorry at Har. (+1)

he was well and] Tan; I was very well and (−1)

where he was] Tan; where I then was Har. (−1)

had good companie,] +Tan. (+3)

Even so much ... Thame &c.] Tan; &c. Har. *AW incorporated in Tan the gist of the marginal note in Har:* He alwaies owned that place that gave him an acad. education & none else (+16)

f. 11ʳ

go he must, and go he did with his Brother] Tan; goe wee must & goe wee did Har. (+3)

Michaelmas following ... sent for them] **Ed;** Michaelmas on a horse or horses that were sent for <u>us</u> Har *the underscoring of* us *indicates that AW intended to change* us *to* them; Michaelmas following Tan. (−9)

After his returne to the house of his Nativity,] +Tan. (+9)

he found Oxford empty] Tan; I found the place Oxon at my returne empty Har. (−5) great store of wealth] Tan; good store of wealth Har.

to have been debauch'd] Tan; to be debauc'd Har. (+1)

belonging to Soldiers] Tan; that belong to Soldiers Har. (−1)

he remembred well that] Tan; I remember Har. (+2)

shall be mention made] Tan; I shall make mention Har.

under the yeare 1668] **Ed;** under the yeare 166— Har–Tan.

several times propose] Tan; several times forsooth propose Har. (−1)

some inferior mechanical Trade] Tan; the trade of a Tinner or Tin-man or a man that makes Kitchen-ware, Lanthorns, and such like trivial things Har. (−15)

very active in framing little trivial things, or Baubles] Tan; active in framing little Baubles Har. (+4)

1647. 26 May.

a certificate that] **Har;** ~ cirtificate ~ Tan.

which he kept by him to the time of his death —] Tan; which I have yet laying by me: Har. (+4)

when he was Masters of Arts and had a full] Tan; when I had the ful Har. (+5)

f. 11ᵛ

18 Oct.

put into the chamber] Tan; put in the chamber Har.

day. Then on Christmas eve] Tan; day, on Christmas eve Har. (+1)

eve, Candlemas day and night] Tan; eve and Candlemas night Har. (+1)

made a little after five] Tan; made at five Har. (+2)

Apothegme, or make a] Tan; Apothegme, make a Har. (+1)

would Tuck them] Tan; would *Tuck* them Har.

the lower Lipp] **Ed;** the ~ Lip Har; the Lipp Tan. (−1)

help of their other Fingers] Tan; help of the other Fingers Har.

(according as Shrovetuesday fell out)] Tan (+5)

to the said summons AWood] Tan; to the summons I Har. (+1)

as the other Freshmen did] Tan; as the others did Har. (+1)

1647/8. 15 Feb.

Shrove-Tuesday:] **Har;** Shrove-Tueday Tan.

Shrove-Tuesday: Feb. 15,] **Ed;** Feb 15 *in margin and* Shrove-Tuesday: Har; Feb. 15 *in margin and* Shrove-Tueday Feb. 15, Tan. (+2)

sooner than at other times] Tan; sooner than ordinarily Har. (+2)

f. 12ʳ

(who was then Principal of the] Tan; who is alwaies Principal of the Har.

Undergraduats and Postmasters)] **Ed;** Postmasters and Undergraduats Har; Undergraduats and F̲e̲l̲l̲o̲w̲e̲s̲ Postmasters Tan. (+1)

the Cook (Will Noble) was making] Tan; the cook would make Har. (+2)

dull nothing was given to him] Tan; dul nothing Har. (+4)

salted Drink, or salt put in college Beere,] Tan; salted beere or drink Har. (+4)

with Tucks to boot] **Ed;** and Tucks to boot Har; with Tucks too boot Tan.

bench not visitabis] Tan; bench not frequentabis Har.

(Penniless bench is a seat ... use to sit.)] **Ed;** Penniless ... sit. *in margin, here inserted in text with single brackets.* +Tan. (+20)

is forgotten and none there are that now remembers it] Tan; I have forgotten and I know not how to retreive it Har. (−1)

was spoken with gravity] **Ed;** was spoken Har; spoken with gravity Tan. (+1)

put on his gowne] po^u^t on ~ Tan.

which AWood spoke while he stood on] Tan; that I spoke while I stood in Har.

band off and uncovered] **Ed;** band off Har; band of and uncovered Tan. (+2)

expect that I should thunder] Tan; expect I should thunder Har. (+1)

f. 12ᵛ

should evaporate with] **Har;** ~ into Tan.

with a tart Satyr of] Tan; with the tart Satyrs of Har.

Phœbus] **Har;** Phebus Tan.

pistoletto Tobacco Pipe,] **Ed;** Pistoletto ~ Pipe Har; ~ Pipes, Tan.

planted in the Academian] **Har;** ~ in Academian Tan. (−1)

who are fed] **Ed;** who fed Har–Tan.

huge Colossus's] **Har;** hugh Colossu's Tan.

a country Bagg-Pudding] **Har;** a Bagg-pudding Tan. (−1)

chop. These are the Mertonian counterscullers that tug] **Har;** chop, that tugg Tan. (−5)

place, as a Dog at Mutton —] Tan; place as *at end of line, then a gap and in margin:* Commons — Har. (+3)

are as acute as] **Har;** are acute as Tan. (−1)

f. 13ʳ

sack, least they should] **Har;** sack, should Tan. (−2)

and their heads turne *round* —] Tan; and so make the heads turne *round* — Har. (−2)

round] Tan, *underscored in red pencil.*

I never came ... absolutely forgotten.] +Tan; Har, *f. 25ᵛ, following 'round' on f. 25ʳ, is blank. See preceding note.* (+175)

of the seniors] Tan, ~~seniors~~ *canc, and corrected in the margin:* seniors

f. 13ᵛ

1648. 12 May.

Friday (May 12) The] **Ed;** May 12 *in margin and* Friday, the Har. (2); May 12 *in margin and* Friday (May 12) The Tan. (+2)

(for the members were] Tan; (for wee were Har. (+1)

this question by one of the ... *this Visitation?*] Tan; the question whether I would submit &c. Har. (+11)

Will you submit ... this Visitation] Tan, *underscored in red pencil.*

and wrot it downe] **Har;** and wrot down Tan. (−1)

on a paper lying on the Table as he was directed] Tan; in a paper Har. (+8)

therefore I am not] Tan; therefore am not Har. (+1)

I do not ... Answer] Tan, *underscored in red pencil.*
and must therefore go] Tan; and must go Har. (+1)
in her husbands house] Tan; in my fathers house Har.
during the time of] Tan; during the life of Har.
and kept in his place] Tan; and kept in Har. (+2)
gon to the Pot] Tan; got to the Pot Har.

Aug.

his Coll*ege* of Ch*rist* Ch*urch*] Tan; his Coll Har. (+3)
against the Rebells there] Tan; against the Rebells Har. (+1)
was this: viz. that he] Tan; was, that he Har. (+2)
other Parliament Garrisons] Tan; other Garrisons Har. (+1)
by one or more of them] Tan; by some of them Har. (+2)
they were in their cups] Tan; they were in their drink Har.
named Edward Adams a Barber] +Tan. (+5)
on the signe post of the Catherine ... of their Plot] +Tan. (+22)

f. 14^r

Mr Francis Croft, whome AW] Tan; I remember one Franc. Croft whom I
    Har. (−2)
first comming thereunto] Tan; first coming that Har.
engaged in the said Plot] Tan; engaged in this plot Har. (+1)
high-flone] Tan, *an old form*; high flowne Har.
in his little paper-book] Tan; in his paper book Har. (+1)
At the first discovery] Tan; I remember also upon the first discovery Har.
    (−3)
plot Mr Croft fled] Tan; plot he sculkd Har. (+1)
supposing that he might] Tan; supposing he might Har. (+1)
his chamber, which joyned ... Room belonging to Merton] Tan; his Chamber,
    which joyned to that room, the common room of Merton Har. (+4)
AW with some of the Juniors] Tan; wee of the juniors Har. (+2)
saw it all] Tan; I remember I saw his Chamber all Har. (−4)
he (Mr Croft) had got] Tan; he had got Har. (+2)
Queens courts in Oxon,] **Ed;** Queens ~ Oxon. Har; Queens c̲o̲u̲r courts in
    Oxon. Tan.
but these, his Books and bedding were not then touched.] +Tan. (+10)

6 Nov.

Edward Wood before mentiond] Tan; My second Brother Edw. Wood Har.
    (−1)
Probationer-Fellow of] Tan; probationer Fellowes of Har.
Arch-Visitor, yet all that were then admitted, submitted to the Visitors.]
    Har; Arch-Visitor. Tan. (−10)
Some Admissions ... and Visitors.] Tan; (some Admissions ... and Visitors.)
    Har.
Some Admissions of Fellows that] **Har;** Some Admissions that Tan. (−2)
Soon after E*dward* Wood] Tan; Afterwards my brother Har; (+1)
next to the Gate of Merton] Tan; of Merton Har (+4)
AW was put into the Cockloft] Tan; he put me in the cockleloft Har.

So then and after his trudging] Tan; So by that means the trudging Har.

· 1649.

AWood's mother (Mary Wood) being] Tan; My mother being Har. (+2)

and taking her son] Tan; and taking my brother Har.

f. 14^v

sojourned in a fair] **Har**; sojourned in fair Tan. (−1)

stone-house then] Tan; stone house which was then Har. (−2)

one John Tipping] **Ed**; one Tipping Har; one —— Tipping Tan. (+1)

from the Vicaridg] Tan; from his Vicaridge Har.

the dau*ghter* of one Willi*am* Dewey who had been] +Tan. (+9)

acquainted with M^{ris} Wood] Tan; ~ with my mother Har.

but now (1649) curat] Tan; but then curat Har. (+1)

to whom Christop*her* Wood] Tan; to whom my brother Christopher Har. (−1)

did go often to ... house to visit] Tan; came often to the same house to Har. (+4)

exceeding loving] Tan, exceeding & loving.

and tender man] Tan; and tender person Har.

AW. did not then in the least think to] Tan; I never then thought that I should Har. (+2)

he sent to him Letters] Tan; I sent him letters Har. (+1)

(a) lib. 2. p. 250.b. See also in *Ath. et Fasti Oxon.* vol. 2. p. [6]33] Har–Tan, *in margin.*

Ath. et Fasti Oxon. vol. 2. p. 633] **Ed**; *Ath. et Fasti Oxon.* vol. 2. p. 533 Har–Tan, *the page on which Sherlock's entry appears (1692) is misnumbered, 533, but it follows 632.*

where the Fault lay] Tan; where the Fault layd Har.

that he was the son] **Ed**; that I was ~ Har; that he was that he was ~ Tan.

of himself and writings] Tan; of himself Har. (+2)

that he gave to Dr Sherlock] Tan; as I did Dr Sherlock Har. (+1)

f. 15^r

(b) See in the second vol. of *Ath. et Fasti Oxon.*, vol. 2. p. 637] Har–Tan, *in margin.*

did, verie joyfull, and] **Ed**; did, very joyfull, and Har; did verie joyfull and Tan.

such a little Junior] Tan; such a little thing Har.

of several folio's for] Tan; of folio's for Har. (+1)

Berks (a ... Cassington)] Tan; Berks, a ... Cassington Har.

See in the first vol. of *Ath. et Fasti Oxon.* p. 893.] Tan, *in margin*; See *om* Har, *in margin.* (+11)

See in the first vol.] See in the see. ^first^ vol. Tan.

their *Terræ filius*] Tan; their Terræ filius Har.

a hansome yong man] Tan; a handsome yong man Har.

contemporarie with AW] Tan; my contemporary Har. (+1)

James Blanks Gent*leman*] Tan; Mr James Blanks Har.

more than a weeke] Tan; more then a week Har.

as the space of six paces of a man] Tan; that I can go over with about six of
  my paces Har. (−2)

man these many yeares] Tan; man many yeares Har. (+1)

away, so that if some care in time be] Tan; away & fall into the Lyde, so that
  if care in time being Har. (−4)

may prove true] Tan; will prove true Har.

In the church here] **Ed**; Tan, ~~Jan. In the church~~ here *smeared but legible.*

In the church here were some] Tan; Here were then some Har. (+2)

in the Windowes,] Tan; in the windows & monuments on the ground Har.
  (−5)

and an inscription or two … notice of —] Tan; but my sense was not than
  arrived to maturity & therefore I did not commit them to writing, as I
  did afterwards things of that nature Har. (+21)

his then capacity, *[f. 15ᵛ]* but afterwards] **Ed**; ~ . ~ Tan, *and canc catchword*
  These.

These] Tan, *AW cancelled the catchword after he added the 1st clause on f. 15ᵛ.*

f. 15ᵛ

1649/50. Jan.

  a generous Requital] Tan; a Requital Har. (+1)

  for the great civilities he shew'd] Tan; for his great Civilities shewd Har.
    (+1)

  in his house last Christmas] Tan; in his House Har. (+2)

1649/50. 16 Feb.

  Parents, as … Bister in Oxfordshire.] Tan; parents (as … Bister) Har. (+2)

1650.

  one of the Bible] **Har**; one of Bible Tan. (−1)

  of the postmasters places] Tan; of their postmasters places Har.

  have been after this time bestowed] **Har**; have been after this time have
    been bestowed Tan.

  make the postmasters places better] Tan; make them better Har. (+2)

  for the clerks] Tan; for the Clerk Har.

  sacraments in the chap*el* were] Tan; Sacraments were Har. (+3)

  there was for them in the Hall] Tan; in the Hall only Har. (+3)

5 Apr.

  5 Apr. Fri. He answerd … opposed him.] +Tan. (+22)

  in the little … Exchequer Chamber] Tan; against the Checquer Chamber
    in the little or old Quadrangle Har. (+1)

f. 16ʳ

Aug.

  Juniors of Mert*on* Coll*ege*] Tan; Juniors of our Coll. Har.

  Ambler, AWood &c] Tan; Ambler &c and my self Har. (−2)

  to Wallingford in Berk*shire*] Tan; to Wallingford Har. (+2)

  let them come into the Castle] Tan; let us in Har. (+3)

  they refused to doe it] Tan; they refused Har. (+3)

  as the scholars supposed, but] Tan; as I suppose, than Har. (+1)

  their number was too great] Tan; our number being larg Har. (+1)

Designe upon them] Tan; designe with us. Har.

seems the Governour] **Har;** seems Governour Tan. (−1)

otherwise, as 'tis believed they might] Tan; otherwise I believe wee should Har. (+1)

return'd to Oxôn.] Tan; returned to Oxon. I had then by [me] all accounterments for a journey, which I kept till I grew too bigg for them. Har. (−19)

14 Dec.

 Castle of Oxôn] Tan; Castle at Oxon Har.

 the yong Poets of the Universitie] Tan; our yong Poets of our University Har.

1650/1. 16 Jan.

 Ambler, Rich*ard*] **Har;** Ambler Rich. Tan.

 were *godly youths*, as] Tan; were godly youths as Har.

 Stane] **Ed;** Stanes Har; Staine Tan.

 Stane &c they afterwards] Tan; Stanes &c they *om* Har. (+1)

 and confirmed them in their] Tan; confirmed in their Har. (+1)

 after the Kings] **Har;** after Kings Tan. (−1)

 after the Kings restoration became] Tan; became after the Kings restoration Har.

 Ambler a minister in] Tan; Ambler a Curat or Minister in Har. (−2)

 Shropshire, and Rich*ard* Philips] Tan; Shropshire, Rich. Philipps Har. (+1)

 after he had taken] Tan; after he had took Har.

 Arts, he became a] Tan; Arts became a Har. (+1)

f. 16ᵛ

1650/1/ 22 Jan.

 Edward Wood Fellow] Tan; My brother Ed. Wood ~ Har. (−2)

 divers pretended miscarriages] Tan; divers miscarriages Har. (+1)

 in that Coll*ege* untill farther Order] Tan; in that house until further order Har.

 than 'twas thought] Tan; than was thought Har.

 at Medley neare Oxôn] Tan; at Medlay Har. (+2)

 junior Fellow of Mert*on* Coll*ege*] Tan; Junior Fellow Har. (+3)

 the said Coll*ege* into] Tan; the said Coll. of Merton into Har. (−2)

 and Independents] **Har;** and Independent Tan.

 Troop raised by the University of Oxôn] Tan; University Troop Har. (+5)

 against K*ing* Ch*arles*. 2 at] Tan; against K. Ch. 2 at Har.

 whilst others that … Opportunity served] +Tan. (+24)

 at Cranfield, express] **Har;** at Cranfield, to ~ Tan. (+1)

 This yeare Jacob … See in 1654.] +Tan. (+56). *See also the textual note at 10 Aug. 1654, f. 20ᵛ.*

1651. 7 Apr.

 for Mʳⁱˢ Wood (mother to AW)] Tan; for my mother Har. (+3)

 to pay, by way of renewing, for] Tan; to pay for Har. (+4)

 Parish; which was soon after paid.] **Ed;** Parish; which was soon after paid, by way of renewing. Har; parish. Tan. (−9)

f. 17ʳ

Newes from the ... Ann Green] Tan; Newes from the ... Anne Green Har.

under the name of AWood] Tan; under my name Har. (+2)

Ital*ic*] Tan, *in left margin with a double bracket on left of AW's stanza, here omitted.* (+1)

I'le stretch ... fell &c] Tan; I'le stretch ... fell &c Har.

Death her self is] **Ed;** Death her self is Har; ~ *her self in* Tan.

1651. Dec.

Thom*as* Wood eldest brother to AW] Tan; This yeare my eldest brother Thomas Wood alias à Wood Har. (−4)

Tredagh in the month of Decemb*er*] Tan; Tredagh in Ireland, but the day or month when I can not yet tell Har. (−8)

om] Tan; He died after the 18 of Nov 1651 Har, *added later, in margin.* (−8)

on the 24 May 1624,] **Har;** *om* Tan. (−5)

kinsman Mʳ *William* Burt] Tan; kinsman Burt Har. (+2)

Battle — see more under] Tan; battle. See under Har. (+1)

See in the second ... p. [692.]] **Ed;** See in the *om* Har, *in margin;* ~ p. *om* Tan, *in margin, here transferred to note 62.* (+8)

from being a soldier] **Ed;** ~ a ~~soldier~~ *canc* ^scholar^ Har; ~ a scholar Tan *Apparently AW intended a further emendation, but he did not make it.*

for a Trooper] **Har;** for a Troper Tan.

See more there p. [742.]] **Ed;** See in *om* Har, *in margin;* See more there p. *om* Tan, *in margin, here transferred to note 63.* (+2)

of Arts, an*no* 1647,] Tan; of Arts 1647, Har. (+1)

under that yeare, (1648) he] Tan; under that yeare, he Har. (+1)

yeare, (1648) he to] Tan, ~ to *altered from* too.

Thame called Colo*nel* Hen*ry*] Tan; Thame Colonel Henry Har. (+1)

afterwards a Captaine] Tan; at length a Captaine Har. (−1)

and, as I have heard ... to be a Major.] Tan; if not Major. Har. (+14)

f. 17ᵛ

About a yeare ... in 1650 he] Tan; In the yeare before his death (1650) he Har. (+2)

Arrears at <u>Ch</u>rist *Church*] Tan; Arrears at Ch. Church Har.

with his Mother and Brethren] Tan; with us Har. (+3)

himself had been engaged] Tan; himself was engaged Har. (+1)

that at least 3000, besides] **Ed;** that at least 3000 besides Har; that besides 3000 at least, besides Tan. (+1)

after the Assailants had] Tan; after they had Har. (+1)

body hack'd to pieces] Tan; body hackd and chop'd to pieces Har. (−2)

up to the Lofts and Galleries in the church] Tan; up the ~ in Churches Har. (+2)

and up to the Tower] Tan; and up to the Towers Har.

to use as] **Ed;** and use as Har; as use as Tan.

all in the church, they] Tan; all in the Churches, they Har.

hansome Virgin, arraid in] Tan; handsome Virgin & arraied in Har. (−1)

kneel'd downe to Tho*mas* Wood] Tan; knel'd downe to my brother Har.

187

with a Profound Pitie] Tan; with a deep Remorse Har.

and to let her shift] **Har;** to shift Tan. (−3)

but then a soldier] **Har;** but a soldier Tan. (−1)

Whereupon Mr Wood seeing] Tan; whereupon my brother seeing Har.

took away her money, Jewells &c and] +Tan. (+7)

Ingoldesbie before mention'd, telling] Tan; Ingoldesbie & telling Har. (+1)

mentioned, telling] ~, he told telling Tan.

AW thereupon did discourse with him] Tan; he discoursed then with me Har. (+1)

Things that the Colonel told him] Tan; things he told me Har. (+2)

soldier, stout and ventrous] Tan; soldier and very ventrous Har.

he buried him in] **Har;** he buried in Tan. (−1)

in a church at Tredagh] Tan; in one of the Churches of Tredagh Har. (−2)

when he died — This Tho*mas* Wood] Tan; when. My brother Har (+3)

f. 18^r

    This yeare AW began ... as well as he] Tan. *At Har, f. 63^r, a slip added at the end of the ms., has an entry by AW which has a similar first sentence:* This yeare I began to exercize a natural & ^unsatiable genie^ I had to musick — I playd by sound without any Teacher on the violin & having an eare, I could play any Tune, but y^o must conceive not well

    Will Boreman Gent. com. of Pembr. Coll (of the Isle of Wight my companion good at the virginall — Will. Bull of Trin. Gent. com.] Har. (+35)

    that others used] **Ed;** *om* Har; that other used Tan. (+3)

1652. 2 July.

    Friday July 2 AWood] **Ed;** Jul. 2 *in margin and* Friday I Har; Jul. 2 *in margin and* Friday July 2 AWood Tan. (+2)

    for the Degree of Bac*helor* of Arts] Tan; for my Bachelaurs degree Har. (+3)

    by Will*iam* Browne] Tan; The person that examined me, was, as I remember William Browne] Har. (−8)

    Har has an entry at 6 July, some of which AW incorporated into 2 July. See next note.

    He had before answer'd twice] Tan; I was admitted Bach. of Arts — I have no certificats by me when I performed my respective exercises, and whether I had any I cannot tell. Sure I am that I answer'd twice Har, *written at 6 July.* (−28)

    under a Bachelaur among] Tan; under Bachelaur, among Har, *at 6 July.* (+1)

    which M*atthew* Bee was] Tan; which Matth. was Har, *at 6 July.* (+1)

    in Oxfordshire: And on the 6 ... of Arts.] Tan; in Oxfordshire. Har, *at 6 July.* (+14)

    And on the 6 ... of Arts.] Tan, *added later to the end of the paragraph.*

26 July.

    Wake as it seems] Tan; wake I think Har. (+1)

    the horse of AW being] Tan; my horse being Har. (+2)

    he had a fall] Tan; I fell from my horse Har. (−1)

him that his Arme was not out of Joynt,] Tan; me it was not out, Har. (+4)

yet notwithstanding this] Tan; yet for all this Har. (−1)

10 Aug.

10 Aug.] **Ed,** *placed at head of paragraph*; Aug. 10 Har, *in margin at middle of paragraph*; om Tan. (−2)

Catstreet who was an expert] Tan; Catstreet, an expert Har. (+2)

look'd on his Arme] Tan; lookd upon my arme Har.

f. 18ᵛ

casting AW's] **Ed;** casting my Har; casting his Tan.

one of his hands ... below the Elbow] Tan; one hand above my elbow and the other below Har. (+2)

and the other] **Har;** and nother Tan. (−1)

being great and unexpected] Tan; was so great and unexpected Har. (−1)

that the veines and arteries] **Har;** that the arteries Tan. (−2)

arteries had been shrunk) he fell] Tan; arteries were shrunke) that I fell Har.

Adams then laid him] Tan; They then laid me Har.

knew what sowning] **Har;** knew was sowning Tan.

was or is] Tan; was or is; which without doubt is as bad as death Har. (−8)

had an estate of] **Har;** had an estate in of Tan. (+1)

took all advantages to do it *gratis*] Tan; take all ~ it gratis Har.

not fit to live in an] Tan; scarse fit to live in an Har.

after he had let out money] Tan; after he had lent money Har. (+1)

to eat, drink and lodg on the Debter] Tan; to grind on his Debter Har. (+3)

Debter: and to this Farmer of] Tan; Debter. And to the Farmer at Har.

to whome he had lent money,] **Har;** om Tan. (−6)

Aug. Sept.

In the latter end of] **Ed;** Aug. Sept. *in margin and* In the latter end of Har; Aug. Sept. *in margin and* In the latter end of Tan.

to angle with] Tan; an angling with ~ Har.

Will*iam* Stane of Mert*on* Coll*ege*] **Ed;** Will. Stane of our coll. Har; ~ Staine ~ Tan.

Bridge and nutted in Shotover] Tan; Bridge and nutted Har. (+2)

and AW sitting and standing] Tan; and standing or setting Har. (+1)

of eating. It prov'd a quartan] Tan; to eat. It was a quartern Har.

it came on him he would be] Tan; it came, I should be Har. (+2)

contracted, he would] Tan. *In Tan:* contracted, he sh̲o̲u̲l̲d̲ *[i.e., canc]* would.

he would on the sick-day] Tan; I should on my sick day Har.

with great wretching] Tan; with great reching Har.

made him grow much taller] Tan; made me grow taller Har. (+1)

Ayre than in Oxôn] Tan; aire than at Oxon Har.

to shake the Ague off] Tan; to shake it off Har. (+1)

1652/3. 15 Feb.

Tuesday (Feb. 15) AW] **Ed;** Feb. 15 *in margin and* Tuesday I Har; Feb. 15 *in margin and* Tuesday (Feb. 15) AW Tan. (+2)

Cassington before mention'd] Tan; Cassington, (mention'd before under the
yeare 1649) Har. (−4)

Quarters in that Towne] Tan; quarters there Har. (+2)

f. 19ʳ

sufficient Farmer] Tan; sufficient Fermour Har.

yet AW had a] **Ed;** yet I had ~ Har; yet he had ~ Tan.

had a very fair Chamber] Tan; had a fair chamber Har. (+1)

therein with a chimney and] Tan; therein and Har. (+3)

1652/3. 21 Feb.

AW had a very sad Dreame in his sleep.] Tan; A very sad Dreame in my
sleep — Har. (+2)

He was in … companion &c] +Tan. (+10)

he would have] Tan; I should have Har.

the plow on his Well-Dayes] Tan; on my well-dayes the plow Har.

and sometimes plowed] Tan, plowed *corr over ployed.*

his most tender yeares an extraordinary ravishing Delight] Tan; my tender
yeares a most extraordinary and ravishing Delight Har. (−1)

practiced privately there] Tan; practiced there Har. (+1)

tuned his strings] **Ed;** tuned my strings Har; tuned in strings Tan.

Eare and being ready] **Ed;** eare and being ready Har; Eare and ready Tan.
(−1)

upon hearing it once] Tan; upon hearing of it once Har. (−1)

1652/3. 4 Mar.

Mar. 4] Har–Tan, *moved from margin at middle of the paragraph to the head
of the entry.*

an Houre or two before] Tan; an houre or more before Har.

and drunk very desperatly] Tan; and drank very desperately Har.

had put in Mʳ Woods Cup Tobacco. —] Tan; had secretly put tobacco in
my Drinke. Har.

that had got within AW] **Ed;** that had got within me Har; that had got
within him Tan.

was none of AW's] **Ed;** was none of mine Har; was none of his Tan.

that sent it out of his Mouth] Tan; that sent it out of mouth Har. (+1)

In this condition he continued,] Tan; In this condition did I continue Har.
(−1)

and grew hotter, and then his Ague] Tan; and then as the weather grew
hotter and hotter, so my ague Har. (−5)

f. 19ᵛ

had he not prevented it] Tan; had not I prevented it Har.

by taking Physick] **Har;** by Physick Tan.

1652/3. 12 Mar.

Saturday March 12 his brothers] **Ed;** 12 *in margin and* Saturday my brother
Har; 12 *in margin and* Saturday March 12 his brothers Tan. (+2)

Edward and Robert Wood, with Mʳ] Tan; Edward and Robert and Mʳ Har.
(+1)

to comfort him … and then departed] Tan; and dined in our House Har.
(+9)

Tan, *gap at end of paragraph, of* 7 *lines.*

1653

persons, he] Tan; persons (whom I cannot now remember) I Har. (−5)

than the other going before] Tan; than the other Har. (+2)

he thought then to be a most excellent] Tan; I then thought to be an excellent
Har. (+1)

but when AW. improv'd … found him not so] Tan; but was not Har. (+10)

Sept*ember* 8, Thursday, he gave] **Ed**, *date integrated into the text*; Sep 8 *in
margin and* I gave Har; Sept. 8 *in margin and* He gave Tan.

and 10ˢ quarterly] Tan; and whether afterwards I gave him 5ˢ or 10ˢ quarterly,
I have utterly forgot Har. (−11)

without a Director or Guide] +Tan. (+5)

and Antiquities stand] Tan; and Antiquities stood Har.

f. 20ʳ

lighted upon] **Har**; lighted up Tan, *catchword* upon.

The Description of Leycestershire] Tan; The Description of Leycestershire
Har.

did this, or] **Har**; did this or Tan.

which he had … his last dayes] Tan; which I have laying by me at this time
Har. (+1)

The Display of Heraldry] Tan; the Display of Heraldry Har.

and in other books of] Tan; and other books of Har. (+1)

could not avoid them] Tan, ~ avoid ^them^.

and could not avoid them;] Tan; and could not avoid it, Har.

Heraldry, Musick and Painting … for lucre sake. —] +Tan. (+57)

crowd upon him that] Tan, ~ ^him that^.

His brother Edw*ard* Wood was much] Tan; but my brother Edward was
Har. (+1)

to each others content, but the same J. W.] Tan; but Har. (+8)

Gent*leman* of a good] Tan; Gentleman of Har. (+2)

per an*num* at least,] Tan; per an, Har. (+2)

debauch'd] **Ed**; debauhed Har; debach'd Tan.

which did not a little Trouble to AW.] +Tan (+8)

which did not a] Tan, which ^did^ not a.

Nov.

Stoke-Lyne neare to Bister] Tan; Stoke-Lyne Har. (+3)

Tan, *gap at end of page, of* 6 *lines.*

f. 20ᵛ

—— Hussey and —— Peck] Tan, *a false start above heading, canc by
erasure.*

1654. 25 July.

two Gentlemen that were lately] Tan; two Gentlemen and lately Har. (+1)

Castle-yard in Oxôn] Tan; castle yard Har. (+2)

commission and employ, and] **Ed;** Commission, Har; commission and employ, Tan. (+2)

money to maintain them] Tan; money Har. (+3)

imprisonment in the Jayle at Oxon] Tan; imprisonment Har. (+5)

Partie John Glynn serjeant at law] Tan; Partie Serjeant John Glynne Har. (+2)

the Eldest, had] Tan; the eldest of the two, had Har. (−3)

Marks of honour] Tan; marks of valour and honour Har. (−2)

who was yonger, was proper] Tan; was yonger, proper Har. (+2)

seemed a stout] Tan; seemed to be a stout Har. (−2)

As soon as they were cut downe] Tan; They were, as soon as cut downe Har.

they were carried away] Tan; carried away Har. (+2)

was on the same day] Tan; was the same day Har. (+1)

of his Studies and Thoughts —] Tan; of my thoughts. Har. (+2)

pittied by all men.] Tan; pittied by all men &c Har. (−1)

10 Aug.

Master of Arts by] Tan; Master in the Natural Philosophy School by Har. (−3)

Will*iam* Bull of Trinity,] Tan; Will. Bull of Trinity Coll, Har. (−1)

Fellow of Alls*ouls* Coll*ege*. —] **Ed;** ~ Allsoules Coll. Har; ~ Allsouls, Coll — Tan.

Weldon of Magd*alen* College] Tan; Weldon of Magd, Har. (+1)

who examin'd the rest … are imbezld and lost] Tan; I have a certificate of this examination by me, but no certificates of any other exercise performed for the said Degree, as being lost or imbezild. Har. (−2)

Cirques Jobson a Jew … 1650 and 1655.] Tan; Coffey, which had been drank by some persons in Oxon 1650, was this yeare publickly sold at or neare the Angel within the east gate of Oxon, as also Chocolate by an outlander or a Jew. Har, *corresponds to an entry in Tan, 22 Jan. 1650/1, f. 16ᵛ.* (−5)

Students, especially MSS, he] Tan; Students I Har. (+2)

Mʳ Tho*mas* Barlow the Head-Keeper of the said Library;] Tan; by the Head-keeper of it named Mʳ Tho. Barlow, Har.

f. 21ʳ

Later end of 1654] **Har;** *om* Tan. (−4)

his companions, W*illiam* Bull, E*dmund* Gregory, J*ohn* Trap, Georg M*ason* were not without silly Frolicks —] **Ed;** his companions* were not without silly Frolicks *and in margin a surname and initials:* *W. Bull.; E. G.; J. T.; and G. M.*] Tan; Har, *see next note.*(+15)

not now to be maintaind —] Tan; Having by this time got some musical acquaintance, a frolick by all meanes must be taken by us; and what should it be but to disguise our selves in poore habits, and like contry fidlers scrape for our livings. Farringdon fair this yeare was the place designed to go to: And all of us five in number lodging in a House in the middle rew in Magd. parish, belonging to one Gregory a chandler wee sate out very early the next morning, and calling first on Mʳ Th. Lattons

house at Kingston Bakepuze, wee bid him good morrow by 2. or 3. Tunes
— He came in the hall among us, listned to our Musick, gave us money
and ordered Drink too, carried to us. After wee had done with him, wee
retired to the In standing on the road going to Farringdon, dined there,
and after dinner wee were entertain by some of the Neighbours, who
dancd as I remember in the Green, gave us some money and victualls,
and I think wee returnd very late that evening to Oxon. The names of
those in this exploit were my self and Will. Bull before mentiond who
played on the violins. Edm Gregorie B. A and Gent Com of Mert. Coll,
who playd on the Bass viol. Joh. Trap of Trinity, on the Citern and
(Georg) Mason of the said Coll on another wyer Instrument but could
do nothing. — Soon after wee took another voyage Northward called at
Hampton Poyle, playd at Mr Wests house, had some money and but more
drink — Afterwards wee went I think to Kidlington got somthing there,
returnd in the evening, and certain soldiers overtaking us they by force
made us play in the open feild, and then left us without giving a penny

Most of my Companions would afterwards glory in this, but I was
ashamed and could never endure to heare of it

at the latter end of 1654 Har. (−319). *AW wrote this on the currently
misplaced f. 41*$^{r-v}$*, a slip of waste paper formerly used as a receipt (someone,
not AW, wrote* 'an acquittance for a subsidie' *on the verso). AW inserted the
slip after f. 42*$^{r-v}$*, and it was there at one time (the transcription by Richard
Rawlinson, MS. Rawl. D. 97 has the correct, chronological, sequence). AW's
handwriting on both sides of this slip is casual and hasty, not formal as on
the leaves before and after.*

Tan] *gap at end of paragraph, of 4 lines.*

1655. 25 Apr.

Edw*ard* Wood eldest brother to AW and] Tan; My eldest brother now living
and Har. (+11)

of the Uni*versity* of Oxôn.] Tan; of the University. Har. (+2)

3 May.

AW made his first ... *perseverant.*] Tan; I spoke my first Declamation in the
Nat. Philosophy school for the degree of M^r of Arts. Har. (+1)

16 May.

AW made his 2^d ... *subire?*] Tan; About Midsomer day I spoke my 2^d Declamation in the Nat Phil. School: A copie of which I having not by me, I
cannot therefore tell y^o the day when twas spoke Har, *AW lined out this
entry at June 1655 and inserted after the entry, 3 May 1655, the marginal note:*
'May 16 I spoke my second Dec.' (−10)

esset Ciceronis libros] **Ed;** *om* Har; ~ Ciceroni ~ Tan. (+3)

quam Mortem subire] **Ed;** *om* Har; ~ subiri Tan. (+3)

22 May.

Edw*ard* Wood died] Tan; My Brother Edward died Har. (−1)

of his Friends and Relations] Tan; of Relations and Friends Har. (+1)

by Ralp[h] Button his] Tan; by Mr Ralph Button his Har. (−1)

Ralph Button his] **Har;** Ralp ~ Tan.

now Canon of Ch*rist*] Tan; but now Canon of Ch. Har. (−1)

and made a most religious End] Tan; and very penitent to the great comfort
of his Relations Har. (−4)

24 May.

hall of Merton Coll*ege*, where] Tan; hall, where Har. (+3)

f. 21ᵛ

last E*dward* Wood had] Tan; last my brother had Har.

money to buy him a] Tan; money to buy a Har. (+1)

among which last was] Tan; Among which was Har. (+1)

Friend thou was wise] Tan; Friend, tho was wise Har.

12 Oct.

This is mention'd] Tan; This I mention Har.

a person as he who] Tan; a person that Har. (+2)

was squint ey'd and] Tan; was squint and Har. (+1)

to Winchester School] Tan; to Winchester Har. (+1)

17 Oct.

f. 22ʳ

which he afterwards ... lib. 2 [. p. 91.]] Tan; which are printed in his — Har.
(+8)

lib. 2. p. 91.] **Ed;** lib. 2 Tan; *om* Har.

17 Dec.

Lancing therof] **Har;** Lancing *om* Tan. (−1)

1655/6. Mar.

In Har *the 1st paragraph of this entry appears at March 1656/7, is there lined out,*
and ends abruptly at the end of a leaf.

of his brother Edw*ard* Wood] Tan; that my brother Edw. Wood Har.

deceased which he had preached before the Universitie] Tan; deceased had
made and publickly preached in the University Har. (−1)

See *Ath. et Fasti Oxôn*, vol. 2. pp. 117–8.] **Ed;** See Har; See *Ath. et Fasti Oxôn*,
vol. 2. p. Tan. (+7)

See *Ath. et Fasti Oxôn*, vol. 2. p[p. 117–8.]] Tan, *in margin, here moved to note*
79.

He dedicated them ... in Gresham Coll*ege*] Tan; I dedicated them Har, *ends*
abruptly at the bottom of f. 46ᵛ. (+58)

Tillyard an Apothecary] **Har;** Tillyard Apothecary Tan. (−1)

and great Royallist] Tan; and Royallist Har. (+1)

now living in Oxôn] Tan; now remaining in Oxon Har.

and by others who esteem'd] Tan; and by some who esteemed Har.

Virtuosi or *Wits*] Tan; Vertuosi or Wits Har.

the chiefest number] Tan; the chief number Har.

Castle, Will*iam* Bull] **Ed;** Castle, W. Bull Har; Castle Will. Bull Tan.

as Joh*n* Lamphire a] Tan; as Mʳ Joh. Lamphere a Har.(−1)

Oxon, Mathew] Tan; Oxon, as Mathew Har. (−1)

and had an Excise set upon Coffey.] +Tan. (+7)

Tan, *gap from end of paragraph to bottom of f.* 22ʳ, *of 6 lines.*

f. 22ᵛ

1656

    had genuine skill] Tan; ~~was a proficient~~ ^had some genuine skill^ Har. (−1)

    the weekly meetings] Tan; the weekly Meeting Har.

    Ellis late Organist] Tan; Ellis the ejected Organist Har. (−1)

    was built.] Tan; was built || Har, *the vertical lines, in red pencil, indicate an addition to be made.*

    The usual company that ... under the yeare 1658.] +Tan (+651)

    Bister, and] **Ed;** *om* Har; Bister and Tan. (+2)

    Brome Whorwood] **Ed;** *om* Har; Brome. Whorwood Tan. (+2)

    Ralph Sheldon] *om* Har; Ralph *later written in blank space in pencil and* ~ Tan.

    Westminster —— 1659] **Ed;** *om* Har; ~ 165 Tan. (+2)

    gent*leman* or singing man] **Ed;** *om* Har; ~ man. Tan. (+4)

f. 23ʳ

    (8) Joseph Proctor] **Ed;** *om* Har; (8) —— Proctor Tan.

    starch'd] **Ed;** *om* Har; starc'hd Tan. (+1)

    yeare 1658.] **Ed;** *om* Har; yeare 16 Tan. (+2)

22 July.

    Joseph Proctor died] **Ed;** —— Proctor died Har; —— Proctor died Tan.

    had been bred] **Har;** had bred Tan. (−1)

    in the faculty of musick] **Har;** *om* Tan. (−5)

    for the Lyra-viol and] Tan; for the Lyra and Har. (+1)

    The Antiquities of Warwickshire] Tan; The Antiquities of Warwickshire Har.

f. 23ᵛ

    in the public Library] Tan; in the Library Har. (+1)

    this time and after was] Tan; this time was Har. (+2)

1656/7, 10 Jan.

    AW, his mother, and his two Brothers Rob*ert* and Christopher Wood] Tan; My mother, my two brothers Robert and Christopher & my self Har.

    Brothers Rob*ert* and Christopher Wood] Brothers Rob. ^and^ ~ Tan.

    up into the Tower] Tan; up in the Tower Har.

    warden in 1421] Tan; Warden 1421 Har. (+1)

    Abendon was put)] Tan; Abyngdon was) Har. (+1)

    of the said Abendon] Tan; of the said Abyngdon Har.

    and to make] **Har;** and to make, and to make Tan. (+3)

    to make the five, six, Bells, that is to put a Treble to them.] so make them six: Har. (+10)

    eight, and Dʳ John] **Har;** eight, Dʳ Joh. Tan. (−1)

    to take order about their] Tan; to order their Har. (+2)

    Master, by some] Tan; Master, & by some Har. (−1)

    and the rather,] and the ^rather,^ Tan.

    because it was said, that he] Tan; because as 'twas said he Har. (+1)

    knowledg of Dancing] **Har;** ~ in ~ Tan.

f. 24ʳ

gained some improvement] Tan; gain'd improvement Har. (+1)

as Griffith and] **Ed;** as Griffin and Har–Tan.

in privat meetings which AW frequented] Tan; in our private meetings Har. (+2)

parts all with Viols] **Har;** parts with Viols Tan. (−1)

with an Organ, Virginal] Tan; with either an Organ or Virginal Har. (−2)

or Harpsicon joyn'd with them] Tan; or Harpsecon with them Har. (+1)

to be an Instrument] Tan; to be the Instrument Har.

endure that it should come] Tan; endure it to come Har. (+1)

vaine and fidling] Tan; vaine or Fidling Har.

restoration of K*ing* C*h*ar*les* 2] Tan; Restoration of K. Ch. 2 Har.

while he was at Meales] Tan; while at Meales Har. (+2)

than Viols.] Tan, *gap at end of paragraph, of 3 lines.*

1657. 27 Mar.

At the funeral of] Tan; I rode to Garsington with the Corps of Har. (−4)

of Garsingdon neare Oxôn Gent*leman* Shee was buried] Tan; of the same place Gent. to see and attend her burial Har. (−3)

by the Remaines of] Tan; neare to the Remaines of Har. (−1)

woman was sister] Tan; woman who was sister Har. (−1)

(of the same Familie with the] Tan; (of the familie of the Har. (+1)

did not then survey] Tan; did not survey then Har.

monuments in Garsingdon church] Tan; monuments of the church Har.

but rode immediatly home to Oxôn —] +Tan. (+6)

14 May.

ring very well at] Tan; ring well at Har. (+1)

f. 24ᵛ

not at all please] Tan; not all please Har. (+1)

critical Hearer] ~ Re*ad*er *i.e., canc and followed by:* Hearer Tan.

afterwards re-cast] ~ re*cast i.e., canc and:* re-cast Tan.

wherein the Ringers stood] Tan; wherein the Ringers ringed Har.

hanged the Ringers stood] Tan; hanged the Ringers rang Har.

againe, this Belfry, that] Tan; again, this, that Har. (+1)

4 Aug.

exceedingly delighted in] **Ed;** ~ delighted with Har; exceedingly in Tan. (−1)

14 Aug.

Joh*n* Drope] ~ Dr*a*^o^pe Tan.

afterwards for giving him] Tan; afterwards giving him Har. (+1)

Those that remaine] Tan; Those that remaind Har.

as also of the Armes] Tan; with the Armes Har. (+2)

and tricked out with his pen the] Tan; tricked out the Har. (+4)

church, cloyster and] Tan; Church and Cloyster and Har. (−1)

5 Sept.

poore supr] Har *only, in the margin at head of the paragraph; meaning not clear.*

of Halton neare Oxôn] Tan; of Hatton neare Oxon Har.

f. 25ʳ

his mother] Har *only, in the margin at the end of the paragraph; a reminder for AW to include here the story of the mother of Brome Whorwood.*

I set this Memoire downe … lets proceed.] +Tan. (+1018)

Hampton Court August 1647] *om* Har; *date entered later in pencil* Tan. (+4)

enclin'd to his] *om* Har; ~ ~~for~~ to his Tan. (+3)

f. 25ᵛ

Hampton Court to acquaint] **Ed;** *om* Har; ~ to acquainst Tan. (+4)

John Ashburnham] **Ed;** *om* Har; —— Ashburnham Tan. (+2)

the Lord George Goring] **Ed;** *om* Har; the Lord —— Goring Tan. (+4)

f. 26ʳ

his only way] **Ed;** *om* Har; his only, way Tan. (+3)

to his Majestie] **Ed;** *om* Har; to to his Majestie Tan. (+3)

to his Majestie yet the] *om Har;* ^ ~ ^ Tan. (+5)

said Lord Say … peace)] **Ed;** *om* Har; ~~the~~ said L̲o̲r̲d̲ S̲a̲y̲ … p̲e̲a̲c̲e̲) Tan, *all canc.* (+14)

peace) did] **Ed;** *om* Har; p̲e̲a̲c̲e̲) ~~his Majestie~~ did Tan. (+2)

send for them] **Ed;** *om* Har; send for him Tan. (+3)

16 Sept.

north walls of the church standing] Tan; walls on the north side standing Har.

with a melancholy Delight] Tan; with ~~very great~~ ^a Melancholy^ delight Har.

or the Lodg,] **Ed;** or the Lodge Har; or Lodg, Tan. (−1)

were soon after pul'd downe] Tan; are since pulled downe Har. (+1)

f. 26ᵛ

24 Dec.

twelve at Noon] Tan; twelve of the Clock in the morn Har. (−4)

what account — He] Tan; what account I was to dine there. I Har. (−5)

He went forthwith with] Tan; I went with Har. (+1)

and ready but Edmund] ~ ready —— *canc word and:* but ~ Tan.

Gregory Bach*elor* of Arts, lately] Tan; Gregory B. A lately Har. (+1)

that morning in the chappel of S.] Tan; that morning at S. Har. (+3)

The company sate downe] Tan; Wee sate downe Har. (+1)

downe to dinner between] **Har;** sate downe between between Tan.

clock in the Afternoon,] Tan; Clock, Har. (+3)

Bride smiling to them] Tan; Bride (smiling) to us Har.

and then went to] Tan; and then returned to Har.

where, or neare it his] Tan; where his Har. (+3)

a good Estate with his yong wife] Tan; a plentiful estate by his wife Har. (+1)

Bagshot neare Windsor] Tan, *written later in a blank space, in pencil;* Bagshot *and a blank space, not filled in* Har. (+2)

was buried there.] Tan, *gap at end of paragraph, of 3 lines.*

1657/8. 14 Jan. *Entry of 14 Jan. om in* Har.

He (AW) went ... monuments there before —] +Tan. (+52)

f. 27ʳ

12 Mar. *Entry of 12 Mar. om in* Har.

Edm. Greg.... School &c.] +Tan. (+19)

the public lib*rary*, Anatomy School] **Ed;** *om* Har; ~ libr. ~ Tan. (+5)

17 Mar.

Soundess neare Nettlebed in Oxfordsh*ire*] Tan; of Soundess Har. (+3)

in S. Andrews church in] **Har;** in S. Andrews-ch. in Tan.

neare to Winchester] **Har;** neare to Wincester Tan.

23 Mar.

23 He walked ... bought of him —] +Tan. (+32)

23 Mar. Tues. He walked] **Ed;** *om* Har. *See the preceding note.*

did in the latter end of this yeare] Tan; did Har. (+7)

as also to the Queen] **Ed;** and to the Queen Har; as also the queen Tan.

in 1669 to Cosmo Prince of Tuscany when in Oxôn] Tan; to the Prince of Tuscany when in Oxon 1669 Har. (+1)

Davis Mell the most eminent] Tan; ~~David~~ Mell the eminent *and in margin:* or Davys Har.

of London]Tan; of London *in margin:* and clockmaker Har. (−2)

AW did give a very handsome] Tan; my self gave him a handsome Har.

Salutation, in S. Maries] **Ed;** Salution in ~ Har; Salutation, ~~own'd by~~ Maries Tan. (−2)

Oxon, own'd by Tho*mas* Wood] Tan; ownd by Tho. Wood a Dancing Master Har. (−2)

to the Father of AW — The company] Tan; to my father — wee Har. (+3)

upon Mʳ Mell to] Tan; upon him to Har. (+1)

as all in London ... beyond him] Tan; could go beyond him as all in London did Har.

Baltser an Outlander, came to Oxon] Tan; Baltzar the out-lander came among us Har.

other thoughts of] Tan; other thought of Har.

who tho he playd farr sweeter ... of the Finger-board] Tan; Some of Mʳ Mells Compositions I have. Mell who had been one of the musicians to K. Ch. 1. & afterwards to K. Ch 2 had a sweet stroke — Baltsars was rough Har. (−6)

Tan, *gap at end of paragraph to bottom of f. 27ʳ of 7 lines.*

f. 27ᵛ

1658. 5 Apr.

in the chancel of Garsingdon church] Tan; in the church of Garsingdon Har. (+1)

13 Apr.

Easter-Tuesday Chr*istopher* Wood (brother to AW) ... Elizabeth Seymour] Tan; My brother Christop. Wood was married to Elizab. dau. of William Seymoure of Oxon. Gent. See in the yeare following — They were married on Easter Tuesday Har, *paragraph lined out.* (−14)

At Cuxham, with other ... Mr Gregory;] Tan; The same day I went with
some of my acquaintance to Mr Gregories house at Cuxham, Har. (−3)

collect Monumental Inscriptions] Tan; collect monuments, inscriptions
Har.

4 May.

William Coniers] **Ed;** —— Coniers Har–Tan.

carried her into Broken] Tan; carried her to Broken Har.

f. 28^r

because that he afterwards broke] Tan; because he afterwards broke Har.
(+1)

See ... 199] **Ed;** See Dr. Plot Nat. Hist. of Ox. 199, *added later, in pencil, barely
legible.* Har; See Dr. Plot Nat. Hist. of Ox. 197 *added later, in pencil, barely
legible.* Tan.

14 July.

with most excellent Musick] **Har;** with with most ∼ Tan. (+1)

name among the Musitians of Oxôn,] Tan; name among us Har. (+3)

entit*led Ayres and Dialogues*] **Ed;** entit. Ayres and Dialogues Har; entit *Ayres
and Diologues* Tan.

Ayres and Di[a]logues... Bass-Viol] Tan; Ayres & Dialogues ... Bass viol
Har.

See *Ath. et Fasti Oxon*, vol. 1 p. 901] Tan, *in margin*; See the first vol. of Ath.
et Fasti Oxon. p 901 Har, *in margin*. (−2)

which they played in their] Tan; which wee used now to play in our Har.
(−3)

24 July.

Tho*mas* Balsar or Baltzar a] Tan; Thom. Baltzar a Har. (+2)

Low lately Organist of] Tan; Low lately now Organist of Har. (−1)

all with alacrity] **Har;** all in alacrity Tan.

which he nor any in England] **Har;** which he now any ∼ Tan.

of the weekly meetings at Mr Ellis's house] Tan; of our meetings Har (+5)

and there played] **Har;** and the played Tan.

of all the Auditory: and] Tan; of us all, and Har. (+1)

Wilson thereupon the public Professor] Tan; whereupon Wylson the Professor Har. (+1)

Judg of Musick] **Har;** ∼ of Musick of Musick Tan. (+2)

f. 28^v

to see whether he] Tan; to feel whether he Har.

a Devil, or not, because ... parts of Man] Tan; not a Devill, &c. Har. (+8)

Whereupon he ... it, he] Tan; Whereupon being not able to avoid it I Har.

as I have before told you,] +Tan. (+6)

came into England and] Tan; came and Har. (+2)

so admired, yet he] Tan; so much regarded yet Mell Har. (−1)

sweeter, was a well] Tan; sweeter and was a well Har. (−1)

and not given to excessive drinking as Baltzar was] +Tan. (+9)

30 Aug.

    See *Ath. et Fasti Oxon*, vol. 1. p. 323] Tan, *in margin*; See Ath. et Fasti Oxon
        vol. 1. p. 323 Har, *in margin*.

6 Sept.

    have been proclaimed] Tan; are proclaimed Har. (+1)

f. 29ʳ

    who stood at a Distance] +Tan. (+5)

18 Oct.

    to his kinsman Charnel] Tan; to my Cozen Charnel Har.

    22 day of the] **Har;** 22 of the Tan. (−1)

    on the 10 of May 1612] Tan; on the tenth day of May 1612 Har. (−1)

11 Feb.

    a Petition to present to] Tan; a petition drawn up to present to Har. (−2)

    Visitors in the University] Tan; visitors of the Universitie Har.

    he set his hand &c The] Tan; I set my hand. Another Har. (+1)

    The Independents ... the Godly Party] Tan; Another party, (the Indepen-
        dents or the Godly party) Har. (+1)

    petition contrary to the former, and said] Tan; petition, & say Har. (+4)

    No person was more ready than] Tan; None more ready then Har. (+2)

    notwithstanding he ... reverence and obedience] +Tan. (+15)

1658/9. 12 Feb.

    Edward Bagshaw] Bagshaw *over Backshaw* Har–Tan.

    Bagshaw M. A and student of Ch*rist* ch*urch*] Tan; Bagshaw of Christ-church
        Har. (+4)

    (ejected his clerkship of] Tan; who had been ejected his clerkship of Har.
        (−3)

    Visitors 1648) living now] Tan; Visitors but now living Har.

    Smith on a certaine Morning] Tan; Smith one morning Har. (+2)

    in or neare to, Bagley] Tan; in or neare Bagley Har. (+1)

    Wood, between Oxon and Abendon, inhabited] Tan; Wood, inhabited Har.
        (+4)

    Lord of Sunningwell] Tan; Lord of Bayworth Har.

    The house called Bayworth is an] Tan; It is an Har. (+3)

f. 29ᵛ

    AW found a pretty] Tan; wee found a pretty Har.

    carpets. There had been painted] Tan; carpets, had painted Har. (+2)

    soldiers (Rebells) in the grand rebellion] Tan; soldiers in the late warr Har.
        (+1)

    He also found there] Tan; Wee also found there Har.

    excellent Organ in the said Oratory: on]Tan; excellent Organ, on Har.
        (+4)

    Smith perform'd the] Tan; Smith executed the Har.

    found him to be a melancholy] Tan; found him a Har. (+2)

    enquirie farther of the person] Tan; enquiry more of the man Har.

    that he built for] Tan; that he builded for Har.

    them to ring when] Tan; them to ring at when Har. (−1)

He had been several] Tan; He was severall Har. (+1)

the mother of AW] Tan; my mother Har. (+2)

and a Sojournour] Tan; & sojourning Har. (+1)

and when he knew that AW was her son] Tan; Upon this account Har (+6)

and AW afterwards frequented the house] **Ed;** and I went afterwards to the House Har; and afterwards ~ Tan. (−2)

and with the retiredness] Tan; and the retiredness Har. (+1)

In the latter ... physick-Drinke] Tan, *in the text*; In the latter ... physick drink Har, *in the margin.*

yeare (in Mar*ch*)] Tan; yeare in Mar. Har.

facultie of musick] **Har;** falcultie ~ Tan.

f. 30^r

company, when he] Tan; company that I found when I Har. (−3)

names of them are set ... yeare 1656] Tan; I have set downe under the yeare 1656 Har. (+3)

that came in after and were now performers] Tan; that now came Har. (+5)

playd, were] Tan; played with were Har. (−1)

(1) Charles Perot ... the yeare 1662] +Tan (+875). *In Har there is a blank verso (f. 55ᵛ) to allow room for an addition.*

See *Ath. et Fasti Oxon.* vol. 2. p. 781.] **Ed;** *om* Har; see *Ath. et Fasti Oxon.* vol. 2. p. *om* Tan, *in margin, here transferred to note 90.* (+8)

See in the same book before quoted p. 465] *om* Har; Tan, *in margin, here transferred to note 91.* (+7)

where he died in 1680] *om* Har; ~ died in *AW later inserted in pencil:* 1680 Tan. (+5)

traveller and belonged ... Office] *om* Har; traveller *AW later inserted in pencil:* and belonged ... Office Tan. (+8)

a Violist and Division-violist —] **Ed;** *om* Har; ~ *in margin, here inserted in the text* Tan. (+4)

f. 30^v

(11) Charles Bridgman] *om* Har; Henr. Bridgman *above the first name AW wrote, in pencil:* ^Charles^ Tan. (+2)

See *Ath. et Fasti* vol. 2. p. 299] **Ed;** *om* Har; ~ Ath. et Fasti vol. 2. p. *om* Tan, *in margin, here transferred to a footnote.* (+7)

and some of the company] *om* Har; and some ~~af~~ of ~ Tan. (+5)

till he went] *om* Har; till he ~~was~~ ^went^ Tan. (+3)

and sce] *om* Har; *below last line, 2 words in pencil, illegible, not reproduced here.* Tan.

f. 31^r

which were first] *om* Har; ~ ~~was~~ ^were^ first Tan. (+3)

chamber of Christop*her*] **Ed;** *om* Har; chanber ~ Tan. (+3)

some Masters of] *om* Har; some Masters ~~af~~ of Tan. (+3)

1659. 2 Apr.

Saturday] Tan; Friday (Good Friday) *lined out and* ^Saturday^ Har.

Stoke-Lyne neare Bister with] Tan; Stoke-Lyne with Har. (+2) to give a Visit to his] Tan; to the house of my Har. (+1)

Petty Esq*uire* and other of his Relations there] Tan; Petty, where I continued a week Har. (+2)

4 Apr.

He went to Middleton-Cheyney ... who was lately] Tan; in which time I took my rambles about the Country to collect Monuments and Armes in churches. I was at the antient and noble seat lately of the Chetwoods, of whome twas bought by Philip Horman of London —— There I found the eldest son and heir of the said Ph. Horman named —— lately Har. (+59)

One John Lewes his kinsman] **Ed;** *om* Har; ~ Lewes AW's ~ Tan. (+5)

f. 31ᵛ

had changed his religion for that of Rome] Tan; wherin he had been reconciled to the Church of Rome Har. (−2)

He was civil to us] Tan; He was civil to me and to Joh. Lewis that conducted me thither Har, *all in margin.* (−8)

and caused the church ... antient Monuments] Tan; In the Church are several Monuments Har. (+8)

Chetwoods, which AW then] Tan; Chetwoods. All these I Har.

on them.] Tan; on them — The said Philip Holman Lord of Werkworth died an. 1669 aged 76 and was buried in the Church there Har. (−19)

the Armes, Quarterings, Crests and] Tan; the Quarterings, Crests and Har. (+1)

in England. At] Tan; Thence I returnd to the place from whence I came viz from the house of my coz. Joh. Cave Rector of Middleton Cheyney, where I lodged that and the next day being Wednesday. Ap. 6. I rod to Har. (−36)

Banbury is a] Tan; Banbury where I saw a Har. (−2)

that were in the Windowes there] Tan; that were therein Har. (+3)

6 Apr.

He returnd to] Tan; I went the next day to Har. (−3)

7 Apr.

Halywell in the suburb of Oxon] Tan; Halywell Har. (+5)

*Mʳ Benjamin Cooper now lives in it] +Tan, *in margin, here transferred to a footnote.* (+7)

Goods, and some money] Tan; goods and money Har. (+1)

9 Apr.

pluckd downe his body much] Tan; pluckd my body much downe Har.

20 May.

Warborow to the] Tan; Warborow at the Har.

He denied him the sight] He denied *illegible canc letters* him ~ Tan.

denied him the sight of it, but Hobbes] Tan; denied me, but Har. (+5)

Rowney an Attorney ... for my use] Tan; Rowney I got that person to bring it with him on a mercate day and leave it with him for a time Har. (−5)

f. 32ʳ

he did the next Mercate day that he came to Oxon] Tan; he did Har. (+9)

in 4°, written on Parchment] **Ed;** in qu. written on parchment Har; in 4°, written in Parchment Tan.

the 8 of June 1555] Tan; 8 Jun. 1555 Har. (+2)

20 July.

This was done to prevent a] Tan; This was in order to suppress the Har. (−1)

Booth and his partie ... to appeare] Tan; Booth in Cheshire, which was to appeare openly in Chesh. and elswhere on the first of Aug. Har. (+5)

31 July.

three stones and some] Tan; 3 stones and Har. (+1)

blown from off the Tower] Tan; blown from the Tower Har. (+1)

to call the soldiers] Tan; to call soldiers Har. (+1)

they in the church cried out that] Tan; they cried that Har. (+4)

Georg Philips] Har–Tan, *AW later added the forename in a blank space before the surname, in pencil.*

of them, were falling on the Heads of people crowding on the Floor to get out of the dores] **Ed;** of them and falling on the peoples heads <u>standing</u> ^crowding^ on the floor Har; of them, falling on the Heads of people, crowding on the Floor to get out of the dores Tan. (+6)

This was on the very] Tan; This was the very Har. (+1)

f. 32ᵛ

Colonel Edward Massey ... an escape into an adjoyning Wood] Tan; Har *has 2 versions. The second is almost identical to* Tan *(see next note) and the first is crossed out:* but their plot being discovered, and Col. Edw. Massey one of their prime leaders being taken, and hurried away behind a soldier on Horsback late this Sunday night, leapt off from the horses back in the dark while they were passing thro a wood & made his escape.

to make an escape] Tan; to make his escape Har.

September.

In the beginning of Sept*ember* the library] Tan; The library Har. *In Har, AW wrote this paragraph after 'Jul 20' 1659 and before 'Jul 31' 1659, f. 58ᵛ. At Sept., f. 59ʳ, he directed the reader, 'See before'.* (+5)

of the learned Selden was brought] Tan; of great Selden being brought Har. (+1)

sorting them, carrying them] **Har;** sorting them carrying them Tan.

which Mʳ Selden had put in, and forgotten to take out] +Tan. (+11)

which he kept in memorie of Selden to his last day] +Tan (+11)

16 Sept.

at the Miter-Inn and faigning] Tan; at the Miter and faining Har. (+1)

Hen*ry* Langley all of] **Har;** Hen. Langley of Tan. (−1)

blessing on his knees which he obtained] Tan; blessing which he did obtaine Har. (+2)

Professor of the University appeared] Tan; Professor appeared Har. (+3)

It was a piece] Tan; This was a piece Har.

instead of an Archbishop] **Har;** instead of Archbishop Tan. (−1)

Archbishop or Bishop, and] Tan; Archbishop and Har. (+2)

Mr Will. Lloyd then ... Lichfield and Coventry.] +Tan. (+115)

f. 34^r

John Backhouse] **Ed**; *om* Har; ——Backhouse Tan. *AW later wrote an incorrect forename, Will, in blank space before the surname, in pencil.* (+2)

Georg Wharton the Astronomer did take notice ... in his Almanack an*no* 1661] Tan; G. Wharton in his Alm. 1661 takes notice of this matter Har, *in margin.* (+4)

Patriarch *Jeremias*] Tan; Patriarch Jeremias Har, *in margin.*

puts the memoire under the XI of Sept*ember* which is false] Tan; puts it falsly under Sept. XI AW was askd to go but he would not Har, *added later, in the margin.* (−4)

under the XI of Sept.] under the —— *canc word and:* XI of Sept Tan.

f. 33^v

29 Sept.

Sept. 29 ... his brethren.] Har–Tan. *In Tan, this paragraph is on the verso only of a small quarto slip, f. 33^v. The recto is blank. The leaf was bound in after f. 32 Tan, and the paragraph follows the entry of 16 Sept. on f. 34^r. The paragraph follows the correct sequence in Har. This is the first of 3 slips inserted into the narrative where AW seems to have initially skipped material (see below, 10 Apr. 1660, f. 36^v, and 1 Apr. 1661, f. 41^v).*

the eldest brother then living of AW] Tan; my eldest brother then living Har. (+2)

Bach*elor* of Div*inity* —] Tan; B. Div. lately Rector of Ardley neare Bister in Oxfordsh. and vicar of Comnore neare to Abendon in Berks. Har. (−16)

It must be now knowne] Tan; It must be here noted Har.

he did by his will leave] Tan; he by his will, left Har. (+1)

therefore Rob*ert* Wood] Tan; therefore my brother Robert Har. (−1)

of the said estate which laid in Oxôn] Tan; of it Har. (+6)

upon Roberts request] Tan; upon his request Har.

the interest he had in the said estate] Tan; my interest Har. (+6)

as surviver or longest liver if it should so happen] Tan; as the longest liver Har (+6)

and this he did without any consideration given to him] Tan; for nothing Har. (+8)

Afterwards he did the like to his brother Christopher upon his request:] Tan; Afterwards my brother Christophor did the like, and he gave me nothing: Har.

f. 34^r

24 Oct.

Tan, *the narrative, 29 Sept., ends on f. 33^v, and 24 Oct. continues on f. 34^r.*

They were taken out thence by] Tan; This favour of perusing them was done by Har. (−2)

of the said House ... satisfied himself with them] Tan; of Ch. ch. and I spent several dayes in perusing them in his Lodgings in the Cloyster of Ch. Church Har. (+7)

collecting matters from them] Tan; collecting matters thence Har. (+1)

Textual Notes

Oct.

in the Cathedral of Ch*rist* ch*urch*] Tan; in the Cathedral Har. (+3)

acquaintance with him] Tan; acquaintance with this person Har. (−1)

of Oliver Cromwell] **Har;** ∼ Cromwel- Tan.

Cromwell the Protector, who] Tan; Cromwell who Har. (+2)

f. 34ᵛ

what shall I doe] Tan; *what should I doe* Har.

To which Quin made answer with great complements] Har–Tan. *Richard Rawlinson's transcript of Har (Bodleian Library, MS. Rawl. D. 97, SC 12915) ends here with 'Cætera desunt.⁄' Apparently ff. 61–3 were not, at that time, with the rest of the manuscript.*

that *your Highness would*] Tan; that *his Highness would* Har.

26 Nov.

His Acquaintance Hen*ry* Stubbe of ch*rist* church] Tan; Hen. Stubb of Ch.Ch. my acquaintance Har.

sitting in ... his Friend] Tan; sitting in my friends upper chamber, Har. (+2)

(Will*iam* Sprigg Fellow of Linc*oln* coll*ege*)] Tan; Will. Sprigg Fellow of Linc. Coll, Har.

Back gate of the Miter-Inn,] Tan; back-gate of the Miter Har. (+1)

thro Stubbe's haire] Tan; thro Stubs his haire Har. (−1)

Dec.

AW was at Cuxham] Tan; I spent some dayes at Cuxham Har. (−2)

house of Edm*und* Gregory] Tan; House of Mʳ Gregory Har.

Mʳ *William* Bull, Mʳ Hen*ry* Hawley &c] **Har;** Mʳ Bull, Hawley &c Tan (−3)

were there also] Tan; were there with me Har. (−1)

1659/60. Feb.

In the beginning of Febr*uary*] Tan; In the beginning of this month Har. (−1)

See *Ath. et Fasti Oxon.* vol. 2 p. 413.] **Ed;** *om* Har; See *Ath. et Fasti Oxon.* vol. 2 p Tan, *in margin.* (+8)

13 Feb.

that then was brought] Tan; that was then brought Har.

should suddenly be a] Tan; should be suddenly a Har.

The Bells rang and Bonfiers were made] Tan; There were ringing of Bells & Bonfiers Har.

into a Bonfier at Qu*eens* College gate] Tan; in a bonfier at Qu. Coll. Har. (+1)

Dʳ Joh*n* Palmer a great Rumper, Warden] Tan; Dʳ Palmer Warden Har. (+4)

very ill and weak, had] **Ed;** ill, had Har; very ill and weak had Tan. (+3)

He had been one ... of Oliver.] +Tan (+14)

AW being resolv'd ... where he was borne] Tan; being resolv'd to set to my study in the house where I was borne. Har. (+9)

in the upper roome] Tan; in the uppermost Rome Har.

205

window next to the street] Tan; window next the street Har. (+1)

things which he] Tan; things that I Har.

with Melancholy by reading] Tan; with a great Melancholy by reading Har. (−2)

entit*led A true and faithfull Narration*] Tan; called *A true & faithfull relation* Har.

f. 35ʳ

on the back-side of the stalls] Tan; on the stalls Har. (+3)

in various ... of K*ing* Hen*ry* 7] Tan; about the beg. of K. H. 7 in various and antique postures Har. (+3)

daubed over ... the command] Tan; daubled over with paint by command Har. (+1)

in two or three yeares] Tan; in 3 or more yeares Har.

pictures quite obliterated] Tan; Pictures quite lost Har.

were performing this work] Tan; were doing this Har. (+1)

and desired them to look after the Offenders] +Tan. (+8)

but, with shame be it spoken,] Tan; but Har. (+5)

not one of them did resent the matter] Tan; none seemed to resent it Har. (+3)

after the sacrilegists, ... poore spirits] Tan; after them Har. (+8)

before this time ... afterwards printed —] Tan; before writ them out, & have since printed them. Har.

Har ends here. From this point, textual notes are to Tan only.

f. 35ʳ

1659/60. 13 Feb.

See *Hist. et Antiq. Univ. Oxon* lib. 2. p. 91.] **Ed;** See *Hist. et Antiq. Univ. Oxon* lib. 2. p +Tan. (+9)

Gap from end of paragraph to bottom of f. 35ʳ, of 20 lines.

f. 35ᵛ *blank*

f. 37ʳ

1660. 30 Mar.

'twas said a man] **Ed;** 'twas a man

1 Apr.

Apr. 1] *in margin, 1 written over 3*

AW] *over canc word(s)*

f. 36ᵛ

10 Apr.

This entry is on the verso of an octavo slip. The recto is blank. The leaf was bound in after f. 35, and the paragraph follows the entry of 1 Apr. on f. 37ʳ. This is the 2nd of 3 inserted slips. See above, textual note at 29 Sept. 1659, f. 33.

looked upon him] ~ him *written over canc* me

f. 37ʳ

10 May.

May 10 Thursday gave] **Ed;** May 10 *in margin and* ~

the Master] **Ed;** the Master the Master

14 May.
> there] *over canc* their

f. 37ᵛ

24 May.
> A<u>lls</u>ouls coll*ege*, Chr*istopher* Harrison of Queens coll*ege*, Franc*is*] **Ed;** *Alls*
> coll. Chr. Harrison of Queens coll. Franc.
>
> Johns Coll*ege*, Thom*as*] **Ed;** Johns Coll. Thom.
>
> Ch*rist* ch*urch*, Hen*ry* Flower of] **Ed;** Ch. ch. Hen.

f. 38ʳ

18 July.
> Jul. 18 ... Jul. 19] *the order of the entries, 18 July and 19 Jul, is reversed in Tan*

19 July.
> in Glocestershire] **Ed;** ~ Glocestershrre

20 July.
> and sculptures of mens] **Ed;** ~ sulptures ~
>
> excellency of them is] ~ them —— *canc word and:* is

30 July.
> of his cheeks, the chang] **Ed;** ~ cheeks the ~
>
> contented] **Ed;** contended

f. 38ᵛ

4 Oct.
> coll*ege*, within a quarter] **Ed;** ~ withn ~

f. 39ʳ

1660/61. 5 Mar.
> Rich*ard* Browne, Dʳ Tho*mas* Clayton] ~ Browne Dʳ ~
>
> stuck not to say] **Ed;** stuck not say
>
> *Gap from end of paragraph to bottom of f. 39ʳ, of 4 lines.*

f. 39ᵛ

18 Mar.
> *Gap from end of paragraph to bottom of f. 39ᵛ, of 34 lines.*

f. 40ʳ

1661. 26 Mar.
> Dʳ Clayton] **Ed;** M Dʳ Clayton *M is the incompleted month of March.*
>
> of Knighthood confer'd] **Ed;** ~ Knighthood ~

30 Mar.
> quarter of an hour before] **Ed;** ~ hour became

31 Mar.
> time the ceremony.] ~ ceremoney

f. 40ᵛ

31 Mar.
> to give it, that the Canopy] **Ed;** to give it, the ~

1 Apr.
> that their Master] **Ed;** that <u>their</u> ~ *(i.e., canc).*
>
> them goe or not goe.] **Ed;** them goe or goe
>
> Treasury-vault, locked] **Ed;** Treasury-vault locked

f. 42ʳ

for the same purpose] *followed by a bar in red ink to denote addition on inserted slip, f. 41ᵛ.*

f. 41ᵛ

About 10 of the ... to Merton.] *This entry is on the verso only of a small quarto slip, f. 41ᵛ. The recto is blank. The leaf was bound in after f. 40, and the paragraph is to be inserted after a red bar following the first paragraph on f. 42ʳ. The last 40 per cent of the leaf is blank. This is the third of 3 inserted slips. See above, textual note at 29 Sept. 1659, f. 33.*

About 10 of the] *preceded by a bar in red ink to denote an addition to f. 42ʳ.*

f. 42ʳ continued

Authority for it?] **Ed**; *Authority for it.*

f. 42ᵛ

unreasonable proceedings and against Clayton] **Ed**; ~ proceedings against ~

desir'd them] **Ed**; desir'd them desir'd them

passed between them] ~ ~~thmm~~ them

where the Keys of the Lodgings] **Ed**; *where Keys of* ~

f. 43ʳ

Thomas in the Eare] Thomas in the ~~yeare~~ Eare

Warden, or words to that effect] **Ed**; Warden. *inserted into narrative from the margin:* or words ~ effect

f. 43ᵛ

that night on which] that night ^on^ which

At length the Appeale] **Ed**; At lenth ~

and seeing that no] **Ed**; and that no

their money, they concluded] **Ed**; their money they ~

f. 44ʳ

3 May.

was admitted at] was admitted ~~was~~ at

he spake a speech] **Ed**; he speake a ~

suffer any thing of it] ~ any ^thing^ of it

f. 44ᵛ

in behalf of Clayton] **Ed**; in befalf of ~

preferment, Clayton told him] **Ed**; preferment, told ~

preferment or other wayes] preferment *canc word and:* or ~

f. 45ʳ

fancying himself to] **Ed**; fanying himself to

Afterwards taking a Lodging] ~ Lodging *d over canc g*

f. 45ᵛ

must not be forgotten] **Ed**; must not begotten

Apothecary to Clayton] Apothecary ~~when~~ to ~

Brent, Savile] **Ed**; Brent Savile

not cost the college] not cost the ~~society~~ college

thought unnecessary] thought *canc word and:* unnecessary

f. 46^r

yet he was often absent.] *over canc words; repeated in right margin*
But Sr Thomas tho] ~ S^{ir} ~
doughty Knight did take] doughty Knight will ^did^ take
tho he used it not] though he use~~th~~^d^ it not
in one yeare threescore] ~ threescore t̲h̲r̲e̲e̲ s̲c̲o̲r̲e̲

f. 46^v

use, it was done conditionally] ~ ^it was done^ ~
usually belonged to the] **Ed;** usually belonged the
for afterwards Clayton disus'd his] for afterwards he ~
into Oxon triumphantly] **Ed;** into Oxon triumphanty

f. 47^r

as twas supposed] as t̲i̲s̲ ^twas^ supposed
of them (the Fellowes)] of them (the *over canc word and:* Fellowes).
which was all the remedy] which i̲s̲ ^was^ all ~
an Enimy to him, E. D., the] **Ed;** ~ him *insert marker to marginal note,* E. D.,
    here inserted into the narrative.

f. 47^v

higher in 1676] ~ 1676 *altered from* 1776
said Bursar G. Roberts] **Ed;** ~ G. Robers.
Vach in Chalfont] Vach in C̲h̲a̲l̲f̲o̲~~rt~~ Chalfont.
    Gap from end of paragraph to bottom of f. 47^v, of 22 lines.

f. 48^v

1661/2. 21 Mar.
    Gap from end of paragraph to bottom of f. 48^v, of 28 lines.

f. 49^r

1662. Mar. ult.
Blechindon in Oxfordshire] **Ed;** ~ in Oxforshire
debauchd person] **Ed;** debauhd person
and having employed a] and b̲e̲i̲n̲g̲ ^having^ employed ~~by~~ a
4 June, in margin.
    vol. 2. p. 194.] **Ed;** vol. 2 p. *om*

f. 49^v

July.
by one Mattthew Jellyman] **Ed;** by one ——Jellyman
10 Sept.
since gone to Ruin] **Ed;** since gone Ruin
11 Oct.
put me off for the] **Ed;** put me off from the
1662/3. 11 Feb.
6^{li} a time] **Ed;** ~ a tine
6 Mar.
    Gap from end of paragraph to bottom of f. 49^v, of 3 lines.

f. 50^r

9 Mar.
Wood, deceased] *Gap at end of paragraph, of 5 lines.*

1663. 23 Apr.

    Chimistry under the noted] ~ unde^r^ ~

    at the west End] at the ~~east~~ ^west^ End

f. 50^v

30 May.

    given 30 shillings] given 30^{li} shillings

    Gap from end of paragraph to bottom of f. 50^v, of 6 lines.

June.

f. 51^v

    afterwards some acquaintance with] ~ acquaint~~ed~~^ance with^

    seriously with him.] *Gap at end of paragraph, of 3 lines.*

27 July.

    under the yeare 1658] **Ed;** under the yeare 16 *om.*

    church in Westminster, see] **Ed;** ~ Westminster see

    before, under the said yeare] ~ the ~~yeare~~ said yeare

f. 52^r

1663/4. 1 Mar.

    death of Dr Holyday] ~ Holyday *altered from Horyday*

    acquaintance of AW.] *Gap at end of paragraph, of 14 lines.*

1664. 21 Apr.

    came to 7^{li}] ~ 7^{li} *altered from* 5^{li}

21 Apr. in margin.

    yeare 1651.] **Ed;** yeare *om.*

21 Apr.

    shewd themselves] **Ed;** shewd themselve

28 Apr.

    schoolmaster of Thame School] schoolmaster *over shhoolmaster* ~

f. 52^v

    lived high] **Ed;** lied high

    and leving him] and leving *over living* him

29 Apr.

    AW assisted] **Ed;** AW. assister'd

    in digesting] **Ed;** in diegesting

    the Evidences, Writings] **Ed;** the Evidences Writings

13 June.

    the cathedrall] **Ed;** the cathdrall

f. 53^r

1664/5. 18 Mar.

    take an Oath before] **Ed;** ~ Ooth ~

1665. May ult.

    at that time perused] at ^that^ time ~

f. 53^v

    11 Jun.

    in his hands] **Ed;** in my ^his^ ~

    Tower. Robert Clerke a fellow] **Ed;** Tower. ——Clerke a fellow

Foulis in the eare] **Ed;** Foulis in the yeare *AW corrected this error earlier, 31 Mar. 1661, f. 43ʳ*

24 Aug.

methodically digested] **Ed;** methodically disgested

f. 54ʳ

21 Sept.

to the E*ast* End] to the E — *canc letter and:* End

where AW perused them] **Ed;** were AW ~

1665/6. 3 Feb.

he would promise] he would — *canc letters and* promise

f. 54ᵛ

1666. 11 Apr.

have seen them] have seen *canc word converted to* them

deal of trouble] deal ^of^ trouble

25 June, in margin.

25] *written over* 26.

30 July.

The Warden of New College with] **Ed;** The Warden with

f. 55ʳ

1666, Aug.

president of S. John's college] **Ed;** president of that college

to do him the favour] **Ed;** to do me ~~the~~ ^him^ favour *AW lined through the wrong word.*

refer'd him to] **Ed;** ~ to to

1666/7. 18 March

K*ing* Willi*am* 3.] *Gap from end of paragraph to bottom of f. 50ᵛ of 13 lines.*

f. 55ᵛ

14 June.

became acquainted with] **Ed;** ~ aquainted ~

f. 56ʳ

21 Jun.

vol. 2. p. 675–6.] **Ed;** vol. 2. p. *om*

Dʳ John Pearson Bishop of Chester] **Ed;** Dʳ —— Pearson Bishop of Chester

f. 56ᵛ

he had business] **Ed;** he had buisness

22 Jun.

occasion'd by the grand] **Ed;** occasin'd by ~

such a vast number] **Ed;** such vast number

few Dayes, he spent] **Ed;** few Dayes he spent

Monasticon Anglicanum, or his *Baronage*:] **Ed;** Monasticon Anglicanum, or his Baronage:

18 July.

perished and become not legible] ~ become *o over canc a and:* ~

third vol*ume* of *Monasticon Anglicanum*] **Ed;** ~ of Monasticon Anglicanum

f. 57ᵛ

and Osney] *Gap at end of paragraph, of 6 lines.*

31 Aug.

in Oxon, with] in Oxon, w̲a̲s̲ with

Notitia Academiæ Oxoniensis] **Ed**; *Notitia* Academiæ Oxoniensis

being afterwards sold] being a̶l̶w̶a̶i̶e̶s̶ afterwards sold

and on Sʳ Joh. Aubrey] and t̶o̶ on Sʳ ~

into the paths of errour] ~ paths *over canc pathe* of ~

Gap from end of paragraph to bottom of f. 57ᵛ, of 6 lines.

f. 58ʳ

Sept.

by the favour of] **Ed**; by the fovour of

put into his hand] ~ m̲y̲ ^his^ hand

1667/8. 24 Mar.

Parishners, 24 Marc*h*, the] **Ed**; ~ Mar. 24. *date in the margin and* the

Gap from end of paragraph to the bottom of f. 58ʳ, of 17 lines.

f. 58ᵛ

1668. 16 May.

Vol*ume* of *Monasticon Anglicanum*;] **Ed**; Vol. of Monast. Anglicanum;

which were the copies] which w̶a̶s̶ were ~

And at some distance] At *canc and written over with* And ~

S̲t̲a̲l̲l̲ ... B̲o̲a̲r̲e̲s̲] *underscored in red chalk, to indicate italics*

f. 59ʳ

seen by them, M*atthew* H*utton*, AW] **Ed**; seen by them M. H. AW

18 May.

Dinner they viewed the Ruins] ~ viewed the̶y̶ ̶v̶i̶e̶w̶ Ruins

21 May, in margin.

entit*led Balliofergus* &c.] **Ed**; entit. Balliogergus &c

under the yeare 10 May 1660.] **Ed**; under the year ———

f. 59ᵛ

30 May.

Caves or Danvers] *blank space, AW later added the names, in pencil.*

hapned in 1680) the] ~ 168 the *AW later added o, in pencil.*

or those that were intrusted with] ~ intrusted *over canc* in-rusted with

f. 60ʳ

1668/9. 18, 19 Mar.

times, eate and drank] times, e̶a̶s̶t̶ eate ~

f. 60ᵛ.

Edward having a] ~ have^ing^ a

Gap from end of paragraph to the bottom of f. 60ᵛ, of 23 lines.

1669. 15 Apr.

(in number about 440] (in number about 3̲0̲0̲^440^

This was done ... then Mayor.] *later added in margin, inserted here in the narrative.*

6 July.

kindly sent for AW] **Ed**; ~ of AW

purposely to deliver] ~ ~~de~~ to deliver
f. 62ʳ

    25 Aug.

    Hist. and Antiq. of the Univ. of Oxon] **Ed**; Hist. and Antiq. of the Univ. of
      Oxon

    Allestrie, Dʳ Thomas] **Ed**; Allestrie Dʳ Thomas
f. 62ᵛ

    glad that there was] *not to himself, opposite 1st 2 lines, in margin:* It[alic]
    Afterwards they all went] **Ed**; ~ the all ~

17 Oct.

    was in 1666.] **Ed**; was in 166 *om*

22 Oct.

    in Anthony Halls house behind] **Ed**; in —— Halls house behind
    schooles, at which were] ~ were *written over* was
f. 63ʳ

    Barlow, Obad. Walker, Alsop] **Ed**; Barlow ^Obad Walker^ *in blank space*
      Alsop

    writing the *Hist. and Antiq. of the Universitie of Oxôn*] **Ed**; ~ Hist. and Antiq.
      of the Universitie of Oxôn

    authority of the book] **Ed**; ~ to the book

    who some time before] ~ before <u>before</u>

    peruse the Book] *Gap at end of paragraph, of 5 lines.*

24 Dec.

    vol. 2. p. 329.] **Ed**; *in margin,* vol. 2. p. *om.*
f. 63ᵛ

1669/70. Jan.

    part of the *Hist. and Antiquities of the Universitie of Oxôn;*] **Ed**; ~ Hist. and
      Antiquities of the Universitie of Oxôn;

    Bathurst his second book] ~ his ~~lib.~~ second ~

    many things relating] many things relat~~ed~~ing

    and whatsoever was] **Ed**; ~ whatsover ~

    wherein they had been] **Ed**; ~ the had been
f. 64ʳ

    for a Notitia of some of them] ~ of some <u>of some</u> of them

    he sent him, Feb. 13, a] **Ed**; he sent him a *in margin,* Feb. 13

    desire of the Author that some] desire of ^the Author that^ some

    Gap from end of paragraph to the bottom of f. 64ʳ, of 13 lines.
f. 64ᵛ

1670. 29 Mar.

    copie of *Hist. et Antiq. Univ. Oxôn*] **Ed**; ~ Hist. et Antiq. Univ. Oxôn

27 Apr.

    Edit*ion* of *Hist. et Antiq. Univ. Oxon.*] **Ed**; ~ Hist et Antiq. Univ. Oxon

1 May.

    Medalls, pictures] **Ed**; Medalls pictures

6 May.

    in his apartment] **Ed**; ~ aportment

works in two folios] ~ in ^two^ folios

at Doway in Latine--] ~ Latine-- ~~see Hist et~~ —— *canc words*

July.

had communicated his] had communicated ~~in MS~~ his

Hist. et Antiq. Oxon in MS] **Ed;** Hist. et Antiq. Oxon in MS

ff. 64ᵛ-65ʳ

Propediem vero, favente ... cicadæ —] *Prope*diem vero, ~ cicadæ —

f. 65ʳ

1670, July

collegii Mertonensis in eadem] **Ed;** ~ in ~~ex~~ eadem

before *Hist. et antiq. Oxon*] **Ed;** before Hist. et antiq. Oxon

11 Aug.

the *Hist. and Antiq. of the Univ. of Oxon* into] **Ed;** the Hist. and Antiq. of the
Univ. of Oxon into

put in what he pleased,] **Ed;** ~ please,

f. 65ᵛ

24 Sept.

first 4 Scotchman] **Ed;** ~ Scothman

did participate in] **Ed;** ~ perticipate of

of Rochester were in Oxford.] **Ed;** of Rochester *om.*

and there liberally] **Ed;** and the liberally

published entit*led om*] *AW did not remember the title.*

Gap at end of paragraph, of 3 lines.

Oct.

entit*led Supplementum Historiæ Provinciæ Angliæ*] **Ed;** entit. Supplementum
Historiæ Provinciæ Angliæ

living in the raigne of Henry III] **Ed;** ~ raigne of *om.*

26 Oct.

of the *Hist. and Antiq. of the University*] **Ed;** of the Hist. and Antiq. of the
University

f. 66ʳ

12 Nov.

Temple Esq*uire* a book] ~ Esq. ~~of~~ a book

such difficult and obscure words] ~ *and* ~~words~~ *obscure words.*

1670/1. 5 Jan.

His son] His son *unfinished sentence.*

21 Feb.

A conference or] **Ed;** A confence or

f. 66ᵛ

1671. 1 June.

The date is in the margin in the middle of the paragraph.

7, 8 July, in margin.

You may see ... entit*led* Boscobel] *in margin, here incorporated in the text.*

You may see many] you may ^see^ ~

f. 67ʳ

Reed a Benedictine] **Ed;** ~ Bendictine

day, July 21,] **Ed**; July 21 *in margin, here incorporated in the text.*
(for he was at the publ*ic* Library) they] **Ed**; (for ~ Library they
should find him at the Miter] **Ed**; ~ find at the Miter

f. 67ᵛ

And seeing that] **Ed**; ~ seing that
horrible thing to be] **Ed**; ~ thing in be
of any one of them.] *Gap at end of paragraph, of 4 lines.*

29 July.

29 July. Sat.] **Ed**; Jun. 29.

17 Aug.

Thom*as* Hallum M. A.] **Ed**; Thom. Allam ~

f. 68ʳ

1671/2. 11 Feb.

over the Water to Lambeth AWood, and] **Ed**; ~ Lambeth AWood. &

f. 68ᵛ

1671/2. 11 Feb.

Ralph Snow to their] **Ed**; *Ralph* Snow ~
libertie of putting in and] ~ in *over canc on* and
owne it.] owne it. —— *canc word, and gap after paragraph, of 3 lines.*

16 Feb.

Gap from end of paragraph to the bottom of f. 68ᵛ, of 4 lines.

f. 69ʳ

1672. 6 July.

his *Hist. et Antiq. Univ. Oxôn*] **Ed**; his Hist. et Antiq. Univ. Oxôn
Gap from end of paragraph to the bottom of f. 69r, of 13 lines.

f. 69ᵛ

Blank, except for a note by Thomas Hearne: 'This MS. belongs to Dʳ. Tanner.
Tho: Hearne. March 11ᵗʰ. 1727.'

NOTES

Introduction

1. The *Diarie* is now British Library, MS. Harley 5409, a quarto of 63 pages (hereafter, Har). The *Secretum* is now Bodleian Library, MS. Tanner 102, a folio of 69 pages (hereafter Tan). Wood revised the passage of his mother urging him to be a tinker in his Diarie when he wrote the *Secretum*, see 24 June 1646, f. 11^r; for his reaction to Dugdale's book, 1656, ff. 23^{r-v}. The 'public Library' is the Bodleian Library. Har ends at 1659/60, p. 70 above.

2. For his models and mentors, see N.K. Kiessling, *The Library of Anthony Wood* (Oxford Bibliographical Society, 2002), pp. xi–xiii. The more complete title of the *Athenæ* is: *The Athenæ Oxonienses. An exact History of all the Writers and Bishops ... in the most ... University of Oxford, from ... 1500, to ... 1690 ... To which are added, the Fasti* (London, 1691–2). The *Fasti* are 'Academical Annals' or lists, sometimes with biographies, of administrators, those who graduated, and incorporations.

3. For two passages concerning the bribery, see above, text p. 152 and note 24. For 'To the Reader', and *A Vindication*, text above at pp. 154–5 and notes 27–8.

4. For a detailed analysis of the differences between the *Diarie* and the *Secretum*, see N.K. Kiessling, 'The Autobiographies of Anthony Wood', *The Bodleian Library Record*, xix, no. 2 (Oct. 2006), 185–215; and the Introduction to the Textual Notes, p. 170. For the reference to his death, Har, f. 40^r and Tan, 1653, p. 42. See also Har, f. 22^r and Tan, 26 May 1647, p. 24 (change of 'which I have yet laying by me' to 'which he kept by him to the time of his death'); and Har, f. 59^r and Tan, September 1659, p. 67 (the addition of 'which he kept in memorie of Selden to his last day'). There are similar entries after 1660, when the first version ended; e.g., his friendship with Obadiah Walker 'continued ... til death parted them', that is, Wood's death, for Walker died in 1699 (Tan, 14 June 1667, p. 104).

5. 26 June 1669, pp. 114–15. On 24 November 1695 Thomas Tanner described in a letter to Arthur Charlett the lengthy meeting of Anthony and Mary 'with whom he [had] been so long at variance', see Tanner's letter above, p. 163.

6. Tan, 26 June 1669, p. 115, and 29 July 1671, p. 126.

7. Hearne, *Thomæ Caii vindiciæ antiquitatis academiæ Oxoniensis* (Oxonii, 1730), ii. 438–603; Huddesford reprinted the Hearne edition and added entries from 1672–95 compiled by Richard Rawlinson, *The Life of Anthony à Wood* (Oxford, 1772); Bliss, *Athenæ Oxonienses An Exact History of All the Writers ...* (London, 1813–20), i. i–cxxv (reissued in 1848, Oxford, for the Ecclesiastical History Society); Clark, *The Life and Times of Anthony Wood* (Oxford 1891–1900), vols i–v, *passim*. All used Har, though not methodically.

Secretum Antonii

1. The heading on top of f. 1ʳ was added later in pencil and is not visible on Plate 2. This simple title replaces the formal title page of the Harley manuscript, see Plate 1. 'Secretum' might be translated as 'a private account'. The '2ᵈ Part', also not visible on Plate 2, may refer to the *Secretum* as the second version of the 'Diarie'. For the MS. note, see Plate 1.
2. Wood's year began on 25 March. See 'Dating' in the Abbreviations and Conventions.
3. à Wood. The 'à' does not appear in any manuscript before 1662, but from that year Wood used it regularly. He at times added it to the names of other members of his family in an attempt to establish his gentlemanly ancestry. See, e.g., 19 Jan. 1642/3, p. 10; and Textual Notes, 1651. Dec., p. 187.
4. 'bought', that is, Thomas Wood bought the lease from Merton College. This took place in the sixth year of James I, who became king in 1603 upon the death of Queen Elizabeth.
5. 1666, that is, 28 Feb. 1667. See above, p. 103.
6. His elder brothers were Thomas, 1624–1651; Edward, 1627–1655; and Robert, 1630–1686. Younger brothers were Christopher, 1635–1684; and John, 1638–1640.
7. The assize is a court which heard cases submitted to it by the Quarter Sessions, the local county courts.
8. 'I here set downe' and 'I shall make mention'. Wood normally, but not always, changed the point of view to the 3rd person narrative in the *Secretum* (Tan) from the 1st person in *The Diarie* (Har). See above, the Introduction to the Textual Notes, p. 170.
9. *E curia Marischalli*. Thomas Wood claimed that, 'by permission of the Marshall' of the College of Heralds, he was exempt from appearing before the Heralds to enter his arms and pedigree. The Heralds charged a fee for their services and in turn kept genealogical records. Thomas Wood did not wish to pay for the service.
10. Three descents was the minimum requirement for certain privileges, including a coat of arms. See 18–19 March 1668/9, p. 113, where the Herald Edward Bysshe dashes off three descents of Wood's family for Anthony.
11. Wood yearned to discover his great grandfather's (Richard? Wood, Croston, Lancashire) and grandfather's records (Richard Wood, Croston and Islington). He left blank leaves at the beginning of his genealogical book for

information of the 'places of their births and burialls and a farther ascent'; This information he would obtain 'by those several meanes & wayes which I have in my mind which I hope in due time will soe come to passe that wee may not be numbred among the ignorant, who scarce, or perhaps not [at] all, like meere brutes, know any thing of their fathers & mothers'. MS. Wood empt. 26, p. 56. He never travelled to Lancashire.

12. From this 'mount' he could look into Fish Street, present day St. Aldate's Street, as the King and Queen proceeded through the Great Gate (before the Tower was built by Wren) to the Great Quadrangle of Christ Church.

13. Wood owned three copies of a ballad by Edmund Gayton describing this entertainment, *LAW* (see above, Abbreviations and Conventions), 500–502.

14. Wood described the whole progress in detail, from August 29 to 31, Monday to Wednesday: the journey from Woodstock and ceremonies near and in Oxford, at St. John's College gate, and at Christ Church gate and in the cathedral. In the evening the university players presented in Christ Church hall a comedy, *Passions Calmed*, or *The Setling of the Floating Island*, by William Strode. The next morning, Tuesday, there was a service in the cathedral, a convocation at the university church, St. Mary's, a visit to the Bodleian Library, dinner at St. John's College library, a second play, *The Hospitall of Lovers*, by George Wild, a return to Christ Church, and in the evening a third play, *The Royall Slave*, by William Cartwright. On Wednesday, the king departed. See *History* (1792), i. 407–12.

15. Wood added the story of the horse that bruised his head to Tan.

16. That is, advancing to exercises in Latin grammar.

17. His master's name may have been 'Wirley', which Wood entered in pencil, in Har. He was, perhaps, Francis Wherley, Balliol, B.A., 3 June 1630.

18. Upon Robert Wood's return from France, his brothers called him *monsieur*.

19. Wood often began his name with the digraph, the joined AWood, or he simply used the digraph alone.

20. A proclamation of 9 August 1642.

21. Called 'Pro-vicechancellour' in Har, because Pink discharged the duties of the vice-chancellor who resigned in June 1642, John Prideaux.

22. The custom of appointing knights, addressed in the coronation proclamation of Charles I, was in 1630 seen as a means to raise money. Thomas Wood avoided the fees but not the fine.

23. Plate which survived in the colleges was displayed in 2004 at the Ashmolean Museum, see *A Treasured Inheritance: 600 Years of Oxford College Silver* (May 2004).

24. For printed items concerning the plague in Oxford in 1643–5, see *LAW*, 2575–7, 3288, 3548, and 4658.

25. The date should be 6 October, a Sunday. 8 October was a Tuesday. See *LT*, i. III.

26. Protobune = pro-tribune, see *LT*, v. 245.

27. Prebends are canons supported by a stipends derived from cathedral revenues.

28. Wood added to Tan details from the source given in the marginal note in

Har, 'as for Blagge see Mon*umenta* Westmonast*eriensia*, p. 186', by Henry Keepe (1682).

29. That is, 7 March 1644/5.

30. Har has the marginal note (not in Tan): 'Puid see Micro-chron. at the end of Quer. Cant an. 1645 in Sept'. Wood owned The *Micro-Chronicon* (1647) by Bruno Ryves, *LAW*, 5679. At September 1645, sig. E2ᵛ, Wood made a mark in the margin at Puide. He also owned *Querela Cantabrigiensis* (1647/8) by John Barwick, *LAW*, 888.

31. Mottos: *Non reos res* [Things are not to blame; or the guilty will not escape]; and *Patria poscente paratus* [Ready at my country's call].

32. Har has 'some of the Parl. troopers'. Wood made several changes in this section to indicate his sympathies with the royalist cause.

33. This paragraph, added to Tan, is from *Micro-chronicon*, sig. E2ᵛ. See above note 30.

34. Wood expanded upon a note he wrote in the margin of Har, in the third person, when he was preparing the second version: 'He alwaies owned that place that gave him an acad. education and none else'.

35. For Theyer, see 1 Sept. 1668, p. 112. Concerning a 'Trade', Wood altered a much more revealing statement in Har of what his mother proposed. See the Textual Notes, p. 181.

36. As the son of a gentleman, *generosi filius*, Wood's fees were minimal and only the son of a plebei, an ordinary citizen, would pay less. Since Wood enrolled before the age of 16, he was not required to take an oath of supremacy. When he was 16, he was required to take a different oath, see above, 12 May 1648. For the matriculation fees and requirements, see Clark, *Register of the University of Oxford*, II. i (Oxford Historical Society, 1887), 6–7, 165.

37. This is the first of several alterations to Tan that indicate that Wood wrote this during his last illness.

38. Wood was made postmaster of Edward Copley, but this, fortunately for Wood, was not confirmed. The postmasters were later expelled, see also, March/April 1650, p. 33.

39. In 1647/8 Candlemas day was 2 February.

40. 'A warm drink consisting of thin gruel, mixed with wine or ale, sweetened and spiced' (*Oxford English Dictionary*).

41. The oath, a parody of oaths required of students, is: 'Item, you will swear that you will not visit the penniless bench'. Wood wrote the definition of Penniless Bench in the margin, here enclosed in single brackets.

42. Wood's speech to the Seniors is full of arcane allusions to classical lore with a few allusions to contemporary life at Merton. For more on the initiation custom, see *LT*, i. 140, and Clark's comments on W. Huddesford's note.

43. Clark, *LT*, misread Tan 'fulminate' as 'sublimate' which reading Bliss followed. Toniturate = thundering.

44. Clark, *LT*, misread Tan 'huge' as 'high' which reading Bliss followed.

45. Seekers of preferment, such as the Puritan 'good saints', were groaning until the parliamentary visitation when they would be awarded positions in the college.

46. In Har, a blank page follows (f. 25ᵛ), and this and the next two paragraphs are in Tan only.

47. Visitors appointed by Parliament examined all members of the college, and all members had to agree to the Solemn League and Covenant (pledging themselves to religious reform and the removal of the episcopacy), swear the Negative Oath (they would not help the king in the war against Parliament in any way), and accept various ordinances concerning worship. If they did not, they were dismissed. See also *History* (1796), ii. 501ff. In Wood's answer to the Visitors, MS. E. Mus. 77, f. 80, the name 'Anthony Wood' was later altered (by Wood himself?) to 'Andrew Woodley'. See A. Gustard, *Notes & Queries*, liv, no. 1 (2007), 83–85.

48. Wood wrote in the margin, '(a) lib. 2. p. 250.b. See also in *Ath. et Fasti Oxon.* vol. 2. p. [6]33.' In the 1813–20 edn (see above, Introduction, note 2), iv. 259–262.

49. Wood wrote in the margin, '(b) See in the second vol. of *Ath. et Fasti Oxon.*, vol. 2. p. 637'. In the 1813–1820 edn, iv. 267–9.

50. Wood wrote in the margin, 'See in the first vol. of *Ath. et Fasti Oxon.* p. 893.' In the 1813–1820 edition, *Fasti*, ii. 501.

51. 'Son of the earth'. Two inceptors in Arts were allowed to speak freely on Act Saturday and Act Monday. They were often punished for what they said. See *LT*, v. 151.

52. The chancel has remained in place until this day (2008) about six paces distant from the drop to the Lyde.

53. A clerk's place required fewer chapel duties than before the arrival of the visitors. AW's appointment as postmaster was apparently blocked by the visitors, see above, 18 Oct. 1647, p. 24. Many appointed as postmasters were soon dismissed, see 16 Jan. 1650/1, p. 34.

54. For 'Generals', see Clark, *Register of the Univ. Oxford.*, II. i. 22, 33. These are disputations which qualified *scholares* to take their B.A. degrees.

55. For the relation of the recovery of Anne Greene, see *LAW*, 1135, 6479–81. In the latter three, among the 'Verses made by the yong Poets of the Universitie' was one by 'Ant. Wood, Schol. of Mert. Coll.' See above, p. 36.

56. AW later obtained this order, or a copy, which is now a slip pasted to p. 1062 in MS. Wood F. 1.

57. A later reader underscored in pencil 'Derbyshire' and wrote the correct 'Bedfordshire' in the margin.

58. See also the entry on Cirques Jobson, 10 August 1654, p. 44, and the textual note, p. 192.

59. In the margin AW made a reference to an earlier fine, 'See in an*no* 163[5] p.', that is, Aug. 1635, p. 5.

60. See above, 14 Dec. 1650, p. 34 and note 55.

61. AW added in the margin of Har: 'He died after the 18 of Nov 1651'.

62. In the margin, AW wrote, 'See in the second vol. of *Ath. et Fasti Oxon.* p. [692.]', where he wrote a version of the above story. See also next note. In the 1813–1820 edn, *Fasti*, ii. 12 and 105.

63. In the margin, AW wrote, 'See more there p. 742'. In the 1813–20 edition, *Fasti,* ii. 12 and 105.
64. Over forty years later, AW could not remember which he had broken.
65. That is, the Bodleian Library.
66. AW never owned a copy of Burton's *Leycestershire* (or of Bosswell or Ferne), but he lent a copy of *The Display of Heraldry* to Obadiah Sedgwick in March 1660, see *LAW,* 3344.
67. AW added this sentence of 57 words to Tan.
68. The initials disguised the name of Warnford, whose death AW noted on 6 June 1662, p. 91.
69. A Jacobite is, here, a monophysite (one who believed in one nature of Christ, not two) Christian group of Syria founded by Jacob Baradaeus, who died in 578. For other references to coffee houses, see 22 Jan. 1650/1, p. 36, and March 1655/6, p. 47.
70. See the Textual Notes above, pp. 192–3, for a lengthy description in Har of one of these 'silly Frolicks', which AW did not wish to include in this second and more formal version.
71. Collector in Austins. 'collectores apud Augustinenses' were two persons nominated by the proctors to arrange for the Bachelor of Arts students to dispute once a year. These disputations were normally held on Saturdays in full term. See A. Clark *Register of the Univ. of Oxford,* II. i. 74–5.
72. 'Anyone may bring about a certain good. But only the best persevere.'
73. 'Whether it would be better to burn Cicero's books than to die'. AW found his second declamation after he wrote a shortened entry in the first version; see the textual note, above, p. 193.
74. The 'ancient' Holyday was 62 at the time of Edward Wood's funeral. He died in 1661.
75. The holograph manuscript of this poem is found in MS. Wood empt. 26, p. 60.
76. That is, wall-eyed and dim-sighted.
77. In the English version, *History. Colleges,* Merton College (1786), p. 27.
78. 'For leading or directing'.
79. Wood wrote in the margin, 'See *Ath. et Fasti Oxôn,* vol. 2. pp. 117–8' (the vignette of Edward Wood). In the 1813–20 edn, iii. 397. AW presented many copies of Edward's book as gifts to others. See *LAW,* 6688. AW added most of the next sentence to Tan.
80. That is, in the year ending on 24 March 1655.
81. Wood here added to Tan a long description (651 words) of the performers in the group.
82. Wood here added to Tan the exploits of Jane Whorwood (over 1,000 words).
83. In the 1813–1820 edn, iv. 30.
84. Wood wrote in the margin, 'See in the 2 vol. of *Ath. et Fasti Oxon* p. 749'. In 1813–1820 edn, *Fasti,* ii. 117. AW added this and the next paragraph to Tan.
85. That is, a disputer.
86. Wood wrote in the margin, 'See *Ath. et Fasti Oxon,* vol. 1 p. 901' (in the

vignette of Thomas Stanley). In 1813–20 edn, *Fasti*, i. 517. *Ayres* was published in 1657.

87. That is, a hoof.

88. AW wrote in the margin, 'See *Ath. et Fasti Oxon*, vol. 1. p. 323'. In the 1813–20 edn, ii. 117–18, Wood made a similar pun, 'He gave *Bond* for his future appearance'.

89. The *festum ovarum*, the Saturday before Shrove Tuesday and Ash Wednesday. See *LAW*, 5047–8, 5062, and pp. xx and xxx; and *LT*, ii. 5. Wood saved the Determinations, that is, disputations, required for the B.A. degree. They took place during Lent. See *LAW*, 5037–62 and p. xxx.

90. Wood wrote in the margin, 'See *Ath. et Fasti Oxon*. vol. 2. p. 781'. In 1813–20 edn, *Fasti*, ii. 175. This list of performers occurs only in Tan (some 875 added words). AW had intended to include it in Har, but the text ends, 'were these', and a blank page follows.

91. Wood wrote in the margin, 'See in the same book before quoted p. 465'. In 1813–20 edn, iii. 1175; for Sylvanus Taylor, see iii. 675.

92. Wood added in the margin 'a violist and Division-violist'; here inserted in the text.

93. Wood wrote in the margin, 'See *Ath. et Fasti* vol. 2. p. 299'. In 1813–20 edn, iii. 819. A Westmonasterian is one educated at Westminster school.

94. According to Har, this would be a day later, since he rode to Banbury on 6 April and 'the next day' he went to Stoke-Lyne. See textual notes, p. 202.

95. Wood wrote in the margin, 'Mr Ben*jamin* Cooper now lives in it'.

96. The Selden books were put in the west end of Duke Humfrey's, still called the Selden End. The books were catalogued as B.S., Bibliotheca Seldoni, and classified by the subjects of Arts, Medicine, Theology, and Jurisprudence, and by size. They were integrated into the general collection in the New Bodleian Library in 1939.

97. Wood added this story of Lloyd to Tan. He did not include it in the biography of Lloyd in the *Athenæ*.

98. Wood wrote in the margin 'See *Ath. et Fasti Oxon*. vol. 2 p[. 413.]' In 1813–20 edn, iii. 1069.

99. See also, *History. Colleges*, Merton College (1786), p. 28.

100. Savage presented a copy to Wood on 21 May 1668, *LAW*, 5763. Wood wrote some critical comments in the volume.

101. That is, the King's brothers, James, Duke of York and Henry, Duke of Gloucester; and George Monk.

102. Wood was too rushed to look at the names he listed in his diary on this date, see *LT*, i. 314.

103. The Selden marbles, along with the Howard, or Arundel marbles, presented by Henry Howard, later Duke of Norfolk, were 'lying' to the north of the west end of the Divinity School. All were taken indoors in 1714 to the Picture Gallery, the second floor above the schools in the Bodleian Library. In 1888 they were removed to the University Galleries, now the Ashmolean Museum.

104. 'On Faireford Windowes', in *Parnassus biceps. Or Severall Choice Pieces of Poetry, Composed by the Best Wits That Were in Both the Universities Before*

Their Dissolution, ed. Abraham Wright (London, 1656), pp. 81, 84. See Wood's entry in the *Athenæ* (1813–20), iv. 275–8. Wood described another visit to Fairford on his way to Bath; see 1679, above.

105. The School Tower is still the headquarters of the university archives, though the major holdings are elsewhere.

106. When the time for the reckoning came, the name of the popular Glendall was thrown out, leaving the others to pay.

107. For more on Clayton's election, see G.H. Martin and J.R.L. Highfield, *A History of Merton College, Oxford* (Oxford University Press, 1997), 212–15.

108. Wood wrote a record of this court case, now MS. Bodl. 594, pp. 35ff; printed in *LT*, i. 372.

109. Wood wrote in the margin 'Savil Bradley'.

110. The Vice-chancellor was Paul Hood.

111. Wood entered a reference symbol here, *, to his note in the margin, 'He [Fisher] made choice of this time purposely to avoid this encounter, because his timorous spirit could not undergoe it.'

112. The first recorded usage of this word, meaning literally, sluggish in the stern.

113. Wood wrote in the margin, 'Rootes of flowers which cost 5 shil*lings* a root'.

114. The initials are in the margin, E., D., are here incorporated into the text. Dickenson was no favorite of Wood, for Wood thought he had made mistakes when he mother was mortally ill; see *LT*, ii. 101, a transcription of MS. Wood empt. 26, f. 69–71, and note 128 below.

115. Minchery Farm, in Littlemore, is still a place name in present-day Oxford. Wood recorded the history of the nunnery in detail, see MS. Wood D. 11, pp. 33–6, and *LT*, i. 404.

116. Wood wrote in the margin, 'See Oxford Obital'. In his Obital, now MS. Wood F. 4, Wood wrote details about when a person died, the lineage, the exact place where the person was buried, and drew the arms which were on the hearse or on the monument. See also *LT*, iii. 443.

117. This charter has remained among Wood's manuscripts (MS. Wood E. 4); Clark printed it in *WCO* (1890), ii. 276. Canterbury College was founded in the late fourteenth century and after the dissolution was assumed by Christ Church.

118. Wood wrote in the margin, 'See Ath. et Fasti. Oxôn, vol. 2. p. 194'. In 1813–20 edn, iii. 577–8.

119. For J.A., see above, Wood's entry of 1653, p. 43. The quotation is from Martial, vii. 96.5–6. 'How has my beauty, speech, and age profited me? Give tears to my tomb, you who read this.'

120. This register is now MS. Rawl. B. 402, a manuscript appropiated by James Bisse, one of Wood's executors, after Wood's death. See above, p. 160 and note 34, and *LT*, i. 446–7.

121. *The Compleat Gentleman* was by Henry Peacham. Wood owned a copy, *LAW*, 5150. Wood at times wrote dialogue in a quaint fashion. What is meant here is: 'Aside from your Lordship, I have read more books than anyone else.'

122. On which to serve pies, or to use as kindling or as toilet paper. See above, p. 159, for an item Wood retrieved from a privy.

123. Wood wrote in the margin, 'See before in the yeare 16[51]'.

124. 'In the year of our lord 1188 in September this church was burned, in the night following the feast of the Apostle St. Matthew; and in 1197, 6 of the Ides of March a search was made in this place for the remains of St. John, and these bones were found in the east part of the sepulchre; and here hidden, and dust mixed with cement found in the same place and hidden.' In the margin, Wood wrote the dates in arabic numerals: '1188' and '1197'.

125. Clark described the custom of keeping money in a bag locked in college towers at a time when there were no banks, *LT*, ii. 38. The bag was sometimes (not here), kept in a locked box. The tower door could be opened by applying three different keys, each kept by a different individual.

126. This is to be taken literally. He lived at a time where this was possible.

127. The colleges were very protective of their records and limited access normally to members only. Publications based on research in the archives could reveal information, especially about property and income, that the colleges would just as soon keep private. At different times Wood was denied access to certain college archives.

128. Wood blamed her physician for her death. Edmund Dickenson 'did extreamly erre in managing the cure, and did, as 'twere, kill her downe-right'. Wood recorded her final sickness under the heading '1666 annus infœlicissimus familiæ nostræ' in his genealogy book (MS. Wood empt. 26, pp. 70–71).

129. The stage coach made it possible for Wood to make thirteen trips to London between 1667 and 1694. The first 'flying coach' took two days. By 1671 the coach made the trip in one day, in 13 hours. Wood collected eleven single sheets, which are known to exist only in his collection, concerning the coaches, see *LAW*, 4920–31. On 26 Apr. 1669, p. 114, the coach began at the home of the licensed carrier Thomas Moore, over against All Souls, at 12 shillings per person.

130. Wood wrote in the margin, 'see more in *Ath. et Fasti Oxon*, vol. 2. p. [675–6]'. In 1813–20 edn, iv. 848–9.

131. Wood himself owned 54 works authored by Prynne, a former member of Oriel College, *LAW*, 5419–73. In the *Athenæ* (1813–20), iii. 844–76, Wood grudgingly conceded some good to a scholar who was theologically and politically his opposite: 'I verily believe, that if rightly computed, he wrote a sheet for every day of his life, reckoning from the time when he came to the use of reason and the state of man.' Wood listed over 180 of his publication in this entry.

132. That is, Repertorium, a hand-list of the manuscripts in the library.

133. Wood annotated his copies of these published in 1673, 1675 and 1676. See *LAW*, 2362–4.

134. That is, Aubrey paid all the bills. Wood used this clause also at 4 Oct. 1660, p. 74.

135. Wood wrote in the margin, 'See before under the year [10 May 1660]', p. 71, above.

136. Wood ended his *Secretum* in 1672, but he apparently had notes before him to continue at least through 1674. See also 29 June 1671, p. 126. Wood's copies, heavily annotated, are *LAW*, 1513–14. Gore's work, before he sent it to Wood, was abysmal; see 'Anthony Wood and Thomas Gore', *The Library* (London), 6th series, xxi (1999), 108–23.

137. Some of Wood's income came from his cataloguing of the libraries of others (e.g., T. Barlow, H. Foules, and R. Sheldon). He generally kept copies of the catalogues for his own use. For an example of a series of such catalogues, see MS. Wood E. 10.

138. When Wood was out of town, at Weston, London, Bath, or in Oxfordshire, he collected information on Oxford events from friends and then compared their versions. See *LT,* ii. 156ff.

139. A reconciliation with Mary Drope Wood, Robert's wife, took place 'when too late', on his deathbed, see above, letter of T. Tanner to A. Charlett, 24 Nov. 1695. Unfortunately Wood could not complete the *Secretum* and 'more herafter' about his loss of hearing. See above, p. 163.

140. Wood owned a copy of the programme for this dedication ceremony, *LAW*, 4914. At the Act, candidates for degrees performed formal exercises. The Act ceremony at this time was 'great and splendid' because it was celebrated along with the Encænia and the dedication of the Theatre. See *LT,* v. 150–51.

141. Here begins Wood's friendships with Catholic bibliophiles and antiquarians.

142. Walker and Stone were rare visitors at Wood's lodging, the attic rooms of Postmasters' Hall.

143. Wood wrote in the margin 'see *Ath. et Fasti Oxon*, vol. 2. p. [329]'. In 1813–20 edn, iii. 881 (a positive portrait of a dear friend).

144. *Et hinc lachrymæ* = 'And hence tears'. After being forced to revise the *Historia*, Wood countered with an unfavourable portrait of Bidgood in the *Athenæ*. In 1813–20 edn *Fasti*, ii. 226.

145. In 1674, for more 'paines', that is, extra work, Wood received a further 50^{li}. See his diary entry, 26 Oct. 1674, *LT,* ii. 296.

146. *Historical Antiquities, in Two Books, the First Treating in General of Great-Brettain and Ireland, the Second Containing Particular Remarks Concerning Cheshire* (1672, 1673). Wood did not own a copy of this history, but he owned several printed items concerning the controversy generated by the book. See *LAW*, 4147, 4148, and 4352.

147. Not now among Wood's books, see *LAW*, 2178.

148. The *Dictionarium historicorum* (Oxonii, 1671) by Carolus Stephanus was edited by N. Lloyd. Wood owned an earlier edition, only, see *LAW*, 2850.

149. 'Shortly, god willing, a splendid book will appear, prepared with great labour and no less judiciousness, in which Oxonia, or rather the entire history of this most celebrated University of Oxford, will be excellently presented by the author, Anthony Wood of Merton College, M.A. of the same university, whose praise, integrity and friendship, special industry and knowledge of these studies I proclaim.' and 'So long as sheep [bees] eat

thyme and cicada, dew'. The error in the quotation from Virgil's *Eclogues* (v. 77), *aves* instead of *apes*, is compounded by Wood's *Oves* instead of *aves* or *apes*.

150. In his proof copy of the *Historia* Wood made well over 1,000 annotations, many of which noted the deletions, additions, and changes made by Dr John Fell. See *LAW*, 6685. Wood does not mention the second translator, Richard Reeves. See above, pp. 134–7 and notes.

151. At this stage, Wood is writing hurriedly and making mistakes. He forgot the title of the book, a gift of the author, *Progymnasmata quaedam* (Edinburgh, 1670), and did not take the time to find it. It has the inscription, 'Donum Autoris viz Joan. Wood philosophiae professoris in Acad. Edinburg. Oct. 3. 1670'. See *LAW*, 6690.

152. Still in Wood's library, *LAW*, 2182 with this inscription: 'Antonii à Wood Oxôn. Ex dono Authoris scil*icet* Franc. à Sta Clara vulgo Davenport, an*no* 1672 ...' Wood wrote in the margin, 'see Ath. et Fasti Oxon vol. 2. p. 487'. In 1813–20 edn, iii. 1226. A manuscript by Eccleston was in Wood's hands at some time; see *LT*, ii. 203, note 4.

153. Wood's copy is missing, see *LAW*, 1011. Wood wrote in the margin, 'see *Ath. et Fasti Oxon.* vol. 2. p. 34'. In 1813–20 edn, iii. 150.

154. In his book of 'Entertainments and Solemnities', MS. Wood D. 19, printed in *LT*, ii. 206ff.

155. Left unfinished.

156. That is, at the cookshop and tavern called Jeanes.

157. Wood wrote the last sentence in the margin. Thomas Blount published *Boscobel* in 1660. Wood owned a copy of the third edition (1680–81), *LAW*, 1015.

158. That is, edited by Joannes Rubeus (John Reed); Wood owned a copy, *LAW*, 5831, with his inscription, 'Antonii à Wood. Oxon. ex dono Sereni Cressey, per manus D. Rad. Sheldon de Beoly, 21. July 1671'.

159. 'He was not found.'

160. *The Rule of Faith* by François Veron, was translated by Edward Sheldon. For Wood's copy, see *LAW*, 6317, where the entry is incorrect. The imprint date is 1672, and Wood's note on flyleaf is: 'Given to me by Ralph Sheldon ... Nov. 3, 1672'. 'Several others' came to 36 copies to be sold at 6^d; Wood received these on 21 Nov. 1672, and he passed twelve on to the bookseller Richard Davis and six to the bookseller, West. See also *LT*, ii. 253.

161. In Wood's copy of the book the 'ninth page' of Blount's manuscript is on pp. 101–2, where it is unmarked. See *LAW*, 1012.

162. Mews thought it unnecessary, if not heretical, to write that conventicles, here secret and unauthorized religious meetings, dated back to Wyclif's time.

163. Wood owned a copy of Echard/Eachard's book, *LAW*, 2388.

164. That is, the Prerogative Court of the Archbishop for the probate and storage of wills.

165. Ashmole's gift was missing in 1695, see *LAW*, 277. Wood's letter of thanks is in MS. Ashmole 1131, f. 281. See *LT*, ii. 248.

Notes

Anthony Wood's life

1. In this section, complete words or phrases or punctuation within a paragraph added by the editor are put inside square brackets. The quotation on 'Truth' is from *A Vindication*, p. 29. Wood's Almanac *Diaries* are referenced to the number, with his first entries in number 1, the 1657 almanac, to 39, the 1695 almanac. See the list in *LAW*, p. 676. All references to Wood's Almanac *Diaries* are followed by locations in *LT*. For Bathurst's comment, 3 March 1673, Wood *Diaries* 17, f. 20^r (*LT*, ii. 258). See also 10 Mar. f. 20^r (*LT*, ii. 259). For Wilkinson's letter, see MS. Wood F. 35, f. 171. For Bathurst's wife, 6 Feb. 1674, *ibid.* 18, f. 2^r (*LT*, ii. 281).

2. The 'commonplace' book is now in MS. Tanner 102, ff. 70^r–129^v. Entries are dated 5 April 1660 to 27 Oct. 1681, with some written as late as 1693. It now follows the *Secretum* in Tanner 102. The 'Almanac' that Wood refers to is his Almanac Diary, see preceding note and 17 March 1673, MS. Tanner 102, f. 108^r.

3. The manuscript has 'chame'.

4. Wood detested the translator Richard Peers. See *Secretum*, above, p. 122. Richard Reeves, the second translator and unmentioned here, was a Catholic friend, see Wood *Diaries* 17, f. 2^{r-v} (*LT*, ii. 259–60).

5. 25 April 1674, Wood *Diaries* 18, f. 23^r (*LT*, ii. 286). 11 July 1674, MS. Tanner 102, f. 109^v (*LT*, ii. 288). The vignette of Hobbes is at *Historia*, ii. 376–7. Wood inserted a copy of Hobbes' letter in his copies, *LAW*, 6684–5, after ii. 444, but I have not found the letter in any other copy. Wood did not insert Fell's rebuttal to Hobbes, normally after ii. [448], 'Quarundam literarum', into his own proof copy (*LAW*, 6685). Clark gave a detailed account of the whole matter, *LT*, ii. 259–61, 290–94; see also Wood's notes at *LAW*, 3616, another copy of Hobbes' letter.

6. The quotations are from 17–27 July 1674, Wood *Diaries* 18, ff. 27^{r-v} (*LT*, ii. 289–90); and MS. Tanner 102, f. 109^v.

7. Wood *Diaries* 18, ff. 34^{r-v} (*LT*, ii. 296–7). 'He desird Mr Lloyd to bring me with him', added later.

8. See *Secretum*, above, 20, 21 July 1671, pp. 125–6 (*LT*, ii. 227–8).

9. For a lost payment, see 6 Nov. 1679, Wood *Diaries* 23, f. 53^v (*LT*, ii. 467). For his tasks at Weston, December 1679, *ibid.* 23, f. 71^r (*LT*, ii. 475). For the promise of £100 for his '*Bibliotheca*', see 13 Dec. 1683, *ibid.* 27, f. 58^r (*LT*, iii. 82).

10. 27 Mar. 1676, Easter Monday, Wood *Diaries* 20, f. 10^v (*LT*, ii. 341) and *ibid.* 22, f. 8^r (*LT*, ii. 401). For Wood and Reeves, see above, note 4. Reeves was forced by his Catholicism to leave his post at Magdalen School in 1673. Sheldon's feigned departures were on 6 Nov. 1679 and 27 Nov. 1680, *ibid.* 23, f. 53^v, and *ibid.* 24 (entry of 12 Aug. 1680), f. 26^r (*LT*, ii. 455, 493).

11. For the events surrounding the death of Sheldon, 8–29 June 1684, and 4 July–22 Aug., Wood *Diaries* 28, ff. 26^r, 27^v, 28^{r-v}, 30^{r-v} (*LT*, iii. 96–8); the £40 for delivering materials to the College of Arms is not counted in the £80.

12. For Sheldon in prison, 28, 29 Nov. 1678, Wood *Diaries* 22, f. 31^v (*LT*, ii. 424); and for Grimstone, 30 Apr. 1679, *ibid.* 23, f. 25^r (*LT*, ii. 449).

13. 28, 29 Nov. 1678, Wood *Diaries* 22, ff. 31^{r-v} (*LT,* ii. 424).

14. 1 Dec. 1678, *ibid.*, ff. 34^{r-v} (*LT,* ii. 424–5).

15. For Clayton's response, 13–17 Feb. 1679, University Archives, WP/11/1, ff. 5, 7 (*LT,* ii. 439–40). For the poem on Dryden, June 1686, Wood *Diaries* 30, ff. 39^{r}, 40^{r} (*LT,* iii. 190–91).

16. 23 June 1676, *ibid.* 20, f. 24^{r} (*LT,* ii. 350). St. Swithins day is 15 July, which would have meant that his return trip, some 68 miles, took two days.

17. 28–9 May 1678, MS. Wood D. 11, ff. 84^{r}–110^{r} (*LT,* ii. 404–7). Creeklade is Cricklade, Wilts. He had visited Fairford on 20 July 1660. See *Secretum*, above, f. 38^{r}. The Oxford *Historiola* is a short history of the University copied in the late fourteenth century into the 'Chancellor's Book' of the University. Brompton's *Chronicle* is attributed to John Brompton, Abbat of Jervaulx, Yorkshire, *c.*1193.

18. 28 June 1678, MS. Wood D. 11, ff. 150^{r}–153^{r} (*LT,* ii. 410–11); and 29 June 1678, Wood *Diaries* 22, f. 17^{v} (*LT,* ii. 412). St. Peter's Day is in late June.

19. 23 July 1680, MS. Wood E. 1, ff. 146^{r}–147^{v} (*LT,* ii. 492).

20. 18–22 June 1691, Wood *Diaries* 35, f. 40^{v} (*LT,* iii. 364–5).

21. June–July, *ibid.* 35, f. 42^{r-v}, 85^{v}–87^{r}, 11^{r} (*LT,* iii. 365, 368–9, 353). For William Warham (and Cranmer), see the *Athenæ* (1691), i. 572, where the passage is in italics, that is, quoted. Bliss did not enter it in italics in the 1813–20 edn, ii. 739. To 'take off 16. copies' meant that Charlett said that he would find 16 subscribers to the *Athenæ*.

22. For the diary entries, 18–24 July, Wood *Diaries* 36 40^{r-v} (*LT,* iii. 395f). The *Liber Matriculæ P.* is: *Matriculation book of the Universitie of Oxôn from the yeare 1648. 49 — To the end of Trin. Terme 1662.* University Archives, S.P. 37, pp. iii–iv (*LT,* iii. 202–3). In his battle with Wallis, Wood had the last word when he prepared additions to the *Athenæ*. On a slip of paper he detailed one of Wallis's battles in the vignette of Henry Stubbe who is there credited with the 'make white black and black white' quotation. Thomas Tanner, whom Wood appointed on his deathbed to arrange his papers and prepare a second edition, omitted this addition though Philip Bliss, the editor of the third edition, added it. See 'Autobiographies', pp. 188–9 and *LT,* iii. 395–6. For Wallis in the *Athenæ* (1692), ii. 816 (in 1813–20 edn, *Fasti,* ii. 245); other examples of Wood's harsh treatment of Wallis are in the description of the Wallis/Zouch competition for the position of university archivist and the Wallis/Ward competition for seniority, *Athenæ* (1692), ii. 415, 627, 785 (in 1813–20 edn, iii. 1073, iv. 248 and *Fasti,* ii.184); and finally, the addition in the *Athenæ* (1813–20), iii. 1073ff.

23. Late July–29 Aug. 1692, Wood *Diaries* 36, ff. 41^{r}–43^{r} (*LT,* iii. 395–9).

24. For statements on 'truth', see, e.g., *A Vindication*, pp. 5–6 and 28. 25 Aug. 1692, Wood *Diaries* 36, f. 51^{v} (*LT,* iii. 400). For Wood's question about the second Earl, *LT,* iii. 400, note 7. The vignette of the Earl is at *Athenæ* (1692), ii. 389–39, and for the brief quotation, ii. 842; in 1813–20 edn, iii. 1018ff. and *Fasti,* ii. 296. For Jenkins and Glynne (1692), ii. 221 and ii. 269; in 1813–20 edn, iii. 643 and 753. Aubrey included the information on David Jenkins in his *Brief Lives* (not published until 1898) and wrote about the bribery in a letter to

Wood. See A. Powell, *John Aubrey* (London, 1948), 223. For the beginning of the suit, *LT,* iii. 407. For attempts to pacify the Earl, see Wood's draft letter, MS. Tanner 456a, f. 37^r, printed in *LT,* iv. 47ff; for a second letter, Oxford Univ. Archives HYP/A52a (olim Wp/26), f. 13.

25. 29–31 July 1693, Wood *Diaries* 37, f. 46^r (*LT,* iii. 429). See also 28 July 1693, *ibid.* 35 (a misplaced entry), f. 18^v (*LT,* iii. 429). For 'Apodyterium', see the Index.

26. 6 Jan. 1694, *ibid.* 38, f. 8^{r-v}, and for Hearne MS. Rawl. C. 867, f. 37^v (*LT,* iii. 440; and iv. 50). The Physick Garden is now the Botanical Garden. For the sentence, see *LT,* iv. 44. In MS. Ballard 14, f. 30, Wood wrote that '2 sheets' of the *Athenæ* were burned, *ibid.*

27. Concerning 'To the Reader', Wood claimed that 'few were printed ...' in *A Vindication*, p. 27. The quotations are from 'To the Reader' in the second edition of *Athenæ* (1721), i, sigs. [2]^v–a^r There the 'booksellers' wrote that it was present in 'very few Copies' of the first edition (1691–2) and 'those only to give away among particular Friends', i, f. [2]^r. John Aubrey distributed 'To the Reader' in London for Wood before 3 December 1692, see his letter of that date to Wood, in M. Balme, *Two Antiquaries* (Durham Academic Press, 2001), p. 141; and 'Autobiographies', 190. Later scholars usually take Wood's self-portrait literally, *ibid.*, 190–91.

28. Gilbert Burnet attacked Wood in a thirty-six page pamphlet, *A Letter ... to the Lord Bishop of Cov. and Litchfield* [W. Lloyd] *concerning ... A Specimen of some Errors ... by Anthony Harmer* [Henry Wharton] (London, 1693). Wood bought a copy on 11 March 1693 and prepared his riposte immediately, sending the manuscript to the London printer on 28 March. The printed copies of the thirty-page *A Vindication* arrived in Oxford on 20 April 1693, Wood *Diaries* 37, f. 24^r (*LT,* iii. 420). A more complete title is: *A Vindication of the Historiographer of the University of Oxford and his Works, from the Reproaches of the Lord Bishop of Salisbury [Gilbert Burnet], in his LETTER ... concerning ... A Specimen of some Errors... by Anthony Hurmer [sic]. Written by E. D.* Wood wrote the date when he acquired Burnet's *Letter* on the title page, *LAW,* 1207. For his copy of Wharton's *Speciman, LAW,* 6533. Wood addressed Burnet's criticisms of the *Historia* in Burnet's *History of the Reformation* (London, 1679) as well. The quotation from *A Vindication* is on p. 29.

29. For Wood's stomach ailment, Wood *Diaries* 37, f. 55^v (*LT,* iii. 433). For letters, 21 Aug. 1694, *ibid.* 38, ff. 2^v–3^r (*LT,* iii. 440); and 1695, *ibid.* 39, f. 1^v (*LT,* iii. 476).

30. For 'William and Mary, 1694: An Act for the Kings most gracious general and free pardon. [Chapter XX. Rot. Parl. pt. 6.]', see *Statutes of the Realm,* ed. John Raithby, vol. vi: 1685–94 (1819), p. 607. For 28 May 1695, 7 June 1695, Wood *Diaries* 39, ff. 26^v, 28^r (*LT,* iii. 484–5). 2 Aug. 1695, *ibid.,* f. 34^{r-v} (*LT,* iii. 487). 11 Sept. 1695, *ibid.,* f. 37^v (2nd) (*LT,* iii. 488–9). 3 and 9 Oct. 1695, *ibid.,* ff. 44^{r-v} (*LT,* iii. 490–91).

31. 10 Nov. 1695, MS. Tanner 456*, f. 45^v (*LT,* iii. 493ff).

32. 16 Aug. 1695, Aug. Wood *Diaries* 39, f. 34^r (*LT,* iii. 487–8).

33. 9 Oct., *ibid.,* f. 41^r (*LT,* iii. 491); 12 Oct. *ibid.,* f. 41v (*LT,* iii. 491); 1 Nov. *ibid.,*

f. 46r (*LT,* iii. 492–3). There is a spurious story that Robert South, a witty and caustic Canon at Christ Church, told Wood, suffering from the inability to urinate, that if he could not make water he must make earth. The angry Wood then went home to write a damning portrait of South in the *Athenæ.* In this portrait, Wood dated certain offices South held, 'to this day (Apr. 1. an*num* 1694)', which indicates that he completed the entry before the onset of his health problem. For the vignette, *Athenæ* (1721), iv. 1045; in 1813–20 edn, iv. 637; for other reservations about the story, see *LT,* iii. 497, note 2. 'Shifting' is to change clothes.

34. For the numbers, see *LAW,* which has a record of 6,760 printed items. For the sources of his printed items, see *LAW,* pp. xv–xix. The printed items are now contained in some 970 volumes and the manuscripts, in some 150 volumes in the Bodleian Library. Not everything ended up in the Ashmolean Museum. Wood's executors had their pick of what they wanted to take, and all the Wood manuscripts now in the Ballard, and Rawlinson collections in the Bodleian Library arrived via the executors James Bisse and Arthur Charlett. The Tanner manuscripts arrived via Thomas Tanner who took manuscripts he thought necessary to prepare a new edition of the *Athenæ.* It was not unusual at that time for academics and collectors to take whatever manuscripts were available, see S. Gillam, 'Anthony Wood's Trustees and their Friends', *The Bodleian Library Record,* xv, no. 3 (Oct. 1995), 187–209. Wood himself took, if he did not purchase, some Langbaine manuscripts in 1658 (Tanner, as the executor, noticed several in Wood's home in November 1695, see p. 162, his letter of 24 Nov. 1695), and Wood definitely took some Sheldon manuscripts when he was hired to oversee their removal to the College of Arms, see I.G. Philip, 'Sheldon Manuscripts in Jesus College Library', *The Bodleian Library Record,* i (Dec. 1939), 119–123.

35. MS. Engl. Misc. d. 10, ff. 3–4 (*LT,* iii. 497–8). S. Gillam suggested that Charlett wrote this letter to bring himself to the attention of the new Archbishop, 'Anthony Wood's Trustees', p. 190.

36. 24 Nov. 1695, MS. Ballard 4, ff. 28–9 (*LT,* iii. 501–2). Charlett answered, 26 Nov. 1695, fol. 92 in MS. Tanner 24.

37. The will was signed by Wood but prepared by a clerk on 24 Nov. 1695, The National Archives (TNA): Public Record Office (PRO) PROB 10/1275. One folio leaf, folded to form f. 1^r, f. 1^v, f. 2^r, f. 2^v. Outside, f. 2^v, the title was written. This copy has not been formally edited before now.

38. MS. Rawl. C. 867, f. 37^v–38^r (*LT,* iii. 499). Hearne copied Charlett's 'Memorandum', 'Out of the matter of University's Copy [formerly Charlett's] of Athenæ Oxon in a spare Leaf at the Beginning:' (original not seen).

INDEX

References for further information, *AO* (*Athenæ Oxonienses*) and *AOF* (*Athenæ Oxonienses, Fasti*); *LAW; ODNB; LT*; and Foster, are cited in full in the Abbreviations, p. x above; only the most complete for each person are included. The abbreviation 'd.' indicates the year of death; 'fl.', 'floruit', gives the year(s) during which a person's existence is documented; directions north, south, east-south-east, are abbreviated N, S, ESE, etc.

Index

Index

Index